A Declaration
of Interdependence

A Declaration of Interdependence

Why America Should Join the World

WILL HUTTON

W. W. Norton & Company
New York   London

Copyright © 2003, 2002 by Will Hutton
First published as a Norton paperback 2004
Published in England as *The World We're In*

Manufacturing by The Haddon Craftsmen
Production manager: Amanda Morrison

LIBRARY OF CONGRESS CATALOGING-IN-PUBLICATION DATA

Hutton, Will, 1950–
    [World we're in]
    A declaration of interdependence : why America should join the world / Will Hutton.—
1st American ed.
            p. cm.
Originally published: World we're in. London : Little, Brown, 2002.
Includes bibliographical references and index.
    ISBN 0-393-05725-9 (hardcover)
    1. Europe—Economic conditions—1945– 2. Europe—Politics and government—1989–
3. United States—Economic conditions—1945– 4. United States—Politics and government—1989– 5. Globalization. I. Title.
    HC240 .H85 2003
    330.973—dc21   2002154392
ISBN 0-393-32560-1 pbk.

W. W. Norton & Company, Inc., 500 Fifth Avenue, New York, N.Y. 10110
www.wwnorton.com

W. W. Norton & Company Ltd., Castle House, 75/76 Wells Street, London W1T 3QT

1 2 3 4 5 6 7 8 9 0

To
Jane, Sarah, Alice, and Andrew

Contents

Preface and Acknowledgments to the American Edition

Ever since Ed Barber, my editor at Norton, agreed that in the United States we should retitle *The World We're In* as "A Declaration of Interdependence," I have been reproaching myself. It is a much better title than I used in Britain. It captures the overriding value that I believe should inform domestic and foreign policy in both the United States and the European Union and it is a call to arms against a conservative, unilateral worldview. It also has a large personal and emotional significance.

This title was my father's suggestion for what I should call my book, and he died unexpectedly, at age eighty-two, of a heart attack, just six weeks after *The World We're In* was published. Thankfully he lived to see the book reach the top ten nonfiction best-seller list in Britain. He had helped on all my other titles, and was adamant that this was my core conception and that the title should reflect it. He was right, and I feel sure he would have been delighted at this choice for the U.S. edition.

My father fought alongside American troops during World War II, an experience from which he drew two fundamental conclusions. First, Britain should never forget its geography; ordinary Europeans hold too many common values to allow crooked ideologies to spawn bitter wars. Democracy is the best defense against both fascism and communism. Second, he concluded that an engaged United States and Europe were essential partners who together constituted the idea of the West. The health of the globe hangs upon an effective, interdependent, liberal, transatlantic relationship. Euro-skepticism in Britain and conservative unilateralism in the United States menaced this interdependence.

So if *The World We're In* attacks Euroskepticism and makes the case for European integration around a reassertion of common European values, *A Declaration of Interdependence* tries to do the parallel job in the United States—insisting that America's interests are still best served by strengthening and modernizing the multilateralist approach that followed World War II. Communism has collapsed and radical Islamic terrorism has arisen as the principal threat to the world's security. Concurrently, American power has grown and with it a capacity to act autonomously. Conservative siren voices argue that the rules are now different. America is on the front line; America is most at risk; America must look after itself.

My view differs—I see multilateralism as more important than ever. Globalization requires an assertion of international law, and legitimate law can never hold that might is right. It must emerge from a consensual, legitimate process—and this extends to the initiatives necessary to combat terrorism. A paradox lurks here, for the more legitimately it acts, the safer America will be, and legitimacy is grounded in a recognition of interdependence.

This flies in the face of American conservative tradition, which holds that America's exceptionalism and economic and social successes are built around independence, individualism, and a ruthless assertion of self-interest.

In modifying my book for an American audience, chapter 1 and the Conclusion have been rewritten, and I have combed through the middle eight chapters, both to update and rewrite where necessary. The last two chapters of *The World We're In,* where I set out the history of the European Union and how European policy might develop from here, have been omitted to keep the book to a more manageable length. Such detail is not of overwhelming interest to American readers. I have been helped by new research from William Davies, and commentaries from Sam Wells, Phillipa Strum, Jerome Karabel, and Nina Planck. Sidney Blumenthal offered wise advice about framing the argument in an American context. Mary Koi did sterling work editing chapter 1 and the Conclusion, and thanks both for that important work and for her comments on the content. Thanks also go to Ann Kirschner, who showed extraordinary care and meticulousness in Americanizing the English text. And of course to Ed Barber, whose steadfastness and faith in the book was remarkable.

The challenges ahead for both the European Union and the United States are formidable. I hope *A Declaration of Interdependence* helps to remind Americans of their European roots and their liberal vocation.

Americans, we Europeans need you back—as reengaged, as generous, and as farsighted as you once were. This is an essential American and, indeed, global interest. I hope this book persuades at least some of you of my case.

—Will Hutton
London
September 15, 2002

Acknowledgments

There are many to thank in the writing of a book this length and with this degree of perhaps foolhardy ambition. At many times over the last eighteen months I have wondered whether I had bitten off more than I could chew, and wished that I had decided on something more modest. But in the writing I became more convinced that one of the book's central contentions—that in today's world it is impossible to conceive of a national economic, political, and social program in isolation—is correct. Developments in Britain are governed to so great an extent by events and ideas outside our borders, particularly by those in the United States, that the only way to capture what is happening is to offer an international context and analysis. Unless we do, we comprehend only a small fraction of the reasons why we make the choices we do and of the political and economic battles we need to fight.

The first person whom I must thank is William Davies, who has worked for me as my principal researcher for fifteen months. Research is a demanding and sometimes solitary activity, and I was lucky to find William, who is intelligent, dedicated, thorough, and capable of sustained research. He understood the thesis and directed his efforts to support it. There is no chapter where his research has not been important. He offered considered feedback and honest criticism as the book unfolded, and I hope he is pleased with the result.

Charlotte Beaupère worked as an additional researcher for some eight months, largely on chapter 2 and the European chapters of the book. I hoped she would bring a distinctive French perspective on Europe, and access to a different literature. I was not disappointed. Charlotte's work was thoughtful and original. Together, she and William provided the depth of research from which the book could be written.

I was also lucky in my friends in Britain, the United States, and Europe who have read draft chapters or sequences of draft chapters and offered invaluable feedback, corrections, and advice. Halfway through I held a seminar at the London School of Economics on the first five chapters (excluding chapter 2), and I owe thanks to Richard Layard, Richard Sennett, Adam Swift, Nina Planck, and David Held for their constructive criticism. Adam in addition read no fewer than three drafts of chapter 2, and his knowledge of political philosophy is awesome. My huge thanks to him; if there are still problems with the chapter then they are wholly mine. David Held, who helped with *The State We're In*, proved to be a no less loyal and wise supporter of this effort. By the end he had read the entire first and second drafts, and I profited enormously from his detailed comments as well as his view of the shape of the overall argument.

None of my American friends should take any responsibility for my thesis or any row that may ensue. It's all my fault. Three seminars in July 2001 on the first half of the book were invaluable. At the University of Berkeley, Jerome Karabel put together a group who gave me intelligent feedback and counsel; my thanks to him, Issac Martin, Michael Reich, Fred Block, and George Lakoff and their detailed written comments afterward. It was Todd Gitlin who led to Jerome; thank you for the suggestion! Laura Tyson and John Zysman at Berkeley took time out of their hectic schedules to offer comment and critical feedback.

Bob Kuttner, the editor of the American *Prospect*, organized a seminar at his wonderful summer house in Wellfleet, on Cape Cod. Robert Reich, Barry Bluestone (and his father), Richard Rothstein, and Bob gave me a concentrated and critical appraisal—thanks again for their comments at the time and afterward.

In Washington, John Judis, Gene Sperling, Larry Mishel, Tom Edsall,

John Schmitt, Roger Hickey, and Kathleen Thelen all offered important reactions and insights. Samuel Wells, a friend of nearly twenty years, kindly organized a seminar at the Wilson Center. This was again an opportunity for constructive critical feedback and commentary, and my thanks go to Martin Albrow, Jodie Allen, Joseph Bell, Matthew Holden, Kent Hughes, Bruce Stokes, Philippa Strum, Michael van Dusen, and Sam and Sherry Wells for investing so much time in putting me if not right, at least less wrong. Philippa Strum and Matthew Holden made detailed comment afterward, and later in December I was lucky to find an insomniac Philippa, who cast an eye over my second draft of the first five chapters, again to my profit. Thanks also to Sidney Blumenthal, who gave a very useful critique of the central thesis.

In October Timothy Garton Ash, and David Miliband joined a small seminar on the European chapters at what was then the Industrial Society (now The Work Foundation); together with commentary from Charles Grant, this was a crucial benchmark in showing where the argument needed to be strengthened. Three of my then fellow directors at the Society—Richard Reeves, John Knell, and Patrick Burns—offered important feedback and comment, as did Robin Cook, Andrew Oswald, Mary Koi, James Long, Ian McEwan, Hans-Friedrich von Ploetz, and Noreena Hertz. My thanks also to the anonymous reader arranged by Little, Brown.

In early November I was privileged to have a short tour of Germany, arranged by Gero Mass, director of the London office of the Friedrich-Ebert Stiftung. My thanks to him, and to Martin Behrens, Ludiger Pries, Hagen Lesch, Wolfgang Streeck, Martin Hopner, and Wolfgang Üllenberg. All provided important feedback and comment on the book, offering a German dimension on the issues raised that came at a critical juncture in my thinking. I must also include the Venice Seminar, which I attended at the invitation of the Italian ambassador to London, Luigi Amaduzzi, and the British/Italian colloquium in Potignano, in March and September of 2001, respectively, as important moments when I was able to test-run some arguments. My thanks for inclusion at both. Jim Garrison of the State of the World Forum and Marcello Palazzi—two doughty campaigners for a better world—offered important encouragement.

Then to my editors. Philippa Harrison at Little, Brown had promised to edit the book, but left the company before it was completed. However, she kept her promise and edited it as a personal favor. I was the beneficiary of a master craftswoman at work. Whether it was the chapter sequence, the structure of individual chapters, or questions of content and style, she was and is superb. And when I was fading toward the end, she and David Held combined to keep up my spirits and insist I find the energy for yet more redrafts. Richard Beswick took over her role at Little, Brown, so that in the closing months I was lucky to have a second fine editor, joined for the final copy edit by the meticulous Gillian Bromley. My thanks to them all; and of course to that great agent and lover of books, Ed Victor, without whom this book would not have been written. My father, as for all my books, was a valued and constructive critic and adviser; many of the views expressed he, and my mother, will recognize as those we have discussed since my boyhood. Roger Alton, editor of the *Observer*, agreed to a month's leave of absence from my column and other writing obligations to help complete the book; and Sir Christopher Wates and the trustees of the Industrial Society, in allowing me to express "time sovereignty," gave me the scope to find crucial writing time in an otherwise crowded working week.

Almost all of these 140,000 words—along with redrafts—were written in 2001 while I was simultaneously discharging my responsibilities to the Industrial Society and the *Observer*. It was physically and intellectually shattering, and inevitably my family bore some of the costs of having to make do with a distracted and obsessed father—especially toward the end. Sorry. My wife, Jane, in trying times was magnificent. All I can say is a profound and intensely felt thank-you for your love and forbearance. I hope you think it's been worth it.

—Will Hutton
March 17, 2002

A Declaration
of Interdependence

Introduction to the British Edition

With the launch of the euro and the hardening of self-confident American unilateralism in the defense of what the Republican party now calls "the homeland," the relationship between the United States and Europe is set to become more tense. These are two enormous power blocs with different visions of how the market economy and society should be run, and with different conceptions of how the great global public goods—peace, trade, aid, health, the environment, and security—can be achieved and maintained. The relationship between the two is the fulcrum on which the world order turns. Managed skillfully, this could be a great force for good; managed badly, it could give rise to incalculable harm.

For the British, for whom this book was first written, there is a fundamental choice. European integration is accelerating: the euro is in circulation, and at the Laeken summit in December 2001 agreement was reached to establish a preparatory convention to examine the outlines of a European constitution before the 2004 intergovernmental conference. The issue will come to a head if and when the referendum on the euro is held. But the question is larger than whether Britain should join the euro. It is: on which side of this argument do we want to put our weight? And that in turn is a question about what values should underpin the building of Britain's economic and social model. How much are we European—and

3

how much do we have in common with an America increasingly in thrall to a very particular conservatism?

This question is posed as British politics drifts around a managerial centrism. There are no great political movements or inspirational causes. Voter apathy is widespread. Our political leaders are well intentioned, but they are at a loss as to how to revive a belief in politics and public purpose. As I write at the beginning of chapter 1, the public realm is in eclipse. It is almost as though citizenship has gone into abeyance.

And yet there remain great issues. The terms of society's social contract remain as vexed and contentious as ever. The rich grow richer while disadvantage remains acute. Equality of opportunity, let alone of income and wealth, remains elusive. Public services are inadequate. And since I began the book, the terrorist attacks of September 11, 2001, are a horrifying reminder of the scale of atrocity that intercultural hatred can spawn—and of the urgent need to find some form of international settlement, along with the necessary policing, that reduces and hopefully eliminates the risk of any repeat.

This book is a response to these concerns. It is profoundly critical of American conservatism, now the dominant political current in the United States, and of its impact on the United States and the world. It sets out to correct the torrent of criticism leveled at Europe as though the United States were a paragon of all the virtues—rather than a country with some severe economic and social problems, whose democracy, where votes and office are increasingly bought, is a reproach to democratic ideals. European capitalism and its accompanying social model—and its democracy—by contrast have much to offer. The old world, contrary to the internationally accepted wisdom, has much to teach the new.

So, in part, this is a book for the idea of Europe. In my view, the quest for European union is one of the great rousing and crucial political projects of our time. It is vital in providing a counterweight to the United States and thus contributing genuine multilateral leadership in the search for securing global public goods. It is a means of advancing core European values. It is also the way to reanimate our politics and the public realm—and, indirectly, to put our economy on an upward trajectory of productivity and to build a less unequal society. We British are more European than we begin to realize, and our alliance with the United States—bound by history and language though we are—needs to be recast in the light of our European vocation. We should, of course, join the euro.

These are not the current accepted wisdoms, and if the book has done its work I expect a vigorous reply. The argument is much needed, and the Euroskeptics have had too clear a run for too long. But one charge that will be made I must refute from the outset. That I am critical of American conservatism and its impact on the United States and the globe does not mean that I am anti-American. I have been careful to distinguish the American liberal and conservative traditions throughout. The world has been lucky over the twentieth century that at key junctures the politicians running the United States, and the dominant discourse, have been liberal. We need them back. It is through a coalition between liberal America and a European Union confident about its values that a benign world order can be constructed. For non-American and non-European readers, this does not mean I neglect your proper claims and interests; I am merely being hardheaded about where power lies and to whom global responsibilities fall.

For this is also a book championing the idea of a liberal America. The United States is a remarkable country. Its noble traditions of democracy, its vitality, and its commitment to the acquisition of education—one of the first institutions each of the new states of the union began was a university—continue to inspire. But all this is now obscured by rampant inequality and an increasingly feral capitalism, together with an overblown conservative rhetoric that prevents self-knowledge and intelligent self-criticism. Indeed, it is my affection for the best of America that makes me so angry that it has fallen so far from the standards it expects of itself. Nor do I share the condescension that some Europeans express for American culture. I enjoy Sheryl Crow and Clint Eastwood alike; delight in Woody Allen, *The Sopranos,* and *Six Feet Under;* love American football; am in awe of the intellectual firepower marshaled at the United States's great universities; and am grateful for Windows 98 (and 2000) and the Internet—only the latest in a long line of inventions the United States has bequeathed to the world.

I have never doubted that the United States had to respond to the terrorist attacks of September 11 by military intervention in Afghanistan; terrorism needs a place to operate from, and the elimination of its physical sites is a crucial precondition for eliminating terrorism. But I have always coupled this support with a demand for genuine economic and social reconstruction and the building of a more just international order less likely to incubate terrorism. What has been dismaying has been the readiness of the United States to embark on the first element of response while substantially neglecting the second. The victors of World War II would not have made the same mistake, spending many billions of dollars on strengthening an already impregnable military position while refusing to increase aid flows to the underdeveloped world to remotely adequate levels or develop multilateral institutions—but that was before the calamitous rise of conservatism.

Moreover, as should be clear from the notes and references, I have said nothing about the United States that Americans have not said themselves. Without the existing body of critical American literature the book could not have been written. Those who try to win this argument by name-calling critics of the current order "anti-American" serve themselves badly. There are plenty of Americans who will find themselves in some agreement with what follows, and as anxious as any European to develop a less one-sided world order. We simply freeze argument and exchange if all criticism gets dismissed as anti-American and thus invalid.

One last point. "Liberalism" means different things in the United States, Britain, and Europe. I have adopted the American usage. Liberalism in the United States is the creed that advocates a rational, universal infrastructure of justice built on complex trade-offs between liberty, solidarity, and equality—and this is sufficiently near European conceptions of liberalism for the term to work in both contexts. "Liberal" or "neo-liberal" economics, however, is free-market economics asserting the primacy of individualism, which I have chosen to call "conservative" throughout to avoid ambiguities over the use of "liberal." American readers will know that there are a number of shades of conservatism; again for ease of exposition I have simply called them all conservative. Neo-conservatives are the animating element in the conservative coalition, but as long as the coalition holds together as a cohesive political and social force it seems reasonable to group the various strands under one rubric.

That's it. "Interdependence" has become a dirty word. This is my attempt at its resurrection.

1
The Reckoning

America's founding fathers proclaimed liberty as the essential value. Liberty and its two associated beliefs, independence and individualism, are what every American holds dear and have made the country an inspiration both to those who live in it and to those who would copy it. It was these beliefs that fired Americans into opposition to the great twentieth-century threats to liberty—communism and fascism—from which the United States emerged as the noble victor. Many millions around the globe have reason to thank America.

Yet, even at the outset of its history, liberty alone could not succor the country. Other Enlightenment values forced themselves upon the framers of the Constitution and the United States's early political and cultural life, notably that all men are created equal. The good society is about more than the protection of individual liberty and promotion of the independence of spirit. It affords possibilities of communal action and expression of the public will. A good society acknowledges that human endeavor is a judicious mixture of independent and interdependent action. It recognizes that a collective agency, the state, should ensure that all citizens may express their talents, guard against life's unavoidable hazards, and have fair opportunity for self-betterment. For these reasons, Americans invented federal and state government and have used them to express the interdependence of its citizens. Independence and interdependence are values that have stood in mutual but creative tension.

At this century's beginning, however, this is no longer true. A notion of "independence fundamentalism" has come close to snuffing out interdependence as an animating value in American life. The validity of the public realm is under assault, and much of what it means to be a citizen is consigned to the sphere of the private. Government and its tools of regulation and taxation are portrayed as coercive and restrictive of liberty—un-American and illegitimate. It follows that the capacity to embrace a common destiny and a social contract has been corroded and diminished.

Inequality of income, already offensive, has leached into and devalued America's proudest asset—its promise of opportunity and social mobility. Wealth is not understood solely as the reward for individual enterprise but also as a badge of individual worth. The poor and disadvantaged often are said to deserve their status. In its dealings abroad, the United States tires of alliances and multilateralism. The same passionate belief in independence and "American exceptionalism" leads it to go it alone in the world. Such autonomy undermines the fabric of treaties and international institutions that need America for their effectiveness and legitimacy, and from which the United States has gained so much.

This very particular brand of conservatism, now a generation old, has spread beyond America's shores to claim scalps across the world, notably in Britain. The great liberal ideas that supported Western civilization and the transatlantic alliance are under siege. Europeans now stand alone in holding that the fruits of a successful economy should be spread around to create a fair society, that inequality of income and opportunity should as far as possible be countered, and that government is the trustee of mechanisms through which social concerns, preferences, and citizenship can be expressed. The West is at odds as never before, and American liberalism has all but collapsed.

The Barren Triumph of Conservatism

Even so, interdependence will reassert itself. America faces great challenges in the next decade—how to restore growth and integrity to the market economy; how to put behind it the stock market bubble and epic scale of corporate corruption; how to promote genuine opportunity for all in a society structured to favor the advantaged; how to use its power to promote a peaceful international order driven by American values such as liberty, democracy, justice, and the rule of law. The new conservative fundamentalism has no convincing answers to these acute problems. Its prescriptions led to the bonfire of regulations so skillfully manipulated by self-serving accountants, bankers, and corporate boards. In the process they enriched themselves and betrayed the confidence of their employees, customers, and mainstream investors. Further, this free-market fundamentalism has left the country with a deadly legacy of personal and corporate debt and a trade deficit so colossal that it is as dependent as a drug addict, strung out on a never-ending inflow of foreign capital. Conservative antistate fundamentalism has eroded America's social contract, and with it avenues to opportunity through education and the university system. In a land preoccupied with upholding a nineteenth-century concept of national sovereignty, with its overwhelming stress on military capability as the guarantor of order, American legitimacy and the international appeal of American values have been menaced.

For in the conservative lexicon, freedom and individualism, especially for business and the propertied, are seen as trumping any assertion of the public interest or social concerns. The law of private property rules supreme. In this climate, taxation is depicted as confiscation, a burden that must be reduced. The collective and public realms are portrayed as the enemies of prosperity and individual autonomy and, worse, as opposed to the moral basis of society, grounded as it should be in the absolute responsibility of individuals to shoulder their burdens and exercise their rights alone.

These principles have never added up to a sustainable or workable philosophy, even before corporate skullduggery exposed their frailties. Public structures and social contract are of profound importance in expressing collective choices: American society today perpetuates that the rich stay dominant and the poor remain trapped at the bottom, tragically nullifying its enduring myth of dynamic social mobility. In the long run, the conservative economic model does not work. For wealth creation *is* a social act. Companies that last and prosper are motivated by a vision of their purpose that transcends the stock price. A productive and creative workforce is not treated as economic chattels but as respected human beings. Business organizations profit from their social and public milieu, in which they are embedded and where they trade; this, and an educated workforce, savvy about social relationships, is good for business. But they don't emerge spontaneously from the interplay of market forces. The stronger a country's society, the stronger its business community. The impact of the collapse of business ethics extends well beyond the boardroom; it threatens the wellsprings of enterprise, because it menaces the integrity of the organizations that deliver wealth.

Nor does the malign impact of privileging market relationships above any other stop there. The supremacy of market contract means that careers, living standards, and relationships are in a permanent state of contingency, dependent upon the next twist in the markets' volatile judgments and increasingly unprotected by commonly held institutions or systems for sharing risk. Civility is under siege as a market society makes strangers of us all. While public horizons shrink, Americans search for satisfaction and contentment in their inner, private lives. This turning in signals a recognition that engagement with the world, on any terms other than those that enthrone market values and diminish those of public citizenship, is increasingly without purpose.

The same economic and social frailties extend to the international system. The so-called Washington consensus, enshrining balanced budgets, a shrinking state, and deregulation, supposes that every country in the world will respond to the same medicine because one conservative remedy fits all of capitalism. Yet economic development is more complex. The world is discovering that markets, especially financial markets, need to be governed if they are to offer a stable platform for growth and investment. Further, the accountability, transparency, and effectiveness of these governing institutions need to be carefully nurtured.

Moreover, capitalist dynamism springs from a multilayered interrelationship between the public and the private. Such subtleties and importance are not understood by conservative ideologists. Developing countries as disparate as Turkey and Argentina are buckling under mountainous debts (in 2001, Argentina's default was the biggest ever recorded). The two countries are unable to mediate between financial-market demands for robust economic performance around the Washington model and their restive populations' wish for better living standards. No support exists, except emergency bailouts, to buy themselves the crucial commodity of time. Amid economic breakdown and the discrediting of their political classes, dangerous ideologies flourish. Turkey witnesses the rise of Islamist fundamentalism; Argentina moves toward ungovernability.

More advanced industrialized countries don't do much better living with the consequences of, essentially, a single global financial market. The stock market bubble of the late 1990s was synchronized in every major Western country. As capital controls declined and Wall Street's speculative instruments proliferated, advanced countries around the world experienced the same bubble, and the consequent crash. No strong instruments exist through which to attempt an internationally coordinated response. The world is paying a heavy price for the frothy 1990s. The legacy of debt, collapse in the confidence of company balance sheets, and bankruptcy may dog our economies for years. There needs to be change.

But is change possible? The triumph of faith in unfettered markets and corporate leadership has had baleful consequences. As the last remnants of the postwar liberal ascendancy inherited from Roosevelt's New Deal have been shattered, American capitalism and society have become harsher, more unequal, less generous. The America that could launch the Great Society program in the 1960s has disappeared as completely as the America that initiated the Marshall Plan after World War II. Of course, American liberalism made mistakes and conservatism has its points. Key social programs, notably affirmative action and some elements of American welfare, had unwanted and undesirable side effects. In championing the interests of minorities in the particularistic and divisive way they did, liberals neglected to nurture the universal values that unite all Americans. Likewise, there have been benefits from the conservative pressure to deregulate. For example, both cheap mass air travel and the rapid development of the information society have been helped by freer markets and deregulation.

Yet for all that, the U.S. economy constructed around fundamentalist conservative principles is too volatile. Also, its underlying performance, despite the claim to a productivity miracle, is not nearly as strong as conservatives pretend. A disproportionate responsibility for successful economic management falls to one institution—the U.S. Federal Reserve, the country's central bank. Personal and business debt have ballooned. The trade deficit cannot continue to expand indefinitely. The social consequences of inequality are impacting social mobility and the integrity of the political system alike. The bottom half of American society is treated wretchedly. Deregulation has contributed to the auditing and financial scandals that plague Wall Street. American conservatism has little reason to boast; it is time for more skepticism about its alleged achievements. Any rational calculation of the overall costs and benefits of the conservative experiment must give a negative result.

The costs mount if the calculation is extended to include what has happened through the extension of conservative principles abroad. No global infrastructure even attempting to govern markets is in place because conservative America has been opposed to it. It has sought to maximize its own freedom to maneuver rather than setting up what it portrays as constraining rules. American national sovereignty—America First—is seen not just as a principle that bolsters corporate economic freedom but as a philosophical and moral imperative.

As early as the 1970s and 1980s the United States looked outside the international framework of treaties and institutions to secure what it wanted by unilateral action. This process has accelerated during the Bush presidency—so that on climate change, on the regulation of international criminality and financial markets, and over the system of international nuclear missile treaties, its stance has been defined by assertion of the U.S. position. Oddly, America's interests and its obligation to extend its values to the rest of the world might be better pursued by persuasion and embedding the rule of law in multilateral processes. But this idea has been mocked and derided. Instead, the new view, challenged by even America's closest allies, is that what America says must rule; that the capacity to act autonomously is more important than respect for law and international process.

Things might have changed after September 11, 2001. The United States, it was said, would reengage with the world as it sought to build and sustain a coalition against terrorism. But its go-it-alone instincts soon returned. Victory in Afghanistan after three months, with the loss of a handful of American lives, proved its vast military superiority and was gained with only token allied support. In the defense of the "homeland," the old conservative urges to secure America behind a unilateralist military shield are rampant. Witness the Bush administration's request in early 2002 for a $48 billion rise in defense expenditure (equivalent to Italy's entire defense budget), despite the fact that disparity between U.S. defense spending and the rest of the world's has already reached unprecedented levels.[1] On the whole, the coalitions America builds are tactical and self-interested. NATO may have offered its collective help in the action against terrorism, but acceptance might have compromised U.S. choices and it was not called upon. Allies may be allowed to help the United States but only by invitation, and on American terms. It was left mainly to the European Union (EU) to provide peacekeeping and the financing of Afghanistan reconstruction. The mindset that fueled unilateralism and built global capitalism on conservative terms remains entrenched.[2]

A profound irony is at play here. No doubt America's military superiority will yield relatively painless victories. In acting unilaterally, however, the United States will have delegitimized precisely those values, especially respect for law, that will be needed in the ensuing political vacuum. Any effort to rebuild nations around democratic principles will be profoundly compromised. A new principle for disorder in the Middle East—the law of the jungle—may well rise. In short, everybody should play by the same rules: observance of international law and refusal to harbor terrorists. Legitimacy is a priceless asset, easily lost and hard to regain. America throws it away at its own peril. It was well advised to seek and gain a UN resolution on Iraq: such multilateralism should be strategic and embedded rather than obviously skin deep.

The big question—how to construct a just international society and a just capitalism—has taken on increased urgency with the emergence of international terrorism. The West needs to build a system in which the ideologies that succor terrorism are less likely to flourish. The leading European countries—Britain, France, and Germany—wish to uphold a framework of international law and reproduce the United States's own generosity after World War II with a new "Marshall Plan." But conservative Washington drags its feet. It obstructs the evolution of international law and accompanying institutions. It objects to the development of an International Criminal Court, not understanding that any loss of American sovereignty (in any case trivial) is vastly offset by American gains in legitimacy and a capacity to build consensus against rogue states and rogue actions. The United States is shamed into making aid contributions rather than leading the process. If Europe is less than full-hearted about opening its markets to poorer countries, the United States sets no better example. Its preoccupations are increasingly militaristic: to repress the symptoms of the problem rather than address its cause. America's intervention in Kosovo in 1999 to prevent ethnic slaughter looks increasingly like the last act of the best of the twentieth-century United States. The twenty-first-century United States, so far, is a darker, less altruistic country.

Justice, and how it is expressed economically and socially, has become the overriding issue of our times. We need a rounded and more humane interpretation than we are getting from American conservatives. We also need firmer mechanisms to regulate American finance and sturdier international governance. A lack of these is not just a democratic offense. It menaces the future.

There can be no durable settlement of the world's problems without America; but without an America that accepts interdependence, there can be no such settlement. The strengthening of the American liberal tradition that will argue for these values is thus central to any such project. It has become a global concern that the liberal tradition reclaim its position as a force in American life. To succeed in its battle with American conservatism, it needs to reconnect to the Enlightenment principles that still dominate Europe, and rediscover a language that works in an American context and can again popularize its appeal among the American majority.

This creed is not dead. It has resisted conservatives' attempts to dictate family and sexual life. America is the home of modern feminism, and among Americans there is a strain of powerful social liberalism that is suspicious of conservative moral absolutism over abortion, sexual preferences, the role of women, and indifference to poverty. There are signs, too, that less vengeful attitudes toward criminal justice and the death penalty are gaining ground. The United States has a proud record of social and environmental movements, and the civil rights movement achieved important gains for blacks. A strong, if currently cowed, tradition of genuine liberal egalitarianism has always championed education for all, a sincere belief in equality of opportunity, and a generous neighborliness. Ordinary citizens have been appalled by the excesses of the 1990s and wonder what was gained; many again are becoming concerned by the silting up of opportunity and the discordance between the conservative rhetoric of opportunity and the reality.

Nor is patriotism as universally aggressive and militaristic as the rhetoric of the conservative cabal would have us believe. There is another American patriotism with a powerful sense of duty not only to America but to the world—the America of Grant, Marshall, and Eisenhower—and whose values still imbue parts of the American military's high command. This group does not consider itself liberal, but it understands and respects interdependence nonetheless. The United States is a continent; there are a multitude of individual states and cities that still guard and protect liberal values and accompanying institutions. Over time, conservative ascendancy has prompted a reinvigorated liberalism in almost predictable cycles; perhaps America stands on the threshold of another such moment.

For the time being, however, a militant conservativism rules. Eyeing the vacuum left by an America less willing to lead and more ready to impose its view, powerful voices in Europe argue that Europe must wear the multilateralist, liberal leadership mantle once assumed by the United States. Indeed this book, written by a European, argues that this responsibility now falls to the EU, however imperfectly it is organized. The EU must protect its own vision of capitalism and its accompanying social contract as well as be the alternative pole around which a more enlightened and liberal global order can be formed.

America, the natural partner of Europe and home of the great eighteenth-century European Enlightenment tradition, should not find itself opposing the development of international law, human rights, and multilateral institutions and governance. It should take its founding principles into the coming century. This will not only serve American interests; it is the right thing to do. America, in short, needs to rediscover the best of itself.

It Can't Go On like This

The United States's 280 million people share the same language, government, market, and legal system. Its companies have organized production on a scale unknown in other countries, taking advantage of the simple rule that as more is cumulatively produced, unit costs go down. Moreover, corporate America benefits from a workforce well aware that as market conditions change, it may be fired at will with minimal compensation and forced to move to find work. In short, it must accommodate to market requirements. Successive waves of immigrants—topped, now, by ten million Hispanic immigrants over the 1990s from Central and South America—have provided a pool of cheap and willing labor; along the way, they've bought into the great American work ethic and a dream that nothing is impossible if you work hard enough. Abundant and cheap land has made Americans unfussy over planning and the environment. Towns and factory sites rise and fall depending on the vitality of their economic base. And Americans are risk takers, culturally dismissing failure and moving on in their large country to new prospects. Always at the ready are a flow of rich investors and markets prepared to support innovation.

Possessing these advantages of scale, cheap land, and cheap labor—coupled with more than a little native enterprise, the United States should be a highly productive economy. To be sure, the United States does enjoy higher average incomes per head than western Europe. But that's not the whole story. In fact, though this is little reported, over the last twenty years output per hour worked in France, the Netherlands, Belgium, and the former West Germany has surpassed that in the United States.[3] Why? Because the Europeans have invested more. Output per hour is only fractionally lower in Ireland, Austria, and Denmark. The only European country not to have significantly closed the productivity gap with the United States is Britain. Any American economic advantage flows from the facts that, proportionally, more American women work and that, on average, American men and women work longer hours. Put another way, Europeans have chosen to invest heavily in order to work shorter weeks, have longer vacations, and still produce the same for every hour they work, if not more, than Americans—a perfectly reasonable choice. True, some larger European countries have a weaker record in generating jobs than the United States (most of the smaller European countries do just as well), but not because they are less productive; rather, it is because fewer of their women, young people in training and higher education, and older people are in the labor market. Again, this is an explicit social choice.

Successful capitalism results from a subtle interplay between forces. On one hand, we have the infrastructure, institutions, and regulations created by government and society; on the other, the incentives and signals that profit-seeking entrepreneurs look for in a market economy. To rely wholly on the "market," without regulation and institution building, is to build upon a false prospectus. We have seen all too clearly how much financial markets need solid and effective systems of regulation. Without them, hype, hucksters, and abuses thrive. Finance left to its own devices is impatient, short term, and volatile; it operates best—and most benefits society—within a framework of smart regulation that limits its own destructive propensities. Too much government and regulation, of course, can obstruct innovation. The task, forgotten in the conservative revolution, is to mix judiciously the roles of government and the market, as Europe does, and which the United States neglects to do.

Where America has enjoyed success, it has profited more from this subtle interplay between state and market than conservatives want to believe. As Barry Bluestone and Bennett Harrison describe in their important book *Growing Prosperity,* the recent rise of productivity in information and communication technology (ICT) was no more than a typical phenomenon of productivity gains working themselves through the economy after a paradigm-changing technological innovation. History has many such examples. Moreover, the ICT revolution was itself spearheaded by government investment, led by the Pentagon; the Internet, for example, grew out of a decentralized networked system developed to coordinate the responses of a multiplicity of military decision-making and operational sites. U.S. leadership in satellite and aerospace technology has been generated directly from defense spending, although recently that has been challenged by Europe's Airbus. Even ubiquitous high-tech "ideopolises"— clusters of high-tech companies and new start-ups around leading universities—are not free-market phenomena. Federal- and state-funded research generates the intellectual capital at their core. And although the venture capital industry, at least until the bubble burst, played a key role in funding the start-ups—it operated in a social milieu and within a set of networks that celebrated technology and risk—it was always singularly short term and greedy. Now that the markets are in reverse and government spending on research is decreasing, this whole delicate mechanism is endangered.

In fact, the quest for high short-term profitability finally set spinning a pitiless and self-defeating vortex. Corporate strategies now embrace aggressive cost reduction, together with investment minimalism and a peripatetic approach to hiring and growth. It is a syndrome uniting most of the Fortune 500, be they oil companies like Exxon or the once lauded GE.[4] As recently as the late 1980s, Americans fretted that their companies were losing ground to European and Asian competitors; education and training of the labor force were poor, the investment record was indifferent, and a weakening capacity to compete internationally across a range of industries was exposed by the growing trade deficit. American companies, it was identified, concentrated more on financial engineering, merger, and takeover than on building value through the patient business of investment and husbanding of human resources. In 1992, for example, Larry Summers, a future U.S. Treasury Secretary, contributed a paper to the Harvard Business School Time Horizons Project confirming that U.S. companies wanted investment to pay back in incredibly short periods and were setting very high rates of return, compared to other major economies; as a result they invested less across the board. During the 1990s those weaknesses were temporarily masked. Now that the economic tide again recedes, they are back in view.

At bottom, this syndrome owes much to the gospel of maximization of shareholder value, a fixation on the stock price that has become the alpha and omega of American corporate life. Its virtue, seen from the boardroom, is that it offers a scale of personal enrichment that beggars belief. Company directors and chief executives did not need to embezzle or defraud to make their millions; such riches emanated organically from a system that awards them generous stock options. Cumulative value of these options in the United States in 2000 amounted to some $600 billion, a tenfold jump in a decade—one of the greatest wealth transfers recorded in world history. In this environment, for example, the $200-million-a-year package achieved at the peak of the boom by Michael Eisner, chief executive of Disney, was no longer remarkable, but merely another temporary benchmark that others aimed to match. America's extraordinarily rule-free system of corporate governance allowed Eisner to construct a board of directors at Disney packed with cronies, who voted him the cash. This board included the principal of his children's elementary school, the actor

Sidney Poitier, the architect who designed Eisner's Aspen home, and a university president whose school received a $1 million donation from the CEO.

The message was and is explicit: Don't mind the gap between rich and poor; play the weaknesses in the system. After all, it's merely part and parcel of "wealth generation"; eventually, everyone benefits. Yet Disney has not performed especially well. This cynicism pervades the American corporate sector; the *Financial Times* reports that the top executives in the twenty-five largest companies that went bankrupt in the eighteen months up to July 2002 amassed $3.3 billion in the months before bankruptcy through stock sales.[5] The notion that the United States just suffers from a few bad corporate apples is wrong; the rottenness is systemic.

Such indifference has strongly driven American income inequality. The gap between the top and bottom 10 percent of earners is so large that those Americans at the bottom are poorer than the bottom 10 percent in most other industrialized countries—the United States ranks nineteenth. Concurrently, the United States has the highest average per capita incomes.[6] But contrary to conservative belief, inequality is not a source of economic or social strength. It reduces social mobility and ossifies the United States into a class society—the rich gain a stranglehold on the elite educational qualifications that pave the way to the top, while those at the bottom are trapped by low skills and low incomes. U.S. social and income mobility is no higher than in Europe, and by some measures, it is actually worse.

Moreover, as Professor Robert Frank details in his subtle and important book *Luxury Fever*, inequality has led to almost baroque levels of personal spending. The United States now has over three million millionaires, and they spend extravagantly on everything from their trophy houses to oversized, overpowered cars to $20,000 vacations. Such largesse lures the middle class. The average new American house is now 2,200 square feet, having expanded from 1,500 square feet in 1970, as the middle class trades up to meet a new standard of opulence.[7]

A paradox lurks here, however. Hawkish companies bent on maximizing value for shareholders are constraining the growth of real wages; it follows that spending nationally on this scale has been sustained only by debt. By mid-2001 personal debt in the United States had climbed to a record 120 percent of personal income; and the net annual flow of credit to consumers has been running at some $800 billion a year at an annualized rate.[8] Astonishingly, in the first three months of 2001 American consumers spent 7 percent more than they earned by using their credit cards and borrowing capacity to the limit. The rationale: if personal borrowing was high, so were the assets against which the borrowing was made. But this was hardly a sustainable position. It depended too much on the feelgood factor or wealth effects generated by rising stock and property prices.

In the mid-1980s Americans held only a quarter of their savings on Wall Street; now the proportion stands at nearly three-quarters, making the relationships between stock-price movements, wealth effects, and spending even closer. As of autumn 2002, the relationship that produced such surges in spending in the 1990s threatens to go into reverse, leaving the economy delicately poised. Wall Street has suffered a dramatic fall, and with stocks still valued high by historical standards—some 50 percent higher in real terms than any other peak over the last 100 years[9]—and the rate of economic recovery weak, the prospect looms of further declines. American consumers are suddenly discovering that the wealth they borrowed against has eroded considerably. Confidence is dropping; so is spending. Meanwhile overborrowed American corporations, many forced into more conservative profit assessments through stricter accounting standards, have pulled back on their own spending and investment plans. Skepticism about the productivity gains of the 1990s contributes to a sense of the economy returning to earth. Will the economy dip again into recession? Whatever the immediate prognosis, clearly neither consumers nor companies will spend so lavishly over the next five years as they did over the last five. The United States is heading for soberer times.

Imports pose another problem. As American consumers spend and uncompetitive U.S. industry fails to meet demand, so the United States has sucked in imports on an epic scale. The U.S. trade deficit reached $477 billion in 2000 and scarcely fell in the two subsequent years. These are incredible numbers—more than 4 percent of gross domestic product (GDP). America can square the financial circle without the dollar collapsing only because foreigners flock to invest in the United States on an equally epic scale, spending more than $100 billion a year directly buying American companies and more than $150 billion a year purchasing American stocks and bonds. Foreign ownership of American assets doubled to $6.7 trillion between 1995 and 2000, equivalent to some two-thirds of American GDP. Without such inflows the U.S. economy could not continue to grow; yet they are unlikely to double again over the next five years.[10] Put another way, the net international investment position in 2000 was minus $2.187 billion, a fifth of GDP: if America achieves only modest economic growth and if trade deficits remain steady and the dollar holds, the United States's international debts will explode to between half and two-thirds of U.S. GDP over the next five to seven years, a completely unsustainable position.[11] The inflow of foreign capital depends entirely on an expectation that good times will continue to roll. In any case, such inflow is dwarfed by the size of the trade deficit and deteriorating international balance sheet. If foreigners come to believe that stock prices might fall, there could be only one consequence: the dollar would drop sharply. It began to do so during the summer of 2002, as precisely this process began. It is a commonplace among economists that the dollar needs to fall by as much as 30 percent to correct the trade deficit. A plunge of this magnitude would trigger potential inflation and a rise in interest rates. This would almost certainly trigger a further deep fall on Wall Street toward more normal levels, and the consequence would be a recession of awesome proportion, as declines in consumer and investment spending become self-feeding. So bleak is this prospect that conservative America will resist it. Trade protection—witness 25 percent tariffs on steel—will be a more tempting option.

Thus the American economy has rested on a confidence trick; and if either of its twin supporters, foreign investors or domestic consumers, were to withdraw their backing, the economy would languish for years while the imbalances work themselves out. Thus policymakers consecrate all their efforts to maintaining growth, and confidence. Hence the 4.5 percent cut in short-term interest rates between autumn 2000 and autumn 2001; hence further proactive easing of monetary policy in November 2002 even with interest rates at a forty-year low of 1.75 percent. Hence the way the incoming Bush administration presented its ten-year tax-cutting package skewed to help the rich as a growth package. And hence, after September 11, the further proposed tax-cutting package, allegedly to stimulate growth. But unless underlying causes are addressed, all that merely defers the reckoning. Clearly, the chairman of the Federal Reserve, Alan

Greenspan, may have helped keep the boom going by his interest-rate policy and his commentary, touting a new source of productivity growth in the ITC revolution. Now he is widely understood to have landed the United States with an even bigger economic headache by not doing more to prick the speculative bubble.

In their rut, the Bush administration and its surrounding conservatives continue to press their case for tax cuts for the rich and corporations, along with minimal reform of company governance and financial systems. The "economic summit" in Texas in August 2002, packed with Republican supporters, sang the same old refrain. Given the nation's challenges—a weakened public infrastructure, widespread poverty and insecurity, a need to sustain overall spending, and declining faith in corporate enterprise in the face of productivity-growth malaise and corporate fraud—this rehashed clutch of conservative ideas seems almost frivolous. The United States's awesome budgetary strength, which the departing Clinton left Bush, has been squandered in under two years. Tax cuts, increased defense spending, and forecasts of lower economic growth have shrunk government budget surplus projections for the decade by a stunning $5 trillion, with precious little to show for it.

Despite these failures and obvious challenges, conservative dominance of the cultural and political agenda remains. The scope of welfare, and access to it, has been pared away with the scarcely subliminal message that the recipients are largely black and the taxpayers who fund it largely white. The United States possesses the best doctors, hospitals, and medical technology in the world, but forty-three million of its people remain without any form of health insurance.[12] The United States has a top tier of world-class universities, but they exist alongside a public education system creaking at the seams; U.S. students achieve among the lowest math scores in international rankings.[13] The country's physical infrastructure is run-down and crumbling.

In one area conservatives consider public spending legitimate—countering crime through building prisons. The United States, with 5 percent of the world's population, houses 25 percent of the world's prisoners, locking up nearly 700 people per 100,000. This is the highest incarceration rate in the world. Here America's repudiation of the social contract under its conservative leadership has reached its apogee. Prison is overtly approved as a means of neutralizing troublesome adults (most of them black) and placing them outside society with minimal opportunity for reentry. There is little attempt at rehabilitation. Only 30 percent of prisoners see a parole board before release. The presumption is that sentences should be fully served, whatever the behavior of the prisoner, because the task is punitive rather than restorative. With those who have transgressed the law, there is no social contract whatsoever. The chance of released prisoners achieving any form of legitimate work is close to nil; two-thirds return within three years. The dehumanization of prisoners has been accompanied by increasing violence in the way they are treated, with guards resorting to chemical and electric shock treatments to achieve restraint. Moreover, the disenfranchising of convicted felons, a withdrawal of citizenship most widespread in the South, has created 4.7 million disenfranchised voters, 2.3 percent of the electorate. Most of them, given the chance, probably would vote Democrat. In Florida 7 percent of potential voters are disenfranchised felons—a key reason why in 2000 George Bush won the state and thus the presidency. Disenfranchisement was a potent political weapon in sustaining white supremacy in the post-Reconstruction south; now it is an important instrument in sustaining Republican rule at the state and national level.

This, then, is contemporary America. Like the nursery rhyme's little girl with a little curl in the middle of her forehead, when America is good it is very, very good—but when it is bad, it is horrid. If it is rich and entrepreneurial, it is also economically volatile, profoundly unequal, and not nearly as productive as it could be, given its enormous assets. Its democracy, one of the great Enlightenment triumphs, at the local level is more genuinely democratic than almost any comparable country. At the national level, however, it now resembles pre-Enlightenment Europe in its dependence on money and private power. This is a country of welcoming neighbors, who routinely accept murderous shooting with little protest. It is a country that proclaims its dedication to opportunity and upward mobility even as they wither—a process about which the country is in total denial. It is a country of well-run cities and world-beating universities sitting side by side with urban squalor and underachieving public schools. This is where worship at church is rivaled only by worship of the shopping mall. It is becoming a land of individual strangers questing for inner happiness because so much beyond them is corrupt and depleted. It is a country losing its sense of self-restraint, obligation, and interdependence. And the whole is overshadowed by a tenacious racism, the legacy of so many centuries of slavery and failed attempts to integrate black and white.

The American dream is of the pursuit of life, liberty, and happiness; but the gap between dream and reality is lived out daily with increasing bitterness. America fails almost half its citizens. Cynicism about public and cultural rhetoric compared with actual experience is profound. Yet American idealism lies just below the surface, ready to be rekindled in the quest to create something better. This is perhaps America's greatest asset: its passionate belief in a positive future and its ready embrace of all that is modern. America needs to look itself in the eye, demand change, and act. The Old World from which most Americans emigrated still has something to offer the New.

There Are Alternatives

All Western democracies subscribe to a broad family of ideas that are liberal or leftist:

- a belief in the primacy of society and respect for its rules and mores;
- concern about the divisive nature of inequality;
- the importance of providing universal public services;
- the need to regulate enterprise, because of its propensity for instability, excess, and monopoly;
- the conviction that all—from minorities to ex-prisoners—have the right to be included in society, implying a stress on tolerance, integration, and rehabilitation;
- the view that workers are assets rather than disposable costs.

Equally there is another broad family of ideas that might be called rightist:

- an honoring of our inherited institutional fabric;

- a respect for order;
- a belief that private property rights and profit are essential to the operation of the market economy;
- a suspicion of workers' rights;
- faith in the remedial value of punitive justice;
- distrust of the new;
- prioritizing liberty above other values of equality and social justice.

These traditions constitute the essential discourse of a democracy. At different times one set of values and policies is more appropriate for the continuing vitality of a country than at others. In Britain, for example, few would dispute that in the early 1980s the country needed conservative Thatcherism to reignite its failing market economy; equally few would deny that in the early years of this century Britain badly needs to rebuild its neglected public services and corroded social contract under the leadership of the Labour party. It is out of this competition between liberal and conservative that a country constructs its political life. In the full heat of political dialogue both sides insist that the other is irredeemably wrong, but there is also a parallel, unspoken recognition that the debate keeps both sides honest, and that democracy needs both political traditions to flourish and do its essential job.

In this respect the United States suffers from a substantive democratic deformation. Compared with the European conservative tradition, the American right is indifferent to inequalities of income, property, and wealth. It massively distrusts the state, except the military. It will not accept the legitimacy or importance of the social contract. It celebrates individualism and the pursuit of liberty but it has no place for the French Revolutionary values of equality and fraternity. It has an extraordinary view of America's vocation in its relationship with the rest of the world. It believes fervently in American exceptionalism, as though Americans are a people apart, with different instincts, needs, and values from others.

Ironically, it is the Constitution that has shaped the character of American conservatism and helped create its unique power. This remarkable document provides an admirable protection of individual liberties, so that from freedom of information to freedom of speech, Americans enjoy a degree of entrenched rights that is a global exemplar. However, the Constitution defines citizenship in essentially political terms: the right to vote, enjoy a fair trial, or, famously, to bear arms. Thus this same Constitution is paradoxically a source of weakness for the liberal wing of American politics. Protecting economic and social rights is beyond its scope, and the political rights it does defend can be easily portrayed as for the individual and against government—a gift to the conservatives. The judicial component of the Constitution, notably the nine-member Supreme Court, defines itself as the protector of this essentially conservative order.

At moments in American life the Supreme Court has sided with progressive elements in American society. Notably it advanced the cause of civil rights in the South during the 1950s and 1960s. But in the main it has been a bastion of conservatism, defending governmental minimalism and the primacy of individual property rights. Its most consummate conservative moment came in the famous judgment on the disputed hand recounts in Florida in the presidential election of 2000. The court in effect gifted the election to George W. Bush by accepting that while hand recounts were reasonable in principle, they were not as practiced in Florida, because, it alleged, recounts in this particular election (but not others) were particularly likely to be subjective. However, it demanded neither a fresh election nor a recount of all the votes cast in Florida. The vote went five to four, reflecting the conservative/liberal split among the judges. Bush would have won on the basis of the votes cast in the disputed four counties anyway (though he would have lost in Florida overall if so-called over votes—where a voter marks their ballot in more than one way to indicate their preferred candidate—had been included).[14] Still it remains, as Vincent Bugliosi has so passionately written, the most partisan legal judgment in recent political history.[15]

The European conception of rights is much broader, and judicial obstruction to economic and social advance is much less. The right to free health, the right to free education, the right to unemployment insurance, the right to fair treatment at work, and so on—all are regarded as key parts of the social contract and as elements of citizenship just as important as political freedoms. Beginning with the New Deal, American liberals have won parallel rights for Americans in education and trade unions, but these are derogations from the basic minimalist, individualistic model. As such, their legitimacy has always been disputed by the political right. Frustrated by conservative opposition, the Democrats have never been able, for example, to develop Medicaid and Medicare into a national health plan for all Americans. A view that such a plan would imply too much federal and government power trumps the social argument.

American liberals champion the great ideas of economic and social citizenship, along with the social contract, so deeply rooted in Western civilization. But they do so against a hostile political and cultural backdrop. This is one reason why there has never been a strong socialist or labor movement in the United States. There have been gains—the United States has had a strongly progressive tax system, for example—and there are periods in U.S. history defined by social advance and concern for social justice. It may even be, as commentators John Judis and Ruy Teixeira argue in *The Emerging Democratic Majority*, that the combination of the liberal values of the New Economy spawned by the information revolution, the dynamic growth in the Democrat-voting Hispanic and black population, and growing concerns about the character of American society presage another period of liberal strength. Certainly there are signs that a new liberalism is struggling to make itself heard. Take, for example, attitudes toward criminal justice. A growing proportion of Americans favor rehabilitation rather than unadulterated punishment for criminal offenders. In 1994, 16 percent of Americans thought the purpose of prison should be rehabilitation; in 2001, the proportion had jumped to 40 percent.[16]

Even so, the framework in which this liberalism is stirring is profoundly different from that of Europe, where left and right alike respect some basic liberal ground rules. Europeans conceive the fair society as comprehending a larger, integrative role for the state in conciliating social partners, providing public services, and regulating business and society. The state is not seen as a mere night watchman or umpire; it is an actor, ensuring that risk and reward are fairly distributed in what the liberal political philosopher John Rawls calls an infrastructure of justice. A powerful system of collective insurance underwrites the risks of poor health, disablement, or unemployment. Workers' rights are supported and entrenched. Risks and rewards are not allocated by chance and market forces; rather, their final balance is settled by an activist state, expressing and enforcing the choices made by the community. Europe has been richly endowed with social and political theorists who accent the primacy of the public realm (as Habermas does in Germany), who insist that capitalism must be enmeshed in society (the great Durkheimian sociological tradition), and who argue that the precondition for a just society is a narrowing of inequality (the British–social democratic tradition embodied by Richard Tawney).

Beneath these political values, moreover, lies also a different conception of religion and morality. Europe has long accepted that reason and science are the twin underpinnings and driving forces of Western society, that religious faith cannot trump or obstruct science but must seek reconciliation with it. No European country would accept that the teachings of Darwin, for example, could not be taught because they challenged the precepts of the Bible or that the Bible may be taught as science. The same is not true of the United States, notably in the South. Early settlers believed that America was a holy country with a special divine providence. The same belief is still alive today, giving American Protestantism its particular evangelical and highly personalized character—reinforced by the country's cultural egalitarianism. Ordinary worshipers come to believe that they can be individually blessed and saved—indeed, their standing as self-governing, God-fearing Americans demands no less. They can be and are "born again." As a result, America's religious culture, or at least its dynamic element over the last twenty years, has stressed the morality of individual self-interest and self-help. Social and public initiatives of the type widely supported in Europe and by liberals in the United States are seen as inimical to morality because they minimize individual responsibility.

These are not simple differences of emphasis; they go to the heart of what lies between American and European culture and of how American conservatism has moved so far from Europe's mainstream. Notions and practices of citizenship, fairness, and justice easily cascade into the European conceptions of property, the role of business, welfare, and inequality, and where Europeans draw the boundaries between the public and private sectors. But the crucial point for Americans, and American liberals in particular, is to recognize that the resulting European economic and social model is not inefficient. A fundamental argument of this book is that Europe, contrary to the barrage of conservative propaganda, boasts both a high-performance corporate sector and a fair society. In other words, liberalism—broadly defined—works.

Yet this is not a commonly accepted position, even in Europe. American conservatism's advance at home has been mirrored abroad. Many European conservatives want to copy it—and the European left has lost heart and self-confidence. The British version of this book is aimed as a wake-up call to Europeans. Stop being so feeble; start believing in the achievement of your societies; use the EU as an instrument to protect yourselves. I argue that if these core European values and outcomes are to be sustained in Britain, then Britain must act with other European countries to advance them. If Britain wants to keep a progressive tax system, for example, one that distributes income more fairly, it must not be undercut by other European countries. If Britain wants to reduce carbon dioxide emissions and not lose international competitiveness, then it better persuade other European countries to follow suit. If Britain wishes to regain some control over its exchange rate and interest rates in an environment where the scale of capital movements can unsettle even continents, it must make common cause and pool sovereignty with other Europeans in creating a single currency. And so on—with defense, or the fight against the Mafia and international criminal cartels. In short, Britain needs to overcome its Euroskepticism and fully commit to the European Union.

In an era of globalization, all nation-states need to cooperate and collaborate if they want to represent their citizens' interests. Such cooperation works well among those who share values and goals; and it works best when entrenched in permanent institutions so that each act of collaboration does not have to start anew as if without precedent. Moreover, these institutions need to be accountable, which is why the EU is moving to turn its processes from those of a diplomatic quadrille into more transparent and politically accountable forms. Of course there will be a leftist/rightist argument within this larger Europe as in any democracy, but it needs to respect the basic ground rules that underpin our European civilization.

Here, I think, is the connection between the political tasks in Europe and in the United States, a connection that could reunite the West. The European case would be easier to make if American conservatism's claims were challenged in America for being eccentric and unworkable. Likewise, it would be easier for American liberals if Europe's example and success were fully understood and explained. In today's environment political ideas travel. For too long, American conservatives have been allowed to make the political weather by insisting that America is so incomparably better than Europe that it proves the conservative case. Now, as the bubble bursts, exposing weaknesses in American capitalism, the American mood is changing. The country is willing to be self-critical, and to move on. The argument presented in the American edition of this book is a second wake-up call; American liberals need to stand up and be counted.

Here American liberalism can learn some lessons from the success of conservatism. If the U.S. Constitution offers conservatism a philosophic advantage, it also offers liberalism a practical advantage—unique possibilities of popular engagement and political action. But these must be exploited to the full in the name of another enduring American value—a cultural egalitarianism that demands everybody should have a chance—which is reflected in the Declaration of Independence itself. The European social contract has complex roots in early Christianity and the experience of feudalism. America, however, has parallel values that allow an even more embedded social contract—belief in justice and opportunity for all. It will require more political daring and activism than in Europe to achieve it, but America, fortunately, is equipped with a democratic framework that encourages activism.

American liberalism must now show how collective and social instruments can achieve enduring American aims that transcend individualism and the amassing of personal fortune. This has been done before by the Progressive movement and the New Dealers; it can be done again. Any reasons why America needed a conservative revival have long since passed. Today's exigencies require a response informed by liberalism. American conservatism is an idiosyncratic creed, with only a tenuous relationship to the core values of Western civilization. Just how idiosyncratic, and why it must be bested, is where our study goes next.

2

Custodians of the Light

European civilization is united by a common set of values with respect to four critical and interrelated areas of human life that are distinct from the canons of American conservatism. European attitudes toward property, equality, social solidarity, and the public realm are different from those that currently dominate the discourse on these subjects in the United States. They express themselves in cultural mores, law, and social choices, which in turn shape the way European economies and societies function. Conservatives allege that Europe does not work. My contention is that there are values inescapably part of the European tradition and that these values provide a better compass toward an efficient, fair, and moral economy and society.

In the first place, property is not seen in Europe as an absolute right, as it is by U.S. conservatives. Rather, it is a privilege that confers reciprocal obligations—a notion captured by article 13 of the postwar German constitution, which specifies that "property imposes duties. Its use should also serve the public weal." Those who hold and own property are members of society, and society has a public dimension to which necessarily they must contribute as the quid pro quo for the privilege of exercising property rights. Nor is this attitude toward social obligation just directed at property holders. Across Europe there is a profound commitment to the notion that all citizens should have an equal right to participate in economic and social life, and that the state is more than a safety net of last resort: it is the fundamental vehicle for the delivery of this equality. It is not just the institutions of social order and defense—for example, courts, prisons, and the military—that it is acceptable to hold in common, as American conservatives contend; Europeans extend the ambition to include hospitals, schools, universities, utility networks, and even scientific knowledge. A publicly founded infrastructure supports equality of membership and participation. This principle of participation extends to notions of social solidarity—or "fraternity" as the French constitution would have it, one of the three values on which the French Republic is declared to rest, along with liberty and equality—a constitutional commitment that in some ways speaks for the continent. Fraternity means that Europeans believe in looking out for one another to insure against life's hazards—the principal reason why social spending in Europe runs some 50 percent above that in the United States.

All this implies a much greater role for the public sphere and the state than conservative Americans could countenance. For Europeans, the state and government cannot be so easily portrayed as enemies of the people as they can in the United States (although there are growing concerns about their efficacy and the shortcomings in their accountability); they are seen rather as upholders of, and means of expressing, public values. Europeans expect the state to finance scientific research or, by owning television and radio companies, to serve a notion of public service broadcasting, just as much as they expect the state to tax and spend to provide public goods like defense and education. The public realm is larger than the state, but the state is its most important component. It protects what society holds in common.

The contention of American conservatives is that this complex of values is economically inefficient, socially counterproductive—and immoral, in that it undermines sturdy individualism and obstructs the natural impulses of competitive capitalism. I argue the opposite. Of course some particular manifestations of these principles may be imperfect and susceptible to reform, but the value system that underpins them is perfectly consistent with a high-performance market economy. In one respect the argument is beside the point; for these values, as this chapter will show, are so deeply embedded that they could hardly be changed even if Europeans wanted to relinquish them. They help to define Europeanness. But there is no need to change them. The conservative American list of complaints, on closer examination, proves to be empty—indeed, the kind of capitalism European values generate is in the long run no less productive than the American kind, while respecting instincts that are fundamental to living in a just and civil social order. Europeans, after all, may be right.

Property—the American Conception

North America was discovered as a wilderness pregnant with riches by settlers who had risked all crossing the Atlantic and who, as fervent Protestants, believed they had a direct relationship with God. They carved plantations and farms out of natural forest under attack by—as they saw them—cruel and barbarous savages. But there was no restraint on their capacity to own land, even if the British, through the "headright" system of assigning ownership, which transferred to the colonies the feudal idea that all land was owned by the Crown, maintained the essentially feudal assumption that property was held in trust for all by the Crown and that it was only the Crown that could assign true legal ownership or freehold. On this view—a view of the legitimacy of ownership that would be of fundamental importance in the American War of Independence—it was not the settlers' land to discover and claim, but the Crown's. But whatever the legal stipulations, the headright system for granting land by the distant British Crown was no more than a titular formality—in practice, land was available to all. And, as they fanned out across the thirteen colonies, the mainly English opinion formers deployed John Locke's famous philosophical dicta to justify the claim that what the settlers found and created was theirs—and had nothing to do with the constitutional and political framework that formally assigned ownership. The seeds of dispute, and of a very different conception of property, were being sown.

"In the beginning all the world was America," Locke had proclaimed.[1] If God had given the world to all men in common, then he had certainly given America to the settlers. They were serving God's purpose by taking possession of it and using it for their own individual good. But this was only the beginning. "Men being, as has been said, by Nature, all free, equal and independent, no one can be put out of this Estate, and subjected to the

Political Power of another, without his own *Consent*," Locke had written. "The only way whereby any one divests himself of his Natural Liberty, and puts on the bonds of Civil Society is by agreeing with other Men to join and unite and into a Community, for their comfortable, safe, and peaceable living one amongst another, in a secure Enjoyment of their Properties, and a greater Security against any that are not of it."[2] It was a message picked up by preachers and politicians alike. The purpose of society was to further the enjoyment of property, and political power was only legitimate if it served this end.

Moreover, as he labored, man created his property with God's blessing. "Every man has a property in his own person. There is no body has any right to it but himself. The labour of his body, and the work of his hands we may say are properly his. Whatsoever then he removes out of the state that nature has provided, and left it in, he hath mixed his labour with and joined to it something that is his own, and thereby makes his property."[3] For an early American settler, the proof was conclusive. God had created America; the settler had labored to create a farm against all the odds. The farm was exclusively and completely his, and he owed nothing to anybody—the Crown, government, or any other settler. The good man was the "rational and industrial man" who followed this injunction.

Locke aimed to provide the rationale for both parliamentary government and the emergent capitalism of late-seventeenth-century England, along the way inveighing against the divine right of kings, the doctrine that had prompted the English Civil War. Protestantism, representative government, and private property went hand in hand. But if this was a useful ex-post justification of what was happening in England, it became the governing ideology of the American settlers, to which today's conservative ideas are linked by a golden thread. Government earned its place to the extent it protected liberty and property.

This early settler culture of the new world escaped all the anguished heart-searching of the old world about what the wealthy and propertied owed to the commonweal—a debate that went back to the early days of Christianity. Clement of Alexandria at the end of the second century had foreshadowed American conservative arguments when he argued that to own property was part of God's design; it was only excessive preoccupation with wealth that was damnable, and as long as the wealthy acknowledged their obligations through charity, inequality of wealth was acceptable.[4] He was on his own. This was not a solid enough doctrine for the early Christian saints and leaders of the church, all of whom challenged the idea that property rights were absolute. St. Augustine declared that "he who uses his wealth badly possesses it wrongfully, and wrongful possession means it is another's property," while St. Ambrose—drawing on Cicero, who took the view that nothing natural justified private property rights—insisted that God's aim was that everything was commonly possessed. Those who held property had an absolute duty to support the poor. John Chrysostom, bishop of Constantinople, was no less radical, calling for the abolition of ideas of "mine" and "thine" and urging—as a forerunner of the best instincts of socialism—that all the Christians in the city put what they had into a common fund so they could achieve the great things otherwise beyond them as individuals.[5] St. Thomas Aquinas argued that part of the obligation of government was to regulate private property for the common good and that "a Christian is obliged to make his wealth available for common needs."

The European feudalism that grew up on a foundation of Christian beliefs thus had at its core the value system that would later give rise to notions of equality before the law and that the exercise of social privilege by the wealthy came with wider social obligations that went beyond charity. Feudal barons might be delegated political authority by their sovereign king, but they held their lands subject to their obligation to offer its wealth to serve the common weal as the king decided. This might take the form of contributing men and munitions to defend the realm, or making regular payments to sustain the cost of administering justice and order. When barons died they could not expect their lands to pass to their sons without the payment of a levy, which today Europeans would call inheritance tax and American conservatives would describe as a death tax. The designers of feudal Europe understood it instead as a life tax—a tribute to the common weal as an acknowledgment that the holding of land was a privilege and that this payment on death was a key means of sustaining the life of the community. It is an important and vital distinction that has relevance today.

And if anyone was in any doubt that the wealthy and propertied were not necessarily the possessors of virtue, in almost every town and village there was the infrastructure of monastic life, where monks attempted to approach the divine by living in a community that produced and consumed no more than it needed. Some, like the Franciscans, went further, insisting that it was only through living in a community of poverty that man could hope to earn God's redemption. Add this to the powerful millenarianism that grew out of St. John's promise in the Book of Revelation that Christ would come again to overthrow his enemies—a claim that was periodically used by dissident clerics to threaten the wealthy with actual or possible revolt by the lower classes if they did not meet their side of the social bargain—and it was well understood throughout the middle ages that property rights were not absolute.[6]

Feudal Europe was not a terrain in which individualism flourished, in particular over religion. The authority of church and state, backed by the nostrums of Catholicism (and eventually in England its compromise version in the Church of England), was suffocating. The English puritans who first settled America passionately believed that they could individually establish a direct relationship with God—and that God-fearing industriousness was the best possible route to God's favor. They had crossed the Atlantic to win the opportunity to express their religious convictions freely. But their encounter with so much virgin land, together with the philosophy of Locke, would trigger the invention of an explosively new and radical ideology justifying an individualist rather than social view of property. God had not given the world to the lazy or even benevolent man, declared Locke: he gave it to the use of the "rational and industrious." Moreover, the property that such industry created was "the best support of that Independency, so passionately desired by all men." Property, ownership, and the virtue of independence were thus indissolubly linked as part of God's plan—a world view that would find renewed legitimacy in the twentieth-century conservative idea that "greed is good" and that the spirit of acquisitiveness benefits all.

Locke had been concerned that too much acquisitiveness might lead to hoarding and avarice, and that any right to appropriation was subject to there being "enough and as good left in common—(of what God had given to the Earth to the Children of Men in common) for others." But 250 years later no such inhibition was felt by his conservative successors. Here is the important conservative philosopher Leo Strauss (of whom more in the next chapter): "Far from being straitened by the emancipation of acquisitiveness," declared Strauss, "the poor are enriched by it . . . unlimited appropriation without concern for the needs of others is true charity."[7] Strauss and the new conservatives built on the logic of Locke's position; if he justified the legitimacy of property as an individual's proper deserts for working on nature's endowment from God, they would justify it as the proper deserts for simply working. It was this tradition that helped form the 1980s conservative dependency theorists and their view that welfare actively increases poverty (see chapter 3), which, rather than springing from social and economic processes, should be seen instead as rooted in the motivational and psychological deficiencies of the poor themselves. They do not do enough to help themselves.

This is the first chasm between Europe and the United States. The radical new world view of the early settlers was cemented into the center of American culture by the writing of the U.S. Constitution. The settlers' rights to enjoy, acquire, and possess their property freely had been usurped by King George III's tyrannous government, went the popular cry, and so they fought the War of Independence to assume responsibility for their own governance—but of a very limited and constrained kind. Their core view, as the citizens of Ashfield, Massachusetts, voted, was that their only true governor was the governor of the universe. This was the Lockean view in the extreme, with some communities insisting that it was not just George III whose governance they disputed, but anybody's: they reserved the right—as self-governing individuals, who had created their own property, owing allegiance only to God—to overturn any state legislation with which they disagreed.

As the war years passed on it became clear that this assertion of individual liberty, under which armed citizens felt justified in threatening state legislatures to do their bidding, could be wildly irresponsible. The principles of independence and individual reverence for God were in direct conflict with that of the proper protection and exercise of property rights. Some of the thirteen states issued paper money to clear their debts; others refused to honor their contracts, wrote off debt, or raised taxes arbitrarily. Indeed, the whole approach was so haphazard that in the early 1780s the very success of the war was threatened, with some states refusing to levy taxes or hand over the receipts to Congress to conduct the war, while others paid up.

The federal state formed after the war was won and the constitution that was written for it were shaped by this tension and its resolution. The pro–central government "federalists" knew that to establish any kind of central government which overrode states' rights, they had to find a way of encompassing the revolutionary commitment to independence and liberty within an apparatus that, despite having the detested central authority, could be presented as promoting—in the words of the Constitution —domestic tranquillity and the general welfare, i.e., the protection of property. It was James Madison who, in coining the famous phrase "We the people" to begin the Constitution, came up with the rhetorical flourish that solved the conundrum; federal government was the means to protect property holders—"we the people"—from the potentially capricious depredations of state government.[8] Madison even wanted a federal veto over state legislatures—which he did not get—but, more important, he insisted that the federal government had to represent the national interest, and as such had to possess some capacity to be disinterested and objective in its deliberations in order to "filter" vested private interests. Hence the powerful office of the presidency to hold the ring between the interests of the haves in the Senate, as Madison saw them, and the have-nots in the House. He could not prevent the states from continuing to exercise as much government power as possible, so that the United States ended up with two sets of checks and balances: one within the federal government, and the other between the federal government and the states. In the wings was an independent judiciary that was to be another source of independent power.

Three years later, in the Fifth Amendment, the Constitution extended constitutional protection to individual property rights, preventing government from depriving an individual of "life, liberty, and property without due process of law; nor shall property be taken for public use without just compensation"—but nowhere is there any notion to parallel the German constitution's stipulation that property imposes reciprocal duties. The federalists counted themselves lucky that they had got their constitution ratified as quickly as they had in a climate in which to acquire and hold property was held to be a necessary and sufficient expression of republican virtue, which a broad strand of opinion felt should express itself in self-governing autonomous units in villages, towns, and member states rather than any federal government. The federalist counterargument was to acknowledge that while property underwrote independence and thus virtue, it was insufficient alone to produce a virtuous order. That required the disinterested arbitration that only federal government might bring—without which the community threatened to break down into warring factions and vested interests. The most practical expression of the principle was the Constitution's commerce clause, drafted in recognition of the evident need to regulate the terms of commerce between states and insist on good transport links.

Government had to be argued for via the back door, not as an expression of a social contract or general will but rather as a means of reconciling the clash of interests disinterestedly. And there was also the ugly question of slavery. To attack this property right in any way would imply that the southern states of Georgia, Virginia, and South Carolina actively expanding their plantation economies through importing slaves could not economically afford to join the new United States.[9] Slavery was thus not forbidden. The new republic would deal with the issue eventually as a matter of federal political authority—but not yet as an embedded constitutional clause. It was a fateful decision that has traumatized American culture.

The American Story Unfolds

From the start, then, the autonomy of private property rights in the United States has been seen as the legitimate consequence of man's interaction with nature; civil society naturally respects property and government is cast as its protector. Any notion that property rights were a concession granted by the state in the name of the common interest—the European tradition, represented in America by the colonial headright system—had been dispelled by the revolution. As for redistribution, that was an even greater offense against nature. The acquisition and holding of property was a private initiative, and what was required of the federal state was that it policed, upheld, and arbitrated between the resulting private contracts between property holders. The Constitution's clause insisting that no state could do anything that might impair the obligations of contracts became the legal lodestar of the Supreme Court, which throughout the nineteenth and early twentieth centuries interpreted the provision as conservatively as possible. Once it had been established, under *Dartmouth College* v. *Woodward* in 1819, that after any state had given a corporation the right to enter into contracts then it had no more right to interfere in its affairs under the contract clause, the stage was set. The Supreme Court would permit the federal government only to regulate commerce between states as it was constitutionally permitted, requiring it to refrain from any other intervention. In *Lawton* v. *Steele* in 1894, for example, the Court ruled that "the legislature may not, under the guise of protecting the public interest, arbitrarily interfere with private business, or impose unusual and unnecessary restrictions upon lawful occupations."

The sanctity of ownership and the rights of property were being spread from the settler farmer to the company. The Supreme Court's extension of the Fourteenth Amendment, guaranteeing the property rights of "persons" in an overt protection from slavery, to corporations, conferred on the latter the same uninfringeable property rights. The federal government should not interfere with how the owner of a company chose to organize his enterprise or how he related to his shareholders—except if he exercised excessive and abusive market power. A company's founding legal document thus became an absolutist expression of property rights in which Washington had no right to interfere.

In any case, even if the federal government wanted to interfere, the registration of individual corporations was not seen as a federal duty, so there was no direct capacity to make any intervention or construct a purposeful constitution for companies; that power rested with individual states, which guarded it jealously—Delaware, the state in which most companies incorporate with the most minimalist requirements, most jealously of all. When New Jersey, in 1896, decided to exercise its rights and drop all restrictions on what companies registering in the state might do, Delaware followed suit three years later—and added in some tax incentives to register with it for good measure. American corporations and the American financial markets developed as they chose.

For the next three decades, up to the Roosevelt years in the 1930s, the Supreme Court and Congress were locked in arguments about what the federal government could and could not do, with the court taking the defense of property interests to what even contemporaries regarded as absurd limits. The court ruled against measures to ban interstate trade in goods produced by children and against state laws limiting work to ten hours a day. The Sixteenth Amendment in 1916 was passed to permit the levying of income tax, which the Supreme Court had ruled as unconstitutional in the 1894 *Pollock* judgment—as it had later ruled against a heavy tax on phosphorus matches, imposed on health grounds. The Court carried on its conservative mandate against key New Deal legislation and it was only (as described in the next chapter) when Roosevelt threatened to pack it with liberals after his reelection in 1936 that it finally backed down and allowed a raft of regulatory measures to be deemed constitutional. As Leo Pfeffer wrote in his history of the Supreme Court, from its inception "the Court deemed its mission to be the protection of property against depredations by the people and their legislature. After 1937 it gave up this mission."[10] The first to make the attempt since the United States's foundation, the New Dealers—as we will see in the next chapter—began to put in place a system of regulation and limits to property rights. But it rested on shaky foundations.

For the Constitution remains explicit. Without powerful popular support and a clear sense of national crisis—as over slavery in the 1860s or unemployment in the 1930s—the American constitutional conception is that government at federal and state level is the custodian of private property rights; and the Supreme Court sees its task as policing that injunction. Thus, as the passion to unwind Rooseveltian regulation has mounted, so the Supreme Court has kept pace. Conservatism's success in promoting shareholder value, the minimalist approach to corporate governance, the objections to capital gains and inheritance tax, the indifference to growing inequality, the detestation of organized labor, the resistance to land-use planning, and even to the reform of campaign finance have all been immensely assisted not just by the cultural belief that private property rights are unassailable but by the constitutional buttresses to this value system. America's rich still believe in charitable giving to an extent unrecognized in Europe—one positive by-product of the Lockean inheritance—but the basic stance is the same. What is mine is mine, and well deserved because otherwise I would not have it.

Property—the European Conception

European attitudes, by contrast, are more complex. Here the notion persists that property is held in trust for all and only delegated to individuals for as long as they accept reciprocal social obligations. This is the legacy not only of the early Christian church and feudalism, but of the fact that Europe was already settled. America's founding fathers operated in an environment where there was almost limitless virgin land; 80 percent of the colonialists were property owners and thus middle class, and there was every expectation that this would remain the norm. When John Adams argued in 1776 that the acquisition of land should be made easy for every member of society in order to achieve equality and liberty, he could disregard European concerns with how the state had to intervene to construct a just society; a continent lay before him waiting to be claimed. As soon as the war was won, the American land survey began. It divided the country's three million square miles meticulously into a grid of about one million squares each. Each square, about six miles long and six miles wide, would then be quartered again and again to form, finally, units of forty acres. Property, a stake for all, was the promise and fundament of America. The same populism about property informs American conservatives today; their continent may now be settled, but by transferring the idea of property for all to the realm of share ownership, so that even small investors should speculate on Wall Street as their sacred right, they have given the notion of property for all without pain new life. The current Republican obsession with making private investment accounts a major part of the social security system comes from the same tradition.

In Europe, propositions about the possibility of individual ownership for all could not be made so easily. Thus when, after the English Civil War, the radicals in the New Model Army—notably the Levellers—wanted equality, liberty, and universal suffrage, informed by almost exactly the same set of Protestant values as the American settlers, the only avenue open to them for the creation of fairness for all was to argue for redistribution and common ownership—and to anticipate, along with the millenarians, that Christ's second coming would bring this about one day even if it was not achieved politically in the here and now. If all property had been created by individual labor, then if the majority had none and the minority a lot the rest of the syllogism was easy to complete. Great private wealth could be accumulated only by exploitation, and the political solution had to be redistribution from the few to the many—a solution validated by a Christian tradition that ran back for centuries. But in the 1650s Cromwell and his son-in-law Henry Ireton, taking the same position as John Adams that individual property ownership should be the foundation of the country, were on the side of reaction rather than revolution. At the Putney debates they resisted the argument for universal suffrage because it might threaten property; England had no virgin land that it could offer the radicals to square the equation by making them property owners without redistribution. Eighteenth-century republican America, however, could be both egalitarian and for private property.

The constitutional compromises reached in England allowed parliament to assume the feudal authority of the monarch, keeping alive the notion that property was a concession that demanded reciprocal privileges in the common interest. The early English corporations, like the East India or Hudson Bay Companies, were exclusive licenses to trade, made by the Crown-in-parliament, that involved reciprocal obligations upon the corporation to pay dividends to the government, conduct trade as directed, and open up lands for English settlement. Indeed, the early American colonies were founded on the same principle of delegated sovereignty and reciprocal obligation—the very principle that the colonialists were to dispute.

It was the industrial revolution that was to dramatize the social weaknesses of unrestrained property ownership and capital accumulation—and the need dramatically to widen the obligations that went with property ownership if the very system was to survive. Adam Smith, the revered godfather of laissez-faire economics, could suppose that a market system would find a natural point of balance only by arguing—along with John Locke—that all value originated in individual labor and that market prices would converge with the natural prices reflecting the labor content. David Ricardo went one step further and argued that value lay purely in the conditions of production; he showed that the lower real wages were, the higher rents and profits would be. Marx's contribution was to argue that common ownership was politically inevitable as the consequence of Ricardo's predictions about falling wages, secularizing the early Christian insistence that property was expropriation, along with its millenarian promise that there would be redistribution on Christ's second coming. Marx instead foresaw revolution.

The secularization of the medieval millenarian predictions about the overturning of an unfair order, together with a highly plausible economics, made Marxism extraordinarily influential. Europe's cities, growing explosively in the wake of industrialization, were social tinder boxes in which the old notions of socially obligated property seemed risible, creating a new class of industrial workers all too ready to listen to the moral content of Marx's message. The conditions of factory work were miserable, and factory owners paid money wages that might or might not offer subsistence. The contrast to life in feudal communities where payments were made in kind—or in towns, where powerful guilds had the power to regulate the labor market to ensure that workers received a just wage—could not have been more marked. The emergence of a mass labor market upon which the enormously new productive factories depended but which respected none of these ancient means of securing justice required an antidote; Europe's new urban working class found it by organizing in trade unions and becoming wedded, if not to Marxism, at least to socialism.

The values that created the European labor movement thus had deep roots, notably in feudalism and Catholicism. Social Catholicism, in this respect, anticipated socialism. It was no less fierce a critic of free-market economics, and over the nineteenth century sought to re-create what it imagined to have been the organic bonds of pre-industrial society through a network of enlightened employers, workers' self-help groups (St. Vincent de Paul societies in France and Kolpings Gesellen circles in Germany), the first mutual funds, and early Catholic trade unions—all inspired by a commitment to Catholicism. In France Leon Harmel, industrialist and devoted Catholic, encouraged his workers to meet and organize themselves collectively, setting up an insurance fund to which he contributed half and creating savings and sickness funds on top. In Germany the Catholic industrialist Franz Brandts followed suit, with Bishop von Kettler providing the religious leadership. Profit, declared Kettler, does not belong exclusively to the owner but should benefit everybody.[11] In France, Austria, and Germany the first tentative regulation of the labor market was prompted not by socialist or liberal members of their national assemblies, but by social

Catholics. Even Bismarck's program of social insurance was partly inspired by a desire to spike the arguments of the growing Catholic movement.

Harmel and Brandts had a British echo in Robert Owen, the inspirer of the British cooperative movement, while the French and German worker circles had parallels in the Victorian friendly societies, created to help workers save and insure themselves but stopping short of being even a shadow trade union. But the social movements that predated socialism were much weaker in Britain. Here the Catholic tradition was virtually extinct, and the marriage between Protestantism and laissez-faire economics that was flourishing in the United States had as firm a foundation in British values. The economic orthodoxy insisted that intervention in the operation of markets would impair their functioning, and that the Samuel Smiles doctrine of the virtues of self-help was the route to individual salvation. There were "laws" of labor and property that simply had to be observed. Yet such was the wealth being generated by the new forces, and such the scale of the poverty created in their wake, that it became increasingly difficult to stand by the maxim that the wealthy deserved to receive their profits in full without incurring any obligation to those who were impoverished other than what charity and Christian instincts might dictate. The nineteenth-century Factory Acts, in any case bitterly resisted, ameliorated conditions for women and children, but left male employment largely unregulated. For that the system had to be recast.

This was what socialism promised. The paradox was that, once the early socialist thinkers had cast aside the Marxist notion of revolution as a consequence of capitalist collapse and accepted that the socialist project was to reform capitalism—the explicit goal of the German Social Democratic Party's 1891 Erfurt program, which became the benchmark for European socialism[12]—socialism was in its values as much backward- as forward-looking. Its attitudes toward property, work, and wealth were strongly influenced by feudal and early Christian notions of the organic community, in which property holders accepted obligations to the common weal—and that work in particular should not be exploitative. The tension was how far those aims could be achieved by legislation, regulation, and taxation through parliamentary action, and how much they would require public ownership of the means of production—and if so, of what industries. Politically, socialism looked for the same democratization and enfranchisement achieved by the American settlers in 1787, but wanted to extend those political rights to the social sphere—notably by securing free education and health care funded by progressive taxation on incomes and wealth. It was a tougher set of demands than the American labor movement, growing at around the same time, needed or wanted to make—but then, the United States had already made more progress in extending suffrage, if only to white males (women of all races had to wait until 1920). Culturally, the American belief that property is natural and more likely to be conferred on individual Americans by the operation of the system is deep-seated. That socialism never happened in the United States is attributable to the differing values of the two continents.

The parliamentary attempt to arrive at a new social settlement in Europe was shattered by World War I and the Russian Revolution. The emerging competition between European parliamentary socialist parties and the first Christian democratic parties growing out of social Catholicism might have delivered a durable social contract without political upheaval. Both traditions championed a curtailing of private property rights and advanced notions of a just wage and the outlines of a welfare state. But the process was never tested. A substantial part of the European labor movement was committed to communism as a more radical solution to the property question. As Europe descended into depression and mass unemployment in the interwar years, fascism emerged as a parallel phenomenon on the right as the democracies and their parliamentary parties of left and right seemed helpless to act before the dictatorial ambitions of communists aiming to confiscate private property. Fascists were content to permit the autonomy of private property, but only, in Hitler's formulation, to produce results "in line with the ideas of the common good under state control."[13] As a German civil servant put it, "at bottom we do not seek a material but a mental nationalisation of the economy."[14] The people, racially pure, would represent their collective will through a strong state. That would suffice to produce socially desirable behavior from those who held property and ran the private enterprise system.

European communism and fascism were thus two extreme routes to the same end: solving the riddle of how property rights were to be exercised for the common good in the face of mass unemployment, poverty, depression, and hyperinflation. The liberal parliamentary system had proved inadequate to the task, and, desperate for prosperity and stability, societies in which property ownership was not widespread readily turned to totalitarian solutions. To complicate matters, German fascism had territorial ambitions as much as Soviet communism had global ideological ambitions. This menacing, evil marriage of ideology and power was to trigger world war.

Beside these developments in Europe the American political settlement, although also challenged by depression and unemployment, was a much more effective defender of liberty and democracy; in the New Deal it proved a creative source of economic and social responses to the problems of the time. The founding fathers had provided a political constitution and value system that could hold a continent together, and in so doing created the country that was to save Europe from itself. Without the United States it is difficult to imagine Hitler being beaten so quickly, if at all—or Stalin's advance into Europe after the war being halted along the Iron Curtain. The inability of Europe's nation-states to provide a durable social and political settlement had put European civilization itself in jeopardy.

But that does not mean that Europe could, or can, solve the property and wealth questions as the Americans have—or that it can freely import the canons of American conservatism. Private property and wealth simply do not have the same legitimacy in Europe as they have in the United States—witness again the qualification in the postwar German constitution that the common will overrides private property rights. If the EU and its members were to copy an absolutist conservative view of government, and say that their only role was to protect private contracts and the right to sack workers at will (see chapter 4), while promoting only interstate commerce, they would be laughed out of court. It is far too limited a conception of property and its obligations for Europeans to accept.

Europe instead has had to continue to develop and protect a distinct model that is true to its values—not only so that it will never again fall prey to communist and fascist temptations, but because that is the only way for European capitalism to win long-term legitimacy. The idea that property must earn its rights through accepting responsibilities to the community of which it is part is deeply embedded in a tradition that extends from John Chrysostom through Robert Owen to the Erfurt program—a tradition that includes Britain. As a result, the notion that companies must earn their license to trade through operating in a socially legitimate fashion and accepting that responsibilities accompany ownership is very much alive in Europe. Property is not a right or a simple network of private contracts; rather, it is a concession made by the society of which it is part that has to be continually earned and deserved. Employees insist on just treatment, ranging from their wages to the acknowledgment that their attitudes and dignity matter in how the organization for which they work develops. Progressive taxation—including tax on property—is an imperative to finance universal health care and education.

Europe's attitudes toward property *are* different from America's—not just because of the experience of war and totalitarianism and the legacy of Catholicism and socialism, but because they are linked ineradicably to distinct European attitudes towards equality, social solidarity, and ideas about the legitimacy and extent of public discourse. The distinction is fundamental—and it is of correspondingly fundamental importance that Europe continue to answer the property question in its own way. Indeed, it may even be that over the next century America has to borrow from Europe.

Equality and Social Solidarity—Utopia in Dispute

The early American settlers prized liberty. It was liberty that allowed them to worship as they chose; and it was liberty that protected them from any coercive constraint or direction on how they acquired, used, and disposed of their property. Governmental minimalism and the free exercise of property rights are thus the bedrock of the good society, a tradition exemplified by the leading American conservative political philosopher Robert Nozick in his *Anarchy, State and Utopia*, where he takes the conservative argument to the extreme. He depicts taxation to finance any minimum income for the poor as a form of forced labor and all forms of redistributive justice as essentially coercive. The reduction of inequality presupposes an authority to discharge the initiative that must of necessity be coercive, and thus endangers the state of liberty which all individuals must prize as an absolute virtue. The quest for equality threatens the onset of totalitarianism, and as a result all citizens must wish for as small a state as possible. This is the utopian condition.

Nozick's propositions strike most Europeans—including mainstream European conservatives—as close to absurd. Of course, pushed to its logical conclusion, what defines state power is that it cannot be resisted, but Nozick sees only the dark side; in the real world the propertyless are coerced through their powerlessness and the state is the means by which many are enabled to do things that would otherwise be impossible for them. Indeed, we accept state authority precisely because we know that the acts of the whole enlarge the possibilities of the parts, just as we accept rules for membership of any club because we are both protected and our interests furthered by membership. The perverseness that denies such self-evident truths begins to make sense only in an American context in which liberty and individualism are so highly valued—and where property has never been associated with any conception of reciprocal social obligation.

Ever since the American constitution banned the conferring of European-style titles associated with aristocracy, feudalism, and monarchy, Americans have believed that theirs is a fundamentally more egalitarian society; but that ostensibly egalitarian culture has only served to mask, as I will argue in chapter 5, massive inequality and disturbingly indifferent rates of social and income mobility, despite the massive propaganda to the contrary. Inherited property and the accompanying titles were properly an offense to the American revolutionaries, just as they were to European radicals, but they had one crucial source of legitimacy that most parties to the debate—with the exception of classic one-nation Tories—missed. Aristocracy contained the notion of noblesse oblige—literally, "nobility obliges"—that in turn is rooted in the conception that property is held in trust for all, and that those who enjoy sovereignty over it exercise their privilege subject to their recognition of their obligations to the social whole. Part of the moral force of the French Revolution in 1789 was the conviction that this explicit social contract had been profoundly abused, and that the overturning of monarchy and aristocracy would permit a new social contract along the lines set out by Rousseau to be established. No such thinking informed the American Revolution, and so it created a culture in which, two hundred years later, clever social nihilists like Nozick can exercise a strong influence in American life.

The European tradition is much more mindful that men and women are social animals and that individual liberty is only one of a spectrum of values that generate a good society; indeed, the pursuit of liberty cannot be considered as an absolute value because at some point one woman's liberty involves a constraint on the exercise of that of another man. As the leading English socialist of the interwar years, Richard Tawney, put it in his famous book on equality: "Every man should have his liberty and no more, to do unto others as he would that they should do unto him." But the instinct of being ready to empathize with others requires in turn some sense of altruism and cooperativeness that itself has to be sustained and nurtured—and which is unlikely to emerge spontaneously from a Darwinian struggle of all against all which necessarily creates a wide spectrum of inequality. To achieve a proper balance of liberties, in short, requires a recognition of the needs of others that comes from knowing you are a member of a social collectivity.

Now I make an explicit European value judgment—but I believe, notwithstanding Nozick, Strauss, et al., that it also applies to Americans. Human beings depend for their humanity on association, and this requires that they participate in a collective consciousness and shared belief system that allows them to empathize with the conditions of others. Membership in an associative conscience is essential to human well-being; but an associative conscience cannot be established if there is not a common culture, which in turn implies that everyone can belong to it on the same terms and has the same chance fully to participate in the civilization that creates it. These are the preconditions for any individual to have the altruistic impulses that underpin human association—and which allow the boundaries of the exercise of liberty to be established.

If these interlinked propositions are to be sustained, they have to be underpinned by a social organization that allows every citizen the equal possibility of participation. To attempt to create this social organization can be described as coercion—as the American right does—only if one is to describe, say, observing common rules of grammar and syntax through which to communicate as coercive. The convention that requires that this sentence finish with a period could be described as coercive, but I observe it because I want to communicate. On the same terms, the tax I pay to ensure that the socially needy can participate in society could be described as coercive, but I pay it willingly because I accept the justice of the transfer. The contrast with American conservatism is that every European country accepts that it needs public organization to achieve the social goals which as an explicit social contract underwrite its civilization, and understands that of necessity the state must be the social contract's trustee. The American conception, pushed to its limits by conservatives, is that no social contract exists or is achievable without an unreasonable extension of state power; the rationale of the state is to protect individual liberties.

This conception of membership in society on equal terms as an intrinsic component of an implicit social contract is fundamental to the European tradition on both the political right and left. It is the reason why across Europe there is much greater popular support for state initiatives to guarantee income and much greater dislike of inequality than in the United States. In *It Didn't Happen Here*, Seymour Martin Lipset and Gary Marks present a table showing that only 12 percent of high-income Americans believe that the state should offer a basic income to all citizens; among low-income respondents the proportion is still only 33 percent. Yet in Britain, the former West Germany (the data are for 1990 and thus pre-unification), the Netherlands, and Italy the proportion of low-income respondents backing the idea is a massive 71 percent, 66 percent, 58 percent, and 80 percent, respectively, with 47 percent, 45 percent, 39 percent, and 53 percent of high-income respondents also supporting the notion. Richer groups in both Europe and the United States are more distrustful of a basic income than their poorer counterparts (they have less need for it), but in Europe three to four times more of even the rich are in favor than their American counterparts.[15]

A similar pattern is evident over attitudes to inequality. An intriguing paper by Alberto Alesina, Rafael di Tella, and Robert MacCulloch shows that Europeans dislike inequality more than Americans, with the poor feeling particularly strongly.[16] In the United States the only group worried by inequality is rich leftists; every other group is indifferent. The authors' view is that the reason the American poor are less concerned than their European counterparts is that they think they have greater chances of upward mobility, the reflex assumption being—as with so many polls of this type—that mobility is necessarily greater in the United States. This is not in fact so, even if it were for the early settlers, but that does not matter; it is believed to be so by almost every American, including most social scientists, and so this perception governs attitudes despite its lack of correspondence with reality. Americans are cultural egalitarians to a degree that makes real income redistribution—and the demand for income redistribution—less necessary than in Europe despite objective conditions that are more or less the same. The American dream underpins egalitarian social attitudes and culture even if it is increasingly hogwash in practice.

The European dislike of inequality and accompanying willingness to support measures that underwrite a minimum income, and indeed a range of social benefits, should not be understood as surrogate communism —the critique leveled by American conservatives. The European acceptance of the need for a social contract is not the same as the communist campaign to redistribute resources exactly equally in a universe in which property is held in common; even some European socialists before the communist revolution (and all of them after it) understood that this approach is economically unworkable and morally undesirable. Tawney, for example, made no such demand, acknowledging not only that individuals would receive different levels of remuneration according to their skills and qualifications, but that such a pattern of differential rewards was necessary to ensure that such skills were acquired. Inequality of that type is ineradicable, and the attempt to abolish it should not be made.

Rather, the objection is to the conservative American justification of inequality as the natural outcome of a process of Darwinian selection, laced with Lockean justifications that obligation-free property rights are natural, leavened only by the need to provide subsistence income for the very poorest if they can prove that they cannot look after themselves. In this universe the losers in the race may be permitted to subsist, but they cannot achieve the broader level of social well-being which allows them to be participants in and members of the whole. Citizens, however, are defined not by mere subsistence, but by the cultural knowledge that they stand in a position of equality with others notwithstanding their low income; they are as much a part of the civilization as everybody else. For this they need their incomes to be higher than subsistence level, and to know that whatever their circumstances they have had an equal right to achieve happiness even if it has not been achieved, and that whatever their current economic and social position they are of equal worth to those more successful, luckier, or better endowed with skills and talents. Tackling inequality is as much about symbolically "stripping inequality of its esteem," as Tawney put it, as it is about providing every citizen with the material means to live above subsistence level.

If this is not even attempted, then the business of creating and sustaining the civilization of which the losers need to be part—and of which the civilization in turn needs to make them part if it is to make the claim to be a genuine civilization—is left to the winners. But this is at best an incomplete civilization, because it accepts that a significant class of its potential members is not eligible to have a stake in the common interest. Unless the working class feel they belong to their society as much as the middle and upper classes, and have a fair chance of raising their status because the odds are not stacked against them, then there is no chance of creating the equality of standing on which social solidarity depends. If that is to happen, then the state has to be vigilant about ensuring that the rich do not exclusively look after their own children and their own networks through inheritance, favored education, and nepotism. In other words, the rich have to accept the legitimacy of the state working to see that they discharge their obligations to the whole. A culture that accepts the principle of egalitarianism, in the sense of acknowledging the legitimacy of some form of social contract, has to be embraced by the better-off as much as the poor if a civilization is to function.

Of course, the degree to which this analysis should be accepted is a matter of political dispute between the European right and left—Christian democrats and one-nation conservatives arguing that the system has to accept a measure of "natural" inequality while social democrats and liberals argue for more redistribution of income and wealth and high levels of basic income. Nor does the exact means by which the social contract is expressed take the same form throughout Europe. My point is rather that these sometimes significant differences should not be allowed to mask the truth that European cultures hold an idea of the social contract in common. If Tawney is among the most eloquent British thinkers to express the concept, the French, for example, can boast Emile Durkheim.[17] The great French sociologist's preoccupation is to identify the importance of social solidarity as not just material but psychic social cement, and in doing so he inverts the arguments made by the proponents of laissez-faire economics. Individual competition, market exchange, and the exercise of liberty do not spontaneously create cooperation and a vigorous social life—on the contrary, they destroy it. It is only when there is strong social solidarity and a powerful collective conscience that individuals have the platform on which to express their individualism; otherwise they risk being isolated by the pressures of the modern market economy and getting lost, resulting in alienation and what Durkheim calls *anomie* or a sense of purposeless anonymity. The task is to make people feel part of the whole, and that requires Tawney's approach of trying to ensure an equal chance of social membership. Durkheim's idea of a collective conscience may now be regarded with some suspicion, but his view that a successful market economy is embedded in a strong society survives. When the former French prime minister Lionel Jospin used the formulation of being for a market economy but against a market society, for example, his ideas descended directly from Durkheim—but then, Durkheim is articulating a common European preference.

The Infrastructure of Justice

Europeans do not have a monopoly on the idea that equality and the social contract are linked. After all it was John Rawls, professor of philosophy at Harvard University, who attempted to prove from the first principle under-pinning American culture—that all citizens are free—that a social contract approach self-interestedly produces the best society, and goes on to outline what the most robust social contract would be. He is trying to reconcile the European notion of a social contract with American preferences for liberty and individualism, as he openly admits in citing his admiration for European social contract ideas. Yet for all its insight and remarkable reception in the world of philosophy and intellectual liberalism, *A Theory of Justice* (published in 1971) has not entrenched itself in the United States with the same force as the new conservatism. It has not informed the policy programs of the Democrats; it has not been deployed to justify any social programs or criticism of America's money-dominated politics. It did not check the conservative advance—indeed, if anything it served only to sharpen conservative arguments in reply. Robert Nozick's *Anarchy, State and Utopia* was written in part as a refutation of Rawls. If a culture is not equipped to hear a philosophy, then it remains deaf.

The Rawlsian thesis is well known and I will review it only in brief. Rawls invites us to indulge in a thought experiment about what would be the nature of the social contract to which we would consent if we were in the "original position"; that is, if we were situated behind a "veil of ignorance," knowing nothing about ourselves and our future life-chances but wanting to live in a just order in which our own and others' liberties were respected. He does not put it this way, but you might imagine you were a new puritan settler imbued with the teachings of John Locke and a love of freedom; what would be the social order you would want to construct in your new land? Rawls sets out to prove that even for liberty-loving individualists, the rational strategy would be egalitarian, subject to the freedom to exercise one's basic individual liberties. Rawls defines these essentially as civil liberties—the right to vote, freedom of thought, and the like—consistent with offering a like liberty for others, which on close examination looks astonishingly like the first amendment.

But in elucidating his second principle—"the difference principle" —Rawls tries to persuade his compatriots that the Europeans are right to be concerned about the conditions of the poorest, if only because anybody could have been one of them. Any individual making a choice about the ordering of society behind a veil of ignorance would want to make sure that the worst outcome that might befall him or her would be manageable and that he or she would still have access to key primary goods—some reasonable level of income and material well-being, access to opportunity, and the exercise of basic rights and civil liberties—which together allow the individual the self-respect on which membership in society depends. The chance of making a very high income should be constrained by the taxation and constraints on the use of property necessary to provide the infrastructure of justice that provides such key primary goods—an infrastructure that ensures that the greatest benefits go to the weakest so that they have no reasonable grievance against the rich. We can only enjoy very high incomes to the extent that we have ensured that the poor are in the best position we could conceive—the yardstick being that were we in their place we would consider the arrangements fair. Equally important, this infrastructure of justice is not only about a minimum level of material well-being; it must also ensure that the disadvantaged enjoy minimum basic civil liberties.

This two-paragraph account only hints at the sophistication of Rawls's model social contract, which he considered superior to other attempts because it guarantees that no section of the community can ever have their well-being neglected, even if that would benefit the general good: unless everybody has primary goods and self-respect (the echoes of Tawney and Durkheim are obvious) then one cannot be said to be living in a just society. What is intriguing is that this attempt to transplant European social contract theory to the United States has not taken off in either theory or practice. When Rawls's broad conception of an infrastructure of justice goes head to head with Nozick's insistence that liberty is so important that it overrides the legitimacy of any attempt to redistribute income, Rawls has emerged the loser. The conservatives have so resoundingly won the cultural argument that in America, and to an extent in Britain, we opt for liberty and inequality. Thus advocates of the Rawlsian position, if they are to gain any ground, find themselves taking the softer position that the good society is simply a meritocracy with a reasonable social floor—rather than the social floor that we would consider fair if we were in that position and that is the very best we could conceive. We would not worry about the discrepancy as long as there is a basic minimum safety net. This is the position of some New Labour theorists. Philip Collins, for example, director of the Social Market Foundation, advances the thesis that the good society is one with a high social floor and a meritocracy with no limits to incomes at the top, looking to Rawls for justification.[18] Rawls's egalitarian liberalism (as we will call it) goes much, much further—but it is the radicalism that currently dares not speak its name.

A Theory of Justice assumes that society is solidaristic enough for us to posit that individuals rank their desires similarly. Perhaps the most expressive sign that his ideas have gained little purchase in the United States is the drumbeat of insistence that in contemporary America minority groups in society will not make the same choices about the level of primary goods they might need because their values are different. A Theory of Justice presupposed a universality of moral choices that cannot be possible, allege the apostles of cultural diversity, given the different world views of say, blacks, or religious groups. In short, in an immigrant society with many subgroups and competing moralities, it is impossible to presuppose a universal morality and commonality of moral codes to guide individual choices behind the Rawlsian veil of ignorance on which the just society is founded.

Here Rawls's thesis is trapped by the character and conservatism of American society; a social contract cannot fly in such an environment, and conservative intellectuals will not let it pass. Even if they were to drop their guard, powerful minority groups in American society would continue to use the protections afforded by the constitution over their individual rights, backed by the courts, to insist on preferential treatment. These are the culture wars that have plagued the United States for the last twenty or thirty years. Blacks, for example, campaign for reparation payments to compensate for slavery, and religious groups insist that their "primary goods" include a commitment to ban abortion: all can use the rights entrenched in the Constitution and the conservative instincts of the Supreme Court to press their cases as minority groups whose grievances must be respected. Thus the United States descends into a cacophony of competing group grievances, with no common view about what the social contract or infrastructure of justice might be that would reconcile them equitably. American blacks are right to argue that they have been systematically discriminated against; the response that would hold American society together would be to redress that grievance over time through an infrastructure of justice that is neutral to all minority groups and mindful only of equivalent disadvantage. If, instead, the claim for hundreds of billions of dollars of reparations ever makes progress, it will poison America's already disastrous race relations for yet more decades. It will be more important to be black than to be an American citizen. Rawls, properly applied, would avoid this social disaster—but destructive conservatism dominates.

Ironically, Rawls's model does capture what is happening in Europe, especially in the Scandinavian states and the countries that practice what Michel Albert in *Capitalism against Capitalism* describes as "Rhineland" capitalism, where there is the necessary egalitarian liberalism to build an infrastructure of justice; and there are shades of this all over Europe as the legacies of social democracy and social Catholicism that form the foundation of the European welfare state. The call to abandon this moral world view by Europeans openly admiring of the United States, and to follow the doctrines of multiculturalism in the name of diversity to reproduce America's approach to recognizing minority groups, is a calamitous mistake. Once group politics trumps the politics of social solidarity, the foundations of further injustice are laid for everyone. Massive inequality and falling social mobility result as it becomes impossible to articulate any sense of a social contract or common purpose once group rights overwhelm the belief in collective efforts and collective responsibilities.

There are plenty of multiculturalists in Britain insisting that Britain should conceive of itself as a community of communities, conceding religious schools to ethnic and racial minorities and all the other social instruments that balkanize and destroy a common civic culture. Indeed, this is declared New Labour policy. But, as Brian Barry, professor of philosophy at Columbia University, argues in his powerful book *Culture and Equality*—probably the best egalitarian argument since Richard Tawney—you cannot create a fair society without a common civic culture committed to some notion of liberal egalitarianism. Lose that, and we are on the road to perdition—legitimizing alike in Britain the noxious politics of the British National Front and the separatist Asian groups protesting that their own subcultures have equal worth whatever their values, with parallels such as anti-abortion groups or separatist black movements in the United States. As the clamor for compensation, reparations, and minority group "separate development" with their own religious schools grows, we have to be clear-headed. A society can hold together only if it stands by universal egalitarian values and a universal infrastructure of justice—and it is within those that we design our responses to racism and poverty alike. Tawney, Durkheim, and Rawls are right in their conception of what produces a just society. Europeans must stand by their values, which underpin the social contract, not give them up. Americans should follow suit. The road to hell is paved with good intentions.

Last but Not Least—the Public Realm

If there is to be a social contract, then there has to be a collective agent that can organize it—and there has to a public space within which the social contract's character and structure can be debated. In short, there has to be a state, and the state has to be part of a wider public discourse in which its actions can be publicly discussed, evaluated, and held to account by the citizenship at large. For any European—or indeed any Rawlsian American—this is a pretty tame lowest common denominator of agreement.

The European tradition of central public authority that can command individual allegiance in the name of the common good goes back to the justification of monarchy as the trustee on earth of God's interest in humankind. While it became obvious during the eighteenth-century Enlightenment that monarchical rule was not consistent with the creation of a free public realm where free argument could be had and debate settled on the objective merits of proposals—not just about politics but across the gamut of human endeavors—the idea of a common interest lived on. Thus the emergence of representative government in Europe had two features that its corollary in America did not. First, political democracy was a consequence of the joyous Enlightenment liberation from the suffocating imprisonment of thought within the limits set by church and monarch. There was a demand for a public realm in which individuals could be free to think as they wanted; the democratic *political* domain was a vital component of this public realm, but it was only a critical subset. Second, the notion of the state as somehow embodying a common interest and thus fundamentally legitimate was handed on to the new world of representative democracy. Thus, as democratic government spread around Europe, the combination of the legitimacy of collective agency as embodying a common interest, the need for public space and public deliberation beyond the state, and the necessity of a social contract together with the requirement of accountability and representativeness became integrated into a European worldview about government that is distinct from the American.

This has been a hard journey, disfigured by the interwar flirtation with fascism and its more radical version, Nazism, and the resulting second world war. As the historian Mark Mazower observes in his powerful book *Dark Continent*, one of the more unpalatable truths for contemporary Europeans is how attractive many Europeans once found the prospect of fascism; had Hitler had been less of a barbarian and less exploitive of the countries he conquered, fascist doctrines might have taken root. The values celebrated in this chapter—basically, that property rights cannot be unqualified—can in different circumstances be exploited for uglier ends.

The emergence of European states with a clear and profound commitment to democracy within a European Union that makes democracy its cornerstone, along with a self-conscious desire to construct a powerful social contract and welfare state, has grown out of the desire never to repeat the experience of the 1930s and 1940s. Europe must never again make the same mistakes.

There were and are important variations in these developments across Europe. Britain, for example, in not writing a constitution that reflected Enlightenment values and merely bolting representativeness onto its old monarchical political system, has a much weaker conception of the public realm than is common on mainland Europe. Its state structures, though, retain immense legitimacy. France has the clearest and most explicit identification of the state as personification of the general will, while the modern German state draws its legitimacy from being the trustee of Germany's complex social contract—the social market economy. But for all their differences, these European states are there to act. Once a course of action has been settled, there is common agreement that each citizen will abide by the rule of consequent legislation or executive action—and has a duty to do so because that is part of the political and social settlement. Individual liberties might be constrained by majority decisions, given the uninhibited nature of state power; but better that than the lack of any capacity for collective action that represents a common interest. Because of its greater legitimacy, the political realm is where normative judgments are made, where political parties compete to tell different narratives about what might or might not produce the good society, drawing from the narratives developed in the wider public realm—and where the state will follow through with prescriptive action.

The American state tradition has significantly different roots, which have allowed the conservative revolution to lead it toward a very different conception. As described earlier, this was never a state constructed to embody any notion of collective will or build a social contract; the contract was the narrower one of protecting the settlers' individual liberties and property rights. As de Tocqueville remarked over a hundred and fifty years ago, American patriotism is not a patriotism that celebrates a common interest; it is a patriotism that celebrates a state that protects individual interests—so that love of property and love of country are united.[19] The state does not and should not embody or represent a common interest, and its capacity to act is restrained not just culturally but by the complex system of constitutional checks and balances that prevent it from acting. This produces the advantage of much more open government and disclosure of information to citizens, because in an important sense they own the state, and its legitimacy resides only in its purpose of serving their individual interests. Its weakness is that, unlike in Europe, it is not supported by any substantial idea of the common interest; there is only a shriveled conception of the public realm, which indeed hardly exists beyond the United States's now chronically impoverished political arena.

For America's conservatives, this is the utopia imagined by their philosophers, like Robert Nozick and the antistate minimalists in the Republican party. Their core conception is that of a virtuous individual unencumbered by obligations or constrained by public regulation: minding one's own business, staying in one's own space, and sticking to one's last. No coercive obligation is laid on others, and none is expected from the state. Indeed, state action that in Europe is seen as a natural outgrowth of any attempt to assert a common interest is quickly labeled coercive by American conservatives—and such is the resonance of this idea in American culture that it has nearly paralyzed the American liberal tradition.

The consequence of this conservative distrust of the state as coercive, antilibertarian, and inefficient, together with American liberalism's reluctance to risk conservative wrath by deploying state power to make morally based collective interventions, has been the collapse of what little capacity the U.S. Constitution confers for constructive state intervention, regulation and institution-building. Indeed, the Constitution itself both creates and compounds the problem. It and the Bill of Rights are seen as the acme of democratic perfection, so that all problems should be solved within their carapace; politics, as the political analyst Daniel Lazare perceptively writes, is conducted by constant deference to what the Constitution says and how it should be interpreted.[20] It thus becomes difficult to use the state to exercise popular sovereignty, for the Constitution was drawn up not so much to check or balance such sovereignty as to deny it. Worse, contends Lazare, because the Constitution is almost impossible to rewrite—it has been amended only fifteen times since 1791—arguments over civil liberties and social progress are frozen, locked in what the unchangeable Bill of Rights asserts. "By externalising civil liberties in the form of an untouchable Bill of Rights," he writes, "US constitutionalism has prevented their internalisation as part of the democratic political process."[21] It is a deformation that bubbled to the fore in the aftermath of September 11, 2001, when Attorney General John Ashcroft, a convinced Straussian, and President Bush adopted measures permitting the private military trial of non-Americans deemed to be a terrorist, along with extensive new powers to wiretap phone calls and e-mails. The scale of this withdrawal of civil liberties to combat terrorism is excessive and hard to justify in terms of potential results; it was a populist response which has become law without any political debate or opposition. Paradoxically, it was the Supreme Court that came later to challenge the legality of the proposals because of its infringement of essential liberties. It was not the political culture but rather the Constitution that came to the rescue. More limited measures in Britain were the subject of intense debate and parliamentary scrutiny, and were substantively amended by the House of Lords.

In the formulation famously coined by Professor Michael Sandel of Harvard University, the United States has become little more than a "procedural republic" which is ever poorer in expressing collective choices and moral preferences.[22] Instead, he argues, the political debate is constrained by a suffocating combination of constitutionalism and the canons of conservatism, leaving wider challenges to be fought out in the bear pit of individuals asserting their individual rights in the courts or through corporate lobbying and allegiance to the latest New Age fad. Essentially, economy and society are now developing according to private choices, with little or no intervention from the political process or wider state except to accelerate the drift toward ever more extreme conservatism.

Those areas of American life that might constitute a public realm for the criticism of government and deliberation about public action have shrunk to almost nothing—not that the U.S. public realm defined in these terms has ever been very vigorous. De Tocqueville, writing of his experience in 1835, found the American press shallow and uninterested in driving public debate; in a country founded on liberty, he observed, the press defines itself as serving liberty by prescribing little.[23] It is a tradition that has continued. The American media wants to portray itself as value-neutral and nonprescriptive, as the state has become—and in any case, the physical space and time devoted to public issues are continually eroded by market and commercial pressures. As a result, writes Sandel, American public life has no capacity to develop political stories with any soul apart from those that celebrate individualism; it is vacuous—much to the delight of American conservatives, who see every impoverishment of the scope for collective initiative as another liberal scalp.

Sandel is part of a growing movement that is fundamentally critical of the way American democracy has developed. The democratic template embedded in the American collective consciousness is of some New England public square in the mid-1750s, in which the colonists are debating how to protect their liberty from George III—the liberalism of what one American commentator has called the "naked public square."[24] It is this image of protecting liberty at all costs that has been captured and permanently bottled in the U.S. Constitution and Bill of Rights, and which explains the attitude of the American media. Newspapers, television, and radio regard themselves as electronic public squares—facilitating debate rather than being active political players.[25] But while the civic republicanism of the eighteenth century was properly concerned with asserting the liberty of the colonists, it is a travesty of its spirit that traps American political debate within incredibly narrow limits, laid down according to a diminished conception of the public interest that in turn shrivels what is politically possible. For Sandel as much as Rawls, a precondition of launching a more determinedly liberal America is to break out of these constraints and recover the ambition of a genuine civic republicanism. Only when this revival is mounted will a foundation be laid for recovering America's social contract. It has been done before and can be done again.

So Europe Points the Way

The United States needs to follow the path postwar Europe has blazed, however uncertainly. From Immanuel Kant's rejoicing in the new freedom for public argument that the Enlightenment offered,[26] to the way Jürgen Habermas defines the public realm today—as any forum where debate and argument can take place—Europe has had, and retains, both an idea of the public realm that transcends the formal institutions of democracy, justice, and government and a recognition that it is legitimate for the state to act purposively to shape economy and society. From the scientific journals where information should be available to as wide a public as possible rather than preserved in secrecy for private clients, to the political stances of its great newspapers, Europeans see a wide range of areas where it is legitimate to insist that public values be expressed and debated. Hence the commitment to publicly owned TV stations with a mandate to provide a universal public service as guarantors that ordinary citizens will have access to core news and comment delivered as objectively as possible—without which participation in the social and public life of the nation is much harder.

The American champion of such an approach is PBS (the Public Broadcasting Service), but it is not offered public revenues or privileges that might allow it to rival the commercial networks in its programming ambitions. Even before the conservative revolution Americans would have hesitated about making such a commitment; now it is impossible. Instead, PBS is a membership organization relying on subscription and public donations from those members of the public willing to join it; it is not a station that has a statutory obligation to broadcast to the universe of American citizens and as a quid quo pro enjoys special state support. This contrast with European public broadcasters encapsulates the different approaches to ideas of the public.

This cuts to the quick of both civilizations. According to a Western tradition that began with Aristotle, the complete individual is one who is capable of expressing in his or her life both the public and the private; but this is a tradition from which the United States is increasingly declaring independence. It is not just a matter of accepting that the state can and should act to build an infrastructure of justice that diminishes inequality, equalizes opportunity, and tries to enlarge individuals' capacity for self-respect. It is, as the German philosopher Hannah Arendt argues, about our needing a public realm to allow the full flowering of our human sensibilities.[27] For, taken to its limits, a society peopled only by conservative "unencumbered selves" jealously guarding their individual liberties and privacy is a denial of the human urge for association and meaning. The musician at the peak of her powers gives a public performance as a celebration of her prowess at which we are delighted to be present. The gardener delighting in his private garden understands its value because it expresses a value a public park cannot; but equally, a public park offers a grandeur and collective space that is a pleasure in itself, complements what is offered by a private garden, and in so doing underlines the character of privacy whose meaning is better comprehended because there is a public park with which to compare it. Similarly, a city needs to have public spaces for us to make sense of and value the private; but if every corner is privatized, those who are offered no access to any-where are reduced to aliens. Contemporary American cities have this feel more and more; their public space diminishes as they become consecrated to the primacy of the private.

In a world that is wholly private we lose our bearings; deprived of any public anchor, all we have are our individual subjective values to guide us. Public parks, public squares, publicly owned television, public museums, public art, public science, and public transportation—to name but a few—should be seen not just as essential expressions of the collective but as vital means for complementing and thus enriching our private choices.

Europeans of both left and right understand this, as do American liber-als—but they are under assault from the values of American conservatism driven by the process of globalization. Arendt, writing in the 1950s, was alarmed that the onrush of a market economy and society was gnawing away at conceptions of the public realm. She warned presciently that the public sphere was becoming reduced, and that as this happened govern-ment was becoming little more than administration and individuals would seek refuge by looking for meaning in their intimate relationships—but that even these would become harder to negotiate successfully as we loaded so much emotional weight on them while simultaneously reducing the anchorage offered by a vigorous public domain. In the first decade of the twenty-first century these processes are much further advanced—and will accelerate if American conservatives have their way. Protecting Euro-pean conceptions of the public realm, the social contract, and the obliga-tions owed by the wealthy and propertied is becoming ever more urgent in both the United States and Europe, not just for wider justice but also for our individual well-being. The most striking evidence for that is what con-temporary America has become—and to explain that, we first need to explore the rise of American conservatism.

3
Waging War without Blood: The Collapse of American Liberalism

American conservatives can be pleased. At the beginning of a new century they have succeeded in binding America's longstanding skepticism about the merits of government, its Protestant religiosity, its belief in its special destiny, and its faith in capitalism and individualism into the country's dominant conservative ideology. To be conservative is to be patriotic—and, even more extraordinarily, to be populist and the champion of ordinary people. Yet only twenty-five years ago this brand of conservatism seemed at the political margins, its fate uncertain before the moral ascendancy of liberalism—which had established a consensual acknowledgment that government was central to the creation of a fair and prosperous society, in particular to dealing with race—and a spreading secularism that seemed set to undermine conservatism's religious strongholds. Today that same liberalism is charged with intellectual incoherence and is placed permanently on the political defensive. To be a liberal is no longer just a dirty word; it is associated with the venal crime of being un-American.

It was not ever thus. In 1960 John F. Kennedy won a closely fought election that was to open up another wave of liberal reform, building on the work begun in the Progressive Era of American politics in the early years of the century and resumed by Franklin D. Roosevelt in his New Deal. It was the Progressives around Theodore Roosevelt who had fought for and won acceptance of the principle of income tax and the trust-busting of monopolies. And it was the New Dealers who later made the banking system more robust, organized long-term credit for farmers and home-buyers, established collective bargaining rights for trade unions, instituted a proper system of unemployment benefits and were ready directly to employ the unemployed or create work for them in huge public works programs. The liberal project in the 1960s was to carry this vision forward; to civilize American capitalism by protecting workers and consumers alike while providing genuine equality of opportunity for all. New Dealers might have relied on votes from blacks, but they had done little or nothing to promote their rights or opportunities. The priority now was to make sure that black Americans could become equal citizens and share in the wealth and opportunity of a dynamic economy and society.

Kennedy's inaugural speech, famously inviting his fellow countrymen and women to ask not what their country could do for them but what they could do for their country, was not just a classic statement of the best in the American liberal tradition but brilliantly identified liberalism with the American way. After Kennedy's tragic assassination Lyndon Johnson was to carry the program forward in his vision of a Great Society, setting out to achieve the elimination of poverty, the genuine enfranchisement of all American citizens regardless of their race, the extension of medical protection to every American, the championing of the environment, massive training of the unskilled, and the establishment of model cities. Nor did this vision represent just the idealized hopes of liberal America; the American business establishment backed the program enthusiastically, and when Johnson left office even the Nixon administration was to establish the Environmental Protection Agency and act to ensure minimum standards of health and safety at work.

Thirty years later, the whole apparatus, together with the thinking behind it, is decried and vilified; it is impossible to imagine a similar impetus being established today, let alone supported so extensively by the business community. George W. Bush is pledged further to emasculate what remains of the New Deal settlement, whether in workers' rights, business regulation, or progressive taxation; his brand of conservatism, masquerading as "compassionate," is the apotheosis of the thirty-year struggle to vanquish liberalism. It is a story so important both to America and the globe that it is worth analyzing in detail.

Sowing the Seeds of Decline: Triumphant Liberalism and Its Weaknesses

When Lyndon Johnson signed the Civil Rights Act in 1964 he made the famous aside that he had just lost the Democratic party the South. This was no casual quip; in private White House discussions over civil rights he had openly conceded that it might destroy the Democrats—but nevertheless maintained that the principle of establishing civil rights for blacks had to be "pressed for as a matter of right." The hope, of course, was that the Democrats could more than compensate for such losses by gaining ground in the North; the fear was that if the huge expanses of the South and West of the United States ever became more fully populated and industrialized, the Democrats might become a permanent minority party.

Johnson's words were prescient: subsequent history has more than borne out his prediction. The states of the old Confederacy are the heartland of American conservatism. Until the last thirty years these had been predominantly agricultural economies—even now, large plantation-style farm units remain at the core of agricultural production—and natural homes for the unique combination of macho individual self-reliance, religious fundamentalism, nationalism, prejudice against blacks, belief in private property and free enterprise together with sexual and social reaction that defines American conservatism. These are the apostles of the states' rights against the reach of the federal government in Washington—the inevitable consequence of the Civil War—and the rights now advocated by the new conservatives as an entrenchment of freedom.

Above all, these are the old slave states, where 250 years of slavery casts its long and ominous shadow into the twenty-first century. The Confederate cause might have been lost militarily in 1865, but thirty years later the condition of southern blacks had scarcely improved, economically, socially, or in terms of citizens' rights. So-called Jim Crow laws enforced a form of apartheid, so that blacks traveled, lived, and were educated separately from whites, and could not exercise basic rights such as voting or testifying in court without the threat of beatings, burning, and even murder executed by the Ku Klux Klan. Even as late as the early 1960s the Klan bombed black churches and killed blacks without any fear of being brought to justice. The racism was endemic; but slavery and its shadow also cemented the cultural view that labor should be cheap, disposable, and without rights. Over the twentieth century the south became the center of anti-unionism as part of the southern ideological cocktail of antifederalism and suspicion of government and its intentions.

The violence lives on, now in the form of scattered, lunatic, but danger-ous militias that exercise their constitutional right to bear arms in the woods and hills, rehearsing armed resistance to what they believe are the dark ambitions of the federal government, or invasion by the UN or communist forces. Nor is this paranoiac element confined to the South. One of the largest of such groups, the militia of Montana, hides out in the hills, grimly warning in its feverish newsletter about how America's white population is about to be overwhelmed and issuing warnings about the anti-American ambitions of the state and the loss of individual freedom. It was this same pathology that drove the mad group led by Timothy McVeigh to bomb fed-eral offices in Oklahoma City in 1995, causing over 160 innocent deaths. Others of this ilk are linked to the sending of letters with anthrax to pro-abortion groups. They may be light-years away from the right-wing think tanks, but they are linked by the same thread.

The picture is not one of wholly unrelieved reaction. Politically the South has necessarily been sympathetic to state-led initiatives for economic development as the only means of alleviating desperate poverty; Louisiana provided the political base for Huey Long's populist economic Keynesian-ism in the 1930s and, for all his segregationism, Alabama's George Wallace was enthusiastically committed to building up the state's public infra-structure. Here social conservatism and racism have sat side by side with deployment of the state to serve the free-enterprise system, but only if the essential pillars of the southern order are left in place—in particular a sub-ordinate role for the black man and woman. It has always been clear that if this culture ever became predominant nationally, the prospects for Amer-ican liberalism would be poor.

In a sense, what has happened to liberalism is the North receiving its due for never properly engaging with the different civilization that consti-tutes the South. The founding fathers of the U.S. Constitution—Washing-ton, Hamilton, and Madison—all knew that a constitution that proclaimed the equality of all men and women could never be squared with slavery. But they also knew that the political necessity of combining all the former

British colonies—even those whose economy was dependent upon slave ownership—into a United States of America trumped the need to offer any constitutional injunction enfranchising the black population. And as Washington and Madison were slave owners themselves they were in any case compromised. So—better leave the issue to the individual discretion of member states. It was a hypocrisy and a betrayal that has bedeviled the United States to this day.

Even after the North under Lincoln's Republicans won the Civil War, the same ambiguities remained. The North turned a blind eye to the devices deployed by white plantation owners and the southern white political establishment to sustain white supremacy after the Civil War—ranging from setting literacy tests for voters to disenfranchising felons. Moreover, the Democrats, then, as the anti-Republican party, holding the advantage in the South, needed to secure their southern base if they were to mount any effective national challenge to the Republicans, on whom victory in the war had conferred a new and immense legitimacy. Add this political calculation to the pork-barrel nature of American politics and the constitution with its checks and balances and it is not surprising that it proved impossible to assemble any national majority in favor of asserting proper civil rights.

The Progressive movement avoided the issue, as did Roosevelt's New Dealers. Their initiatives were aimed at improving the condition of American working people as a class against the rich and powerful rather than championing individual rights—an approach that poor southern whites and the Democratic southern establishment were happy to support, given their own willingness to use the state to promote economic development, just so long as the racial question was not raised. Louisiana's Huey Long, for example, was in economic terms more radical than Roosevelt. In an American context the creation of the Progressive coalition was something of a political triumph, implying as it did and does that the minorities who together formed the coalition put aside the advocacy of their individual rights and instead made common cause. All politics in democracies is about the art of coalition building; it inevitably involves compromises, but as long as there is a sufficiently large core group and a robust enough sense of overall mission, the coalition will hold. In the United States the task is made more difficult because necessarily in a polity that encompasses a continent the core group in any coalition is smaller; coalitions are more a plurality of minorities than an anchored political grouping. In addition, all interest groups in the United States are versed in the language and culture of rights, which makes them intrinsically less willing to make common cause around a common agenda.

The Progressive and liberal approach was to borrow the European center-left language of a working-class interest that needed to be asserted against the rich and business, but rather than use the language of socialist transformation, instead campaign for practical ways of improving working people's lot in a capitalist society that would remain capitalist. With a tacit silence on the civil rights question (for example, the New Deal Social Security Act conveniently excluded agricultural and domestic workers, who were predominantly black), southern Democrats could sit as easily as northern trade unionists in the liberal coalition—which thus encompassed a range of religious beliefs that stretched from Catholicism through to southern fundamentalism.

Eisenhower's election in 1952 did nothing to threaten the new consensus. The new Republican administration respected the essentials of the New Deal framework, at least in part solidly to bind in the American working class to the Cold War confrontation against communism and head off the potential appeal of left-wing ideas to organized labor. In any case the experience of World War II, together with the New Deal, had immensely enhanced the authority of the federal government. It had been government contracts that had underwritten the immense increase in U.S. production and scientific leadership during the war; and it was the government's GI Bill that guaranteed every American serviceman the chance to acquire the skills, education, and housing necessary to succeed in civilian life. Laissez-faire and free markets meant depression, unemployment, and lack of opportunity for all; government meant growth, work, new life-chances.

With business accepting the enlargement of the government's role, the liberals felt that the coalition they had built to support activist government was solid. The next phase in the Progressive journey was to back the growing civil rights movement in the south, agitating to end segregation and discrimination, and to complete the task that should have been finished in 1865. The United States was the richest and most productive economy in the world. It was an age of extraordinary optimism and self-confidence; there was nothing that the United States could not attempt and succeed. It was politically impossible not to include southern blacks in the fruits of the postwar boom—and the country, it seemed, could comfortably afford the necessary social expenditures.

The resulting Civil Rights Act of 1964 in many respects marked the beginning of the high tide of American liberalism that would end a decade later with the Supreme Court's judgment legalizing abortion in 1973. Federal spending on the poor during these years more than quadrupled and there was liberal progress across the board, with the distribution of guns by mail order being limited in 1968 and states like Arkansas and Mississippi finally losing the right to ban the teaching of Darwinian theories of evolution. By the time Congress passed the Equal Rights Amendment (ERA) in 1972, outlawing sexual discrimination, the liberal advance seem assured; but the liberals were beginning to be overconfident and the conservative anti-ERA forces were determined to kill the measure. Too few states ratified it and it failed to become law.

The most important and politically potent initiative of this period was the launch of affirmative action, the concept that was to prove the fateful trigger to a massive conservative reaction. The Civil Rights Act itself, together with the Voting Rights Act that followed, carefully and explicitly avoided positive discrimination in favor of blacks as a group. Rather, the acts sought to outlaw any intervention that obstructed individual blacks from exercising their individual constitutional rights as citizens in elections. In 1964, for example, only 7 percent of blacks in Mississippi had succeeded in registering to vote; by 1969, after the passage of the two acts, the proportion had grown to 61 percent. There were parallel improvements across the South whose fairness and legitimacy it was impossible to contest.

But black disadvantage extended well beyond their lack of citizen rights; poor farm workers in the South, they were the ghetto dwellers of the north. Redress demanded that the economic and social stigma of having a black skin be taken on directly, which was to give blacks privileges as a group in order to give them the same proportional opportunities as whites. Thus employment quotas were established in the public sector and for public contractors; there were quotas for a fair share of good housing and special preferences for educational places. At the time, the movement to redress blacks' position was supported by the Republicans (the party, after all, of Lincoln), with Richard Nixon in 1969 fighting for affirmative action quotas against opposition from Democrats influenced by a trade union leadership that was fearful that white jobs would be stolen by blacks. However, affirmative action was ultimately to prove fatally divisive.

Doubts about affirmative action were not just rooted in racism; they went—and go—to the heart of the twin incompatibilities that form the basis of the American credo. Egalitarianism and citizenship demand affirmative action for blacks (or women) as a group; individualism and equality of opportunity mean that any help should be given only to individual Americans who earn their advance by merit, and those who try to achieve the American dream should not have their progress blocked by administrative fiat favoring a minority. If American liberalism had used the social contract framework to address the black issue, as argued in chapter 2, it could have avoided the political skewer on which it impaled itself and kept the white working class in the liberal coalition. It should have adopted Rawls's formula of creating an infrastructure of justice for every American. Blacks, of course, would have benefited disproportionally, but on the objective justice of their claim for help. Instead, affirmative action created a tremendous sense of injustice. As it was, liberalism never sorted out its own ambiguities over the question—leaving an opening which conservatism was to exploit murderously to help end the liberal ascendancy.

Conservatism's Revenge

For the first half of the 1960s conservatism seemed trapped. The U.S. economy was strong; productivity and growth rose on average by more than 3 percent a year. There seemed no problem in simultaneously financing the massive Great Society program and the military competition with the Soviet Union. Indeed, this competition made the great civil rights and social programs even more imperative. America's racial tensions and poverty were a gift to Soviet propagandists, so that even Republicans could share liberal concerns—if only as a tool in superpower rivalry.

But by the late 1960s severe strains were beginning to show. The United

73

States had decided after 1945 that its own security interests would be best served by throwing a military and diplomatic cordon sanitaire around the entire Euro-Asian littoral, thus constraining the possible geographical advance of communism to the Pacific and Atlantic seaboards. Hence NATO, the Berlin airlift and the Korean War. When communism gained ground in Indochina the doctrine demanded that the same stance be taken in South Vietnam in the 1960s to stop its conquest by the North and assimilation into a communist Vietnam, not least as a demonstration to America's Asian and European allies—and to Moscow and Beijing—that the United States was not in the business of appeasement.

As defense expenditure jumped to nearly 10 percent of GDP at the height of the Vietnam War, inflation moved toward 5 percent and the trade deficit reached hitherto unprecedented levels. The dollar began to come under strain as the linchpin of the international financial system. In 1971 Nixon was forced to break the U.S. currency's fixed linkage with gold and preside over the dismemberment of the Bretton Woods system of semifixed exchange rates, pegged to the dollar and thus to gold, that had held since the late 1940s. The United States could not, it found, support the dollar, the Vietnam War, and its Great Society program simultaneously.

It was this failure that created the intellectual opportunity for which conservatives had been preparing. Kennedy had chosen to prime the American economy with Keynesian-style tax cuts in the early 1960s, and the economic consensus was that the federal government should manipulate demand in the economy by changes in taxes and public spending in order to sustain the growth of employment or lower inflation, as the case might be. In essence the proposition was that the state could and must direct the economy to achieve public goals—anathema to the American right. In the mid-1950s William Buckley's periodical the *National Review* had begun to marshal a coherent anti-Keynesian, pro–free-market position articulating the philosophy of Friedrich Hayek, in which any extension of state activity was the thin end of a wedge destroying the functioning of capitalism and was literally *The Road to Serfdom*, as Hayek titled his book of 1944. For Hayek, wealth creation was the product of economic freedom, which had to be protected from any kind of state intervention. But in the 1950s he had few listeners in the United States. The archconservative Barry Goldwater suffered a landslide defeat in the 1964 presidential election, with

Johnson dismissing him as nutty as a fruitcake—but his winning of the five states of the deep south was a harbinger of what was to follow.

As the 1960s wore on, the economic background became more favorable to conservative preoccupations, and conservative intellectuals intensified their case for free-market economics, linking its precepts to libertarianism and the case for minimal government which conservatives believed underwrote the responsible, and thus virtuous, citizen. These two streams of thought—economic and philosophical—were interwoven through the 1960s in the University of Chicago under the tutelage of the philosophy professor Leo Strauss, a refugee from Nazism who blamed the liberal Weimar Republic for the Holocaust, and the economics professor Milton Friedman. Strauss was to win the largest and most devoted following—or collection of disciples, as one of his students called them[1]—in American academic life. The good society, he insisted, was constructed upon virtuous, morally centered citizens of good character, and the case against state-led attempts socially to engineer more freedom or equality was that they undermined such virtue by relieving individuals of the necessity of facing the consequences of their individual actions. He thought that religion and nationalism helped to entrench such virtue, and that liberalism and secularism undermined it—and that unless the United States was watchful it faced the same fate as the Weimar Republic. Even if religion was bunk and its moral codes impossible to maintain, said Strauss, the task of the educated elite was to keep quiet and maintain the fiction in the name of order. Although Strauss died in 1973, twenty years later the Republican Newt Gingrich was to claim that his "Contract with America" of 1994 was inspired by Strauss—and almost every strand in current American conservative thought, from dependency theory to incorporating the evangelical movement into the Republican party, can trace its lineage back to him. Today the most militantly conservative members of the Bush administration—Deputy Defense Secretary Paul Wolfowitz and Attorney General John Ashcroft—are committed Straussians. When Wolfowitz insists on the United States's right to strike militarily, unilaterally, and pre-emptively against "rogue" states believed to threaten U.S. security or Ashcroft composes and sings hymns in praise of American nationalism, their philosophical and intellectual patron is Strauss. It is a lethal legacy.

However, it took Friedman and the University of Chicago's conservative ultra-free-market economics faculty to put some practical policy bite into the philosophy. Friedman's intellectual bridgehead was his explanation of inflation, which rose steadily over the 1960s and emerged in the 1970s as the leading economic problem. Friedman's proposition, which came to be known as monetarism, was that the rate of inflation was set automatically by the growth in the supply of money, which in turn could be generated only by the state, which has a monopoly of money creation. If inflation was rising, then either the government had mistakenly set interest rates too low, or it was spending too much and financing that expenditure by printing money—all in the attempt artificially to prevent the economy from doing what it "naturally" wanted to do. The cure was to curb the role of the state and its associated spending, and thus the growth of money—and in the process inflation would settle at low levels and economic growth would be rekindled. Behind this view lay the judgment that a free-market economy was essentially self-regulating and generated wealth spontaneously, and that government got in the way of these natural processes and damaged the vitality of capitalism.

A few lecture rooms away, Strauss was insisting that such a government-free environment created the virtuous citizen, especially if it was reinforced by powerful religious sentiment. The very particular brand of American conservatism began to take off in earnest.

Friedman and the so-called Chicago school purported to be "scientific" economic theoreticians, but behind the panoply of monetarism and the associated theoretical toolbox that made it work, notably the theory of rational expectations, and of the rational economic man, lay a Straussian and highly ideological conception of the world. In order to prove that markets tended to work perfectly, the Chicago school had to guarantee that individuals could be relied upon to respond to price signals and, if they made mistakes, immediately to change their behavior—that is, they were rational, formed rational expectations, and adjusted those expectations rationally—despite the overwhelming evidence, furnished by liberal economists, to the contrary. For example, it is simply unrealistic to assume that every market actor has perfect information and that the cost of acquiring information is equal for all, as the Chicago economists claimed. It is perfectly possible for, say, unemployed workers not to find available work because they do not know it exists—so that as a result wages get pitched above what they otherwise should be. Equally, bankers may ration credit to perfectly creditworthy borrowers because they are ignorant or have imperfect information about them—or, equally, lend to uncreditworthy borrowers for the same reason. In short, there is market failure.[2]

But the Chicago school could not admit this. At the center of its universe was the conception of the self-interested, profit-maximizing individual who definitionally cannot make systematic mistakes—first cousin to Strauss's virtuous citizen, and thus the coping stone of a healthy, free-market American republic. It was this ultimately ideological conception that made the narrow economic critiques of the Chicago/Friedman position so ineffective, even though the Chicago school was largely wrong and the implementation of its ideas has weakened the U.S. economy, as we will see in the years ahead. Ideology protected Friedman from the mounting concerns that his methodology, automatically and mechanically linking money supply growth and subsequent inflation over America's economic history, was wanting.[3] The monetarist theory had to be right, because it had to be right to minimize the role of government. The criticism that markets are not self-regulating, nor ever have been, was simply dismissed. It might be true that stock markets, for example, are well known for their bubbles and irrational depressions, or that capitalist firms rig markets to their advantage if they can. But the conservatives, instead of acknowledging these phenomena as inherent in the operation of markets, insisted they arose because some obstacle had been erected—usually by government or unions—that hindered their free operation.

As for the conservative claim that individuals are all-knowing, the human condition is that we face an unpredictable future that can engender irrational fears or hopes which then dictate our actions; the ridiculous expectations that generate irrational outcomes like a stock market bubble can make it rational to buy even in the middle of the bubble. For conservative economists such a suggestion is a logical impossibility; the theoretical framework cannot permit such heresies, for if admitted they would bring down the whole ideological house of cards. No less seriously, the conservative perspective that market economies are solely and completely about the capacity to exchange goods and services in a series of contingent, potentially reversible market contracts is a very limited conception of wealth generation and innovation. The market may be a necessary precondition for wealth generation, but by itself it is insufficient. It does not, as argued in later chapters, take any account of the necessary role of organizations in integrating and marshaling physical and human capital—people whose strategies and capabilities are determined by their histories. Innovation is not switched on like a light bulb inside an entrepreneur's head at the prospect of profits, as conservative economists hypothesized. Its roots are much more complex, as this book will explore.

The Chicago school view that markets are held together and wealth generated by no other means than mere economic self-interest is bunk. But conservatives are obliged to play down or ignore the complicated truth that markets depend upon webs of reciprocal obligations, trust, and social capital that are created by conceptions of fairness and natural justice to which self-interest stands in tension rather than harmony. They cannot accept any criticism on these lines, or even allow it to dent the monetarist, free-market thesis, because to do so would fatally weaken their objective—to delegitimize government, the social, and the collective.

Because of the enormous care and effort expended by conservatives to make sure that their propositions were intellectually coherent, once the foundations were accepted conservative economics could be contested only if the philosophy and politics upon which it rested was challenged root and branch—but this American liberals failed to do. This is why Hayekian and Straussian ideas were so important. Hayek made the linkage between economic and political freedom; Strauss made the fundamental moral proposition that the good society depended on moral individuals—and that individual morality was a higher good than either equality or opportunity. Thus any economics that relied, as Keynesianism does, on the notion that government expresses the common will and public interest is automatically devalued—even if it produces results—first because it enlarges the role of the state and second because it represents a value system that attacks and undermines a superior universe of moral individuals. Conservatives do not even admit that any collective initiative should be taken to minimize inequality, for example, because in the last resort poverty is evidence of "poor" character—that is further morally degraded by accepting welfare.

It was Robert Nozick, as we saw in the previous chapter, who took the conservative argument even further. All state action was characterized as coercive. If, in the name of fairness, the state tries to alleviate poverty, it must perforce confiscate part of some individuals' income as tax to support the incomes of others. The notion that tax is the payment citizens make for the public goods, ranging from pensions to health, that the market is incapable of providing, cannot be accepted.

This combined conservative philosophical stance that the state is amoral, inefficient and coercive was the platform for a savagely effective attack on American liberalism. It has been, in short, the ally of a new barbarism even while it purports to keep barbarism at bay, the sponsor of economic degeneration even as it advertises its commitment to wealth creation. But liberalism never understood the totality of the ideology it confronted, the persecution complex of those who developed it, their fanatical determination to press home their advantage, or the degree to which America's cultural tinder would aid conservatism's advance.

Laying the Conservative Foundation

The South did not need to learn from Straussians that religion was vital social cement; it knew that already. It did not need to learn that individual states' rights were part of America's natural constitution of freedom; that was the basis of the Confederate case. It understood what politicians meant when they spoke of welfare queens, family breakdown, and the dependency culture; they were talking about feckless black sexuality and sponging off whites. The South was the natural political base of the National Rifle Association, Christian Coalition, and ideological businessmen who would drive even the centrist Business Roundtable to the right; and its willingness to mobilize behind the ideological openings offered by the great right-wing intellectuals—Ayn Rand, Milton Friedman, Leo Strauss, Irving Kristol, et al.—has been at the heart of the conservative revival.

Even so, this ultraconservative critique that aimed to destroy the postwar consensus and the foundations of American liberalism might have remained at the margins of debate if the United States had continued to prosper in the 1970s while healing its social and racial wounds. It did not. The Democratic coalition, incorporating northern blue-collar workers of all religions and ethnic backgrounds, southern blacks, and the liberal professional classes, was already fraying before the advance of the right and its attacks on the implications of the civil rights revolution. Race was working its poison in American politics. For northern Catholics the issue might be abortion; for blue-collar workers in the South the flashpoint was affirmative action; suburban whites everywhere recoiled from busing to limit educational segregation. As the political analysts Ruy Teixeira and Joel Rogers observe, 55 percent of American voters are white working class, and over the 1970s they deserted the Democrats in droves; to them, the party seemed more interested in helping blacks and gays than its traditional base.[4] At just this moment liberal America faced a gathering economic crisis. Inflation mounted; growth and productivity slowed. Imports soared; the dollar weakened. Unemployment grew—and blue-collar America was hurting, with its traditional champion apparently no longer focused on its core voters' interests. And if that were not enough, there was the ignominy of losing the Vietnam War. Liberalism at home and abroad seemed to have reached a dead end.

And, as the assumptions of the postwar era were progressively challenged, Nixon resigned over Watergate—his attempted impeachment by the Democrats an event which the Republicans would never forgive or forget, and which they determined they would one day repay in spades. For that they would need a dominance of Congress that had so far eluded them, and for which the necessary precondition was the building of a conservative coalition as strong as the liberal one they sought to demolish. The 1970s were to offer them five simultaneous advantages. The apparent failings of the economy gave Friedman and the Chicago school their chance to open up the entire economic argument, and with it create the space for conservative ideas deploring welfare and the state to enter the arena. Losing the Vietnam War added to a growing sentiment that government was flawed just as winning World War II had enhanced government prestige. The growing sense that the 1960s movement for civil and equal rights had gone too far allowed the right to play the subliminal race card—not always, indeed, very subliminally—thus detaching the white working class from the Democrats. The shift of the United States's center of economic gravity to the South and West offered a natural strong hinterland and secure political base. And finally, the increasing role of the media made money ever more important in U.S. politics, giving conservatism, richer than liberalism, an advantage upon which it has ruthlessly capitalized for more than a generation. The foundations had been laid for the conservatives' march to power.

By the middle of the 1970s the United States was mired in stagflation, the rate of productivity growth was falling sharply, and the dollar was consistently weak, reflecting in part the growing and persistent strength of Asian exports to the United States, particularly from Japan. Nixon's wage and price controls had failed to curb inflation, and the Keynesian mainstream seemed to have no solution that would address the gathering sense of economic pessimism and evidence of failure.

In reality, America's economic problems were rooted as much in the way the international economic system it had created was now developing as in any domestic shortcomings—although this was never to be admitted by the right. Inevitably the rapidly growing Asian and European economies had gained a competitive advantage in some key manufacturing sectors—notably cars and consumer durables—through a heavy program of investment in state-of-the-art technology that necessarily lifted them to the frontiers of productive possibility, and were taking advantage of the liberal world trade regime the United States had devised to exploit the narrowing of their productivity gap with the United States and raise their exports to the world's biggest market. They were responding to no more than the order the United States had constructed for its own geopolitical purposes. Kennedy had pioneered a major round of tariff reduction in the 1960s—the so-called Kennedy round—largely to help consolidate the Asian and European economies into the American-led capitalist West. Khrushchev, the Soviet premier, had boasted that Soviet production and standards of living would overtake those of the West by 1970, saying that "When we catch you up, as we pass by, we will wave to you."[5] The Americans' angry response was to use free trade as a mechanism for spreading American living standards to Europe and the rapidly industrializing countries of Asia in order to limit any potential appeal from a successful communism. Thus part of U.S. industry's difficulty in the 1970s was simply that of adjusting to the new international division of labor as production in Asia and Europe grew to the maturity that the United States had wished into being. America's share of global manufacturing fell by 23 percent between 1970 and 1980—a decade in which the foreign share of the U.S. car market rose from 8 to 22 percent.

Similarly, the problem of inflation which began to loom large in the 1970s needs to be interpreted against the trends of the international financial system the United States had created. Although the British (especially Keynes)[6] had lobbied hard during World War II for an international system less dependent upon the dollar, the Americans had insisted that their currency should be central—a position that in the immediate postwar years was almost unavoidable given that the U.S. economy constituted nearly half the world economy. But the consequence of a generation of American trade deficits and the accompanying emergence of a vast offshore market in dollars (eurodollars) around which London rebuilt its preeminence as a world financial center was to create a vast pool of dollar liquidity. The world had too many dollars chasing too few goods.

When the discipline of the Bretton Woods system collapsed between 1971 and 1973, Europe, Asia, and the United States all stimulated their economies apparently free of an exchange rate constraint, and it was against this background of surging demand and billions of footloose dollars that the OPEC countries were able to make the quadrupling of the oil price stick. Other commodity prices jumped in sympathy. As a result, American inflation rose sharply and the share of profits as a proportion of GDP nosedived because the oil-dependent structure of production could not be changed overnight; wealth was being transferred from the oil-dependent United States to largely third-world oil producers. Investment fell, and the lower trajectory of output growth implied slower productivity growth.

But the intellectual and political argument in the United States was—as it is today—extraordinarily America-centered. Rather than describe the problems of the U.S. economy as arising from a very particular international conjuncture, the conservatives saw their opportunity to press home their view of the world. In essence, as Jude Wanniski argued in *The Way the World Works*, one of the defining texts of the resurgent right, published in 1978, the natural productivity of the so-called supply side of the U.S. economy had been fatally undermined by a burden of regulation and taxation that obstructed the pattern of incentives that go-getting Americans needed to deliver wealth generation. In the free-enterprise system, enterprise had to be free—it needed to declare independence from the postwar bargain with government and return to the truths of the American way.

Together with the monetarist propositions of Milton Friedman, this protest amounted to a full-scale conservative assault on the liberal economic worldview; it was liberalism, rather than the trends in the global economy, that was causing America's travails. If the United States wanted lower inflation, it should generate less money supply growth, which meant reducing budget deficits—not by raising taxes, which would damage the supply side, but by cutting back federal spending, which had jumped by 5 percent of GDP over the 1970s. Indeed, Wanniski and a little-known economist, Arthur Laffer—championed by a Republican congressman, Jack Kemp—argued that cutting taxes would so stimulate vital economic growth and boost accompanying tax revenues that the budget deficit could be cut—one of economic history's more famous delusions about having your cake and eating it. Laffer posited his famous "Laffer curve" on a napkin in a Wall Street restaurant, and a theory that had no empirical or theoretical support took off. Conservatism had become the new orthodoxy so quickly that even its more absurd propositions could suddenly be inserted in the policy mainstream. For the first time since the gold standard and laissez-faire, the right had a complete economic theory with which to contest the liberal consensus. Moreover, as the Californians had proved in 1978 with Proposition 13—a measure halving the state's property taxes which became the forerunner of similar antitax laws in more than half the states—it was connecting with a popular mood.

The great right-wing think tanks—the reconstituted American Enterprise Institute, the Hoover Institution, and the Heritage Foundation, set up in 1973—promulgated this worldview with the fervor of ideological zealots. Their most reliable outlet were the op-ed pages of the conservative *Wall Street Journal*, run by the obsessive Robert Bartley, sponsor of the Wanniski-Laffer supply-side coalition; the number of anti–big-government leaders in the *Wall Street Journal* exploded in the first half of the 1970s.[7] Business in general began to shift its position. It had given the Goldwater campaign in 1964 a wide berth, but by the early 1970s there was a readiness to find cash to support the new think tanks, and even begin to lobby for a more "free-market" approach to economic management. The Business

Roundtable, founded in 1975 as inflation topped 10 percent, brought chief executives together for the first time to make the business case directly rather than through the medium of trade associations; already some CEOs felt that the postwar readiness of business to accept regulation, taxation, and trade unionization was now outmoded. Their initial particular obsessions were the need to challenge the power of organized labor and the growing consumer movement, whose most conspicuous and outspoken advocate was Ralph Nader. But as the 1970s progressed they began to think there might be something in the wider ideology of the right-wing think tanks.

Nowhere was the need to assert conservatism felt more keenly than in the South, paradoxically the beneficiary of the adjustments being forced upon the United States by the world economy. While the high-wage factories of New England, the Great Lakes, and industrial Midwest suffered from foreign competition, the low-wage, cheap-land economies of the South found themselves the object of new interest. The center of economic gravity in the United States moved south and west, aided and abetted by massive federal defense spending: during World War II 60 of the country's 100 new army camps were located in the capacious South, and by the 1970s it boasted more than half the United States's defense installations. California, already the home of high-tech industries related to defense, began to develop Silicon Valley, while high oil prices made Texas an El Dorado. Over the 1970s more than one and a half million Americans migrated south. The men and women behind a new class of growing young businesses—the Sunbelt entrepreneurs—made overnight fortunes apparently independently of the efforts of Washington, tripartism, and the culture of the New Deal. They keenly appreciated the arguments of the new conservative think tanks and the Straussian, Hayekian, and Friedmanite intellectuals, and were ready to back them with time and cash.[8] They believed that such a small investment to fight and win the war of ideas would have a bumper payoff, and so it has. In the conservative heartlands of the South and West, the American way was alive and kicking.

For the first time in the twentieth century the South was making sustained economic advances in relation to the North, and as a result was gaining in self-confidence. Newly and increasingly prosperous, the South felt able to associate its own longstanding prejudices with the intellectual nostrums of the new conservatism. Southerners delighted in the pro quota, antiwar Democratic presidential candidate George McGovern losing every state except Massachusetts in 1972; the cluster of ultraliberal views associated with McGovern and his electoral failure has cast a shadow over the Democrats that lasts to this day. In 1977 the National Rifle Association moved its headquarters out of New York, dropped its image as primarily a lobby for field sports, and instead, after an internal coup, decided overtly to copy the civil rights movement, campaigning for gun ownership as an individual's constitutional right.[9] After the famous 1973 *Roe* v. *Wade* ruling in the Supreme Court, abortion became one of the most divisive issues in the country, with southern Protestants establishing themselves as the leaders of a "pro-life" movement that included northern Catholics. The poisonous divide on abortion marked the politicization of American religion—again overtly borrowing from the civil rights movement—and in 1978 Jerry Falwell established the Moral Majority, whose prime aim was to persuade evangelicals to register and vote. The term he chose was a further extension of Nixon's "silent majority"—the forgotten Americans, in his characterization, who worked, saved, and cared. Neither Nixon nor Falwell needed to say it overtly, but the moral and silent majority were white—it was blacks who did not work, did not save, and relied on welfare. Here again race was being deployed for conservative ends. Formidable new forces were abroad in American politics, before which the Democratic coalition consolidated by Roosevelt and Kennedy began to wilt and fragment.

The last piece of the jigsaw was money. American politics has always been unapologetically about money chasing influence, but one of the paradoxes of the reform of campaign finance that followed Watergate, including the prohibition on direct funding of candidates and campaigns by corporations and unions, was the legitimization of the political action committee (PAC)—a dodge that allowed corporations and unions alike to give money indirectly to support their candidates and causes. The result was a quadrupling in the number of PACs by the 1980 presidential election, the vast majority of them vehicles for the newly politicized business class to give cash to the Republicans.[10] In 1979–80 the Democrats received 21.7 percent of the level of Republican donations; four years earlier both parties had received the same.

By 1979, when the Business Roundtable published its manifesto, essentially arguing for what was later to be dubbed the "Washington consensus" (balanced budgets, tax cuts, tight money, deregulation, anti-union laws), with the Moral Majority and NRA campaigning hard on conservative social issues, the conservatives—spearheaded by the intellectual shock troops of the right—were on the move. They had cash, ideas, and a background of economic stagflation. The center of political and economic gravity was moving to the South and West. The liberal coalition was fragmenting before the charges that it was pro-black and anti-white, and that its economic and social policies did not work—and, worse, promoted the poverty and amorality that they intended to alleviate. Government did not work and produced self-defeating results. What the conservatives needed was a leader, a man who could do for Republicanism what Kennedy and Roosevelt had done for liberalism; somebody who could translate their disparate ideas into an attractive political rhetoric, and then identify them with the American way. Enter Ronald Reagan.

The Long Conservative Ascendancy

Reagan is one of the most underestimated political figures in modern times. Mocked by his opponents as a forgetful B-movie actor with a few folksy lines, a mouthpiece for policy ideas scripted by somebody else, through the 1980s he provided the platform for the consolidation of conservative ideas and policies and created a political coalition in support of them that survives to this day. Even if he vastly overestimated the size of the Soviet Union's military arsenal, he saw more clearly than any of his circle the strategic possibility of bringing communism to its knees through ratcheting up defense spending to a rate the Soviet Union could not match—and if that, combined with the result of the other strategic necessity, tax cuts, was to produce an impossibly high budget deficit and an early recession, then so be it. Reagan was playing for high stakes, and with victory in the Cold War in 1989 and conservatism ascendant in the early 2000s he can claim to have won. In that sense he must rank as one of the most significant political figures of the second half of the twentieth century.

Yet despite all his advantages his winning margin over Carter in 1980 was comparatively tight, dependent on the 70 percent of the southern white vote that went his way. Johnson's eerie warning back in 1964 about destroying the Democrats resonated ominously. From the outset Reagan conceived his mission as reestablishing what he saw as solid American values at home and contesting communism abroad, heavily laced by his romantic attachment to religion and the American way. The Soviet Union was a godless evil empire, while in the American heartland—weighed down by too much government and needy of spiritual revival—"lives the hope of the world."[11] He rarely talked about capitalism or markets, preferring instead to make a moral, spiritual, and religious pitch in which the state was bad and individual freedom good. Reagan may never have read Strauss, Hayek, and Nozick, but many who worked in his administration had; the president was their popularizer.

After the initial depression in the early 1980s, brought about by sky-high interest rates trying to undo the twin inflationary effects of tax cuts and sharply rising defense expenditure, Reagan's government began to get into its ideological stride. By the mid- to late 1980s a consumer boom was under way, driven largely by an explosion of consumer credit after a massive round of financial deregulation. Americans saved less because they could borrow more easily, especially from the savings and loan associations (S&Ls) that had been given more freedom to lend even while their deposits remained guaranteed—a right they abused, ending up confronting the American taxpayer with a bill recognized to be in excess of $200 billion for the subsequent bailout (see chapter 4). But tax cuts and spending increases left the United States with a persistently high budget deficit, while imports poured in to produce an equally large trade deficit—the famous twin deficits. Still, Reagan's sunny optimism remained undented; it was morning again in America.

His vice president, George Bush senior, comfortably saw off the Democratic challenger Michael Dukakis in 1988 by portraying him as an unreconstructed liberal who in particular was wobbly on capital punishment. An effective TV advertising campaign reminded voters that Governor Dukakis had released from jail on parole a convicted killer, Willie Horton, who had murdered again; Horton, inevitably, was black. With some 30 percent of all violent crimes and 60 percent of robberies committed by blacks,[12] the message was explicit: liberals and Democrats, wedded to affirmative action, could not face up to what was really happening in the United States. It was this command of the cultural, racist, and religious arguments that allowed the right to control the agenda irrespective of economic mishaps and disasters. This, after all, was the year Operation Rescue was founded, aimed at blockading abortion clinics throughout the country; it was to prompt 1,500 arrests. Reagan had throughout his presidency maintained a drumbeat of pro-family, pro-life rhetoric, passing a largely tokenistic act gagging abortion counseling. He stroked the prejudices of the Moral Majority and the gun lobby alike, and in 1986 famously legalized interstate gun sales. In these years, too, the impact of money and lobbying in American politics exploded; it was in the 1980s that the lobbying industry based on Washington's K Street bedded down. Officials and cabinet members moved from government to lobbying company and sometimes back again with amoral ease, so that policy increasingly became determined by the relative financial power of the various lobbyists—a situation that benefited the right. The conservative ascendancy was complete.

In hard economic terms Reagan and then Bush presided over twelve years of indifferent economic performance in which the imbalances of the U.S. economy grew more acute. The wages of blue-collar workers stagnated under the pressure of international competition and growing pressure on U.S. corporations to maximize their returns to stockholders. This was the era of corporate raiding, merger mania, and Wall Street excess. Financial deregulation was to leave most Americans with colossal debts. Income inequality began to take off, so that over the 1980s the top 1 percent of families saw their incomes double while the bottom 20 percent suffered a 10 percent decline.[13] Meanwhile the country's infrastructure rotted. The competitiveness of the old industrial heartlands declined as investment stagnated and R&D expenditure was sacrificed for short-term profit maximization. Steel, cars, shipbuilding, and chemicals gave ground to foreign competition, while the Japanese threatened to dominate the emerging new technologies based on the microchip.

As Paul Krugman wrote in *Peddling Prosperity*, the verdict on the supply-siders, monetarists, and economic conservatives has to be a resounding indictment. Most Americans suffered declines or negligible increases in their living standards while little growth in productivity was achieved. Investment languished. Even the monetarist propositions of Milton Friedman proved to be wrong. There was no supply-side revolution at all; just a scale of enrichment at the top that beggared belief. By the end of the 1980s the national debate was beginning to change. In the universities conservative economic propositions were being comprehensively demolished, while discussion in the media was dominated by heart-searching about whether U.S. economic power was sustainable—and whether the United States, like Britain in the nineteenth century, was to suffer relative economic decline as a result of imperial overstretch.[14] A new consensus grew up around the need to develop a smart industrial policy, focusing on strategic trade initiatives, and to lower the budget deficit, if necessary by tax increases—a direct challenge to the conservative orthodoxy. After all, in 1987 the United States became a foreign debtor for the first time in the twentieth century, and the national debt—propelled by an apparently unclosable budget deficit—climbed back to levels that hitherto had been produced only by war. Something had to be done.

During the Bush (senior) presidency, under pressure from economic and social reality—especially the ballooning trade and budget deficits—the conservative coalition began to fragment. The fundamentalists wanted to press home the cause; the religious wing of the coalition despaired at the lack of any real initiative over abortion, restoring family values and "reforming" (i.e., phasing out) welfare, while the supply-siders wanted yet more tax cuts and resisted tax increases as an offense against nature. But the pragmatic wing of the coalition, especially those associated with business and Wall Street, began to argue that the primary task was to close the budget deficit as a precondition for anything, and in 1990 Bush—who a decade earlier had described supply-side economics as "voodoo economics"—gave way to the pragmatists. Having declared at the 1988 Republican convention: "Read my lips: no new taxes," in 1990 he initiated tax increases.

The supply-siders and libertarians were appalled. A Republican president had turned his back on the conservative holy grail. Bush might be the president under whose watch the Soviet Union collapsed and who was to win the Gulf War, but his foreign successes counted for nothing beside the scale of this betrayal. Although his formal poll ratings were high, the underlying coalition he had inherited from Reagan was in disarray. Was the future pragmatic or ideological conservatism? Trade policy produced another split, with Pat Buchanan, Reagan's former speechwriter, championing trade protection and fewer overseas adventures as the response both to the trade deficit and to the stagnation of blue-collar wages. By the 1992 presidential election the independent candidate Ross Perot could exploit the divide, marrying a conservative economic program focused on reducing the budget deficit with a libertarian approach to social issues, suspicion of the religious right, and a readiness to protect American jobs. Reagan's coalition had lost its glue. Perot picked up 19 percent of the popular vote, largely from disaffected Republicans, thereby opening up the presidency for the Democrat Bill Clinton. The conservative revolution had lost its way, it seemed; surely now the liberals could mount their long-awaited fightback?

Clinton—the Eisenhower Republican

The conservatives might have been at odds, but conservative beliefs and values, along with the United States's new electoral geography, continued to determine the political agenda. Christian conservatives extended their grip at the local level across the South in the 1992 elections; in South Carolina alone they distributed 840,000 voter guides before the presidential election.[15] The defining economic arguments during the election were for deficit reduction and tax cuts. If Clinton talked about establishing a national health insurance program, he was careful to make sure he talked lower taxes and a shrinking federal payroll at the same time. Although he was to win an overwhelming majority of the black vote, he positioned himself as pro-white; welfare reform and toughness on crime were clearly directed at blacks, although never stated in those terms. He did not challenge the conservative agenda, but rather worked within it, advocating long-standing Democratic aims only on the three consensus "e's"—education, environment, and the elderly. But even so he won only 98 of the country's 435 congressional districts. Without disaffected Republicans voting for Perot, Bush would have won, notwithstanding the 1991–92 recession.

Eight years later, the valedictory comments on Clinton's presidency all agreed that, whatever his misadventures with the Starr inquiry and the Lewinsky case, one of his enduring legacies is that he firmly repositioned the Democrats in the political center. The truth is that he had no alternative. From the outset of his presidency he never had a political coalition strong enough to do anything other than tack within an overarching conservative consensus; indeed, he famously remarked that he was little more than an Eisenhower Republican, and that the choice confronting America was between that and Reagan Republicans.[16] The Christian Coalition, the National Rifle Association, and the right-wing think tanks continued to press their fierce ideological offensive—aided and abetted by a new generation of right-wing talk show hosts (notably Rush Limbaugh) who taught their audiences to hate liberals as un-American. If there was a consensus that closing the U.S. budget deficit—close to 5 percent of GDP when Clinton took office—was an economic priority, there was none about how it should be done. For conservatives the deficit was just proof positive that central government was too big and too little had been done to reduce welfare and the dependency culture. That Reagan's tax cuts and recession might be to blame was beyond their recognition.

For the incoming Clinton administration, the issue was thus how to reduce the deficit while still retaining an economic and social program that still had some Progressive ambitions, notably increasing investment in social, human, and physical capital—but within an overwhelming conservative consensus. Clinton's response was to raise taxes, partially rescinding the tax cuts Reagan had given to the rich; lower expenditure on defense; and launch new tax incentives for the working poor to find work—but he never dared take on the violent conservative reaction head to head. There was no increase in public investment, even in education and training, despite his ambitious talk. Indeed, over his two terms spending on education, transportation and science—all initially earmarked for substantial additional investment—was in each case to fall dramatically as a proportion of GDP.[17] Without cash he could not lubricate his plan to establish a national health insurance system; so he tried to co-opt business. Business responded by using the new lobbying structures to oppose his proposals to devastating effect, portraying them as communist. The plan collapsed.

Clinton was, in short, able to develop only partially the qualified, so-called modern Progressivism he had played a part in formulating before taking office, and then not convincingly or with a powerful rhetoric. The Democratic Leadership Council, of which Clinton had been a founding member, had been attempting since 1988 to redefine the liberal agenda in the face of three lost presidential elections and the emerging changes in the U.S. economic structure—eventually coming up with a position that Clintonites were later to characterize as the "third way." The conception was three-pronged: to reinvent and so relegitimize government; to recast support for the unemployed and the poor, through massive investment in their education and training, so that they could help themselves to be less dependent on the welfare state; and to reenergize civil society through, for example, the launch of a new national service program. At the same time the Democrats tried to inoculate themselves against conservative attacks by tactically moving to the center on contentious issues like capital punishment or affirmative action.[18] The ambitions of the Roosevelt-Kennedy-Johnson tradition to reshape American capitalism and society around nobler ideals were jettisoned wholesale. As a strategy it may have helped win Clinton power, but it collapsed under the pressure of governing within a conservative consensus that the Democrats had not challenged and, in the absence of a sufficiently robust coalition to rely on as a counterweight, could not face down. Health reform, as we have seen, got nowhere, and even the token concession toward liberal opinion of recognizing the rights of gays in the military had to be withdrawn.

But it was the tax increases that drew the hottest fire. The ideological right—the direct heirs of Strauss, Wanniski, and Friedman, now in the hands of antitax activists like Grover Norquist—had been stung by the Bush tax increase to organize every incoming Republican member of Congress in 1993 to sign a pledge that they would not vote for any tax increase. Norquist, who had come to hate Clinton obsessively, assembled the "Leave Us Alone Coalition" to bring all the elements of the right under one umbrella—and to coordinate opposition to Clinton and support for the Republicans in their bid to capture Congress in 1994. They worked closely with the Republican leader of the House of Representatives, Newt Gingrich, who brilliantly caught the mood with his "Contract with America"—a wish list of populist Republican measures that would allegedly strengthen the family and America's defenses, and simultaneously weaken Washington insiders, cut taxes, and balance the budget. In the 1994 congressional elections the Republicans won control of both the House of Representatives and Senate for the first time since 1952.

Prompted by two years of the most modest and compromised liberalism, the conservatives had healed their divisions; they had reunited the Reagan coalition and were back, even more nakedly fundamentalist than before. Moreover, they were livid that their temporary disarray had been so clearly exploited by Clinton in the 1992 election. The conservative cocktail—against black welfare queens, for white gun owners, and anti-abortion, all laced with a generous dose of tax cuts, religion, and the flag—was still triumphant. From then on the Clinton presidency became an exercise in holding off the resurgent right, securing the center at all costs, and making what Progressive gains he could. This task he prosecuted with tactical genius. And yet, in political truth, the only prospect of substantive legislative success lay in initiating those measures with which a Republican Congress could agree—hence the creation of the North American Free Trade Agreement, the deregulation of banking and telecommunications, and, famously, welfare "reform" in which welfare benefits became time-limited to five years.

But, startlingly, the Republicans overreached themselves. An overconfident Gingrich openly invited commercial concerns to write Republican pro-business legislation through the network of K Street political lobbyists, a surrender of political integrity that even Washington insiders found unacceptable. Most important, he and the Republican leadership were to find that America's appetite for tax cuts did not extend to finding the savings from cutting medical assistance to the elderly, Medicare. As Republican plans ran into public dissent, Clinton brilliantly turned the bombing in Oklahoma City to his advantage, associating Gingrichian fundamentalism with the lunatic antigovernment fringe. Later in 1995 he was to maneuvre the Republican Congress into shutting down the government for six days by vetoing the Republican plans for tax cuts paid for by Medicare cuts. In his memoir, Gingrich later acknowledged that "we mistook the [right's] enthusiasm for the views of the American public."[19]

As the economic recovery continued in 1996 it became obvious that, while Clinton was not strong enough to do anything of which the conservatives did not approve, he was powerful enough to block Republican fundamentalism. He comfortably won the 1996 presidential election, locating himself as both the pragmatic willing to steal Republican ideas when they worked and also a sound steward of the American economy who put the interests of ordinary working people first when he could. But his 1996 State of the Union address, declaring that the age of "big government" was over, and his declaration later in the same year that his aim was to "end welfare as we know it" only further underlined the strength of the conservative consensus.

"Triangulation"—the policy of taking the best of both parties' positions and adopting them as your own, as the pollster Dick Morris coined it—might have been a brilliant tactical ploy for reelection, but as a tool for serious coalition building or constructing a coherent political narrative it was useless. As the 1990s wore on Clinton was the beneficiary of an extraordinary boom—whatever its ultimate lack of sustainability (see chapters 1 and 4)—that validated the fiscal conservatism that had been thrust upon him in his first term. In truth, U.S. economic success in the 1990s had as much to do with the way the world system was now working in America's favor—allowing low inflation and the financing of colossal trade deficits, as it had with any indigenous economic dynamism: the mirror and opposite image of the 1970s. The Democrats' position was strengthening despite their inability to challenge the conservative hegemony—yet the Republicans were unable, to their growing frustration, to capitalize upon their control of the intellectual and political agenda. Their most effective strategy was to intensify their efforts to destabilize Clinton personally, a front they had opened in 1993 with the Whitewater investigation into alleged irregularities when he was governor of Arkansas, and which they were to widen with the Starr inquiry leading to the Lewinsky affair and the presidential impeachment hearings in 1998 and early 1999. David Brock, one of the conservative journalists who led the assault on Clinton's reputation with fake allegations of sexual impropriety, abuse of power, and even drug running, has recently openly admitted that there was a coordinated effort by conservative interests to denigrate the President.[20]

The Whitewater affair threw up no proof of any wrongdoing, and conviction was always bound to fail (there was not the necessary majority in Congress); but for Republican strategists that was not the point. Conservative fundamentalists were genuinely outraged by the president's private peccadillos, notwithstanding the numerous parallels within their own ranks. He seemed to personify the moral decadence they were pledged to reverse. Moreover, the opportunity for paying back the attempted impeachment of Nixon was too juicy to pass up. Politically, it would pose any Democratic presidential candidate in 2000 with a political conundrum. To claim credit for the Clinton boom by association would invite the accusation that the candidate condoned the president's behavior; to dissociate himself from Clinton would legitimize the Republican accusation that the president lacked moral integrity while simultaneously neutralizing the Democrats' greatest advantage, the performance of the economy. Gore fell into the elephant trap and ran a campaign distancing himself from Clinton. Further, Gore's lack of an overriding and urgent political message caused the liberal coalition to fragment. One fragment, a small but significant minority, voted for Ralph Nader and thus gifted key states to Bush. The Republican determination to stake everything on victory was starkly revealed by their astonishing capacity to outspend Gore on political advertising in the most costly ever presidential election; but even so, Bush was to lose the national poll by 537,000 votes. Without their cash and the calculated destructive shock waves of impeachment, the Republicans would not have won back the White House.

Back on Top—but for How Long?

American conservatives had come to believe that liberalism in any guise was a mortal threat to the American way and that it was accelerating the drift to amorality of an already overly secular society. Sacred American rights—ranging from the right to bear arms to the right to do whatever a property owner wants on his or her land (e.g., drilling for oil in a conservation area)—required to be reasserted. Nor should the extension of individual civil rights be accorded to any group en masse—certainly not to gays or blacks. The American way was to live in a free market, to seize opportunity, and to enjoy the fruits of one's work unoppressed by taxation or regulation, while offering due obeisance to God and country. This is George W. Bush's credo, and for all the talk of healing America, compassionate conservatism, and bipartisanship, his administration is driven by the same conservative animus that propelled Gingrich and Reagan. And it is, as we have discussed, no less unilateralist after September 11 than before; indeed, it is arguably more so.

The condition of the U.S. criminal justice system is perhaps the best indicator of the new ascendancy of conservatism, the retreat of liberalism, and the repudiation of ideas of the social contract. It was Winston Churchill, after all, who observed that a good barometer of a civilization is its approach to and the condition of its prisoners. By those criteria, the United States does not perform well. Although approaches necessarily vary from state to state, the trend toward repression is universal. Programs for the rehabilitation of offenders have largely disappeared; parole is increasingly limited, and attempts at education and training have been largely given up. Over 1,000 new prisons have been built over the last twenty years and yet overcrowding is endemic. The prison system now houses more than two million prisoners, and official figures show that prisons were operating at 19 percent above capacity in 1998. Sentencing is increasingly "determinate," with state and federal laws insisting on mandatory minimum sentences for given offenses. Bill Clinton himself, in the starkest repudiation of his party's liberal tradition, famously legislated in 1994 that "three strikes and you're out": that is, the offender must suffer a mandatory long-term sentence. In California, after a third offense as trivial as stealing a pizza the sentence is twenty-five years' imprisonment.

The conservatives have pointed to a falling crime rate as justification for this harshness, but the degree to which its achievement can be directly linked solely to a penal and repressive sentencing and prison policy is unproven. The fall in unemployment, the aging of the population so that there are fewer in the crime-prone younger age group, more effective gun control, and more effective community policing—all elements in the liberal explanation for falling crime—are obvious contributory factors. However, they are neglected in the conservative rush to claim sole credit for the success of conservative measures. This "success" may prove all too illusory all too soon. As the leading criminologist Professor James Alan Fox of Northeastern University in Boston has noted, the rise in the prison population provides only "temporary relief . . . because those people will come out of prison and many will still have inadequate skills and bad attitudes." With over half a million prisoners now being released every year, of whom on current recidivism rates some two-thirds are likely to be rearrested within three years, the "gains" from conservative penal policy look fragile. Indeed, there are already signs that crime is beginning to rise again in some cities. And while violent crime may have fallen, homicide rates remain dramatically higher than in any comparable country; but still conservatives refuse to concede that this may have anything to do with that central article of their creed—the freedom of Americans to carry guns.

The conservative worldview rules; yet there are cracks in its dominance. The United States is dividing, even over crime. The long-standing division between two cultures—the culture of the orderly 1950s and that of the rebellious 1960s, in Gertrude Himmelfarb's formulation—is becoming more marked. Some half of the population—roughly the proportion that voted for Gore and Nader in 2000—is increasingly secular, tolerant, accepting of the role of government, willing to make common cause, concerned about the weaknesses of America's social contract, and growing more suspicious about the death penalty and free use of guns. Despite the persistence of conservative penal policy at state and federal level, recent opinion polls show a growing interest in the rehabilitative role of prison and an increasing awareness of the self-defeating nature of the conservative approach. Other surveys of American opinion show an almost European readiness to spend extra on education, health, and social security.[21] The new ideopolises, as identified in chapter 1, are much more likely to be Democrat than Republican. Surveys of American values show a remarkable stability in adherence to the core principles of freedom, equality of opportunity, the importance of hard work and achievement, fairness, belief in religion, and equality before the law that at a deep level underpin American culture.[22] These could be deployed to serve the liberal cause, as they have been in the past, if the American liberal tradition could marry its core intellectual propositions with American values and real interests as successfully as conservatives have done.

Conservatism may be in the ascendant now, but a powerful American liberalism lies beneath the surface of American life—and it is increasingly uneasy about the direction in which America's society and economy are developing. As we will see in the next two chapters, it has good reason.

4

Greed Isn't Good for You

In the United States private property is king, and the quintessential expression of this philosophy is the corporation. The American corporation, from the early business charters to the great monoliths of the early twenty-first century, has driven the rise of American capitalism; and it is in this corporate representation of individual property rights that the rise of American conservatism has had its most forceful impact. At the beginning of a new century the attempts to legitimize and constrain the exercise of those rights—from regulation in the public interest to the notion that companies should have a wider responsibility than profit maximization to the communities in which they trade—have never commanded less support. The object of the U.S. corporation is now naked and unashamed: it is to maximize financial gain for those who own it. Accordingly, it is to be freely traded, like any other commodity, on the stock exchange. Every corporation in America is not merely seeking to make as much money as possible as fast as possible, it is permanently up for sale.

These are the basic principles of American capitalism; but they are also a source of economic weakness, and the vulnerability of the philosophy underlying them is now being exposed by harder economic times. Companies are more complex than financial poker chips, and the extension of this philosophy over the last twenty years has gradually undermined corporate America in ways we will explore in this chapter. The spate of executive wrongdoing and recent corporate and financial scandals is but the most exposed element of a generalized malaise. But the conservative infrastructure of ideology that has driven this movement has had more pernicious effects still. It has obscured and deliberately neglected the real drivers of much U.S. growth—for example, the importance of high-quality, government-funded scientific research; the impact of education, which at its best in the United States is world-beating; the crucial role played by local and regional banks in supplying patient finance; and the importance of physical infrastructure—choosing instead to celebrate simplistic nostrums of entrepreneurship and to deify capitalism and markets. As a result there is widespread ignorance within the United States about what has propelled its growth, a vast exaggeration of what has been achieved, an uncomprehending dismay at the consequences of the pricking of the epic 1990s financial bubble—and equal incomprehension of how something so irrational could ever have taken place.

In particular, the introversion of American conservatism has massively downplayed the importance of the United State's hegemonic economic role in the globe, which allowed the buildup of unsustainable economic imbalances—notably the disappearance of saving and the emergence of a colossal trade deficit—that no other country could or should copy, and the redress of which threatens even the United States with a period of prolonged economic underperformance, possibly even stagnation.

The Unbinding of the Corporate Leviathan

Americans may have thought carefully about their political constitution, but they have never taken the constitution of their companies and the responsibilities of those who own and finance them as seriously. As noted earlier, companies were seen as no more than vehicles for the expression of individual property rights, and as such essentially unassailable. The view of the financial system is that it accommodates and facilitates the needs of property. Banks, for example, are not conceptualized as instruments for husbanding the growth of American companies; their historic role has been to supply trade credit and keep their distance—so that even when more fruitful relationships develop, these are felt to break the proper rules and are rarely admitted. Nor has the stock market's principal purpose been to raise money for business expansion, where the cumulative sums concerned are trivial; rather, it has been to allow founders of companies to capitalize on their success by selling their companies as a whole or in part to outsiders. This is before anything else a market in property rights and corporate control.

For nineteenth- and early-twentieth-century America, unlike the countries of continental Europe, Japan, or the Asian tiger economies, never had to use the financial system as an instrument of economic development. Growth was driven by the floods of innovative immigrants entrepreneurially combining cheap land and labor to exploit continental-scale market opportunities. Profits were high, and companies were largely self-financing. Wall Street in the first thirty years of the twentieth century resembled a gambling den more than a forum for mobilizing risk capital for enterprise—a tradition to which it has recently returned with a vengeance.

This attitude bubbled to its climax in the stock market boom of the 1920s, when the entire nation was playing financial poker with its companies in a casino that seemed to guarantee profits as long as you speculated aggressively enough. This was a rule-free environment. Lack of creditworthiness was no bar to speculating in company stock by paying only a fraction of its worth and borrowing the rest—so-called margin trading—while companies themselves could report and account for their financial performance almost as they chose. Banks could use their capital to support lending or stock market speculation. It was a market free-for-all—and the natural culmination of the republic's attitude toward property and the sanctity of markets over its first century and a half.

Famously, the boom came to a shuddering halt in the Wall Street crash, whose financial losses spread first around the financial system and then through the rest of the economy as a cancerous, depressive contagion. The Great Depression was above all the result of a massive credit crunch; the financial system imploded. Roosevelt's New Deal was as much about the reconstruction and reorganization of the hitherto self-governing and self-regulating American financial system as it was about the things for which it is more famous—establishing the foundations of the U.S. welfare system, for example, or recognizing trade unions and launching great public works programs. There had been over 9,000 bank failures that had inflicted incalculable harm on the economic life of the nation; firewalls had to be constructed to prevent the same thing from happening again. For the first time the federal government took it upon itself to dictate how the self-governing autonomous corporation should be run—and above all, how the financial system was to operate.

The Glass-Steagall Act of 1933 forbade commercial and investment banking to be undertaken by the same company. Never again should losses in the stock market pollute the ability of the commercial bank to lend—the two functions should be kept separate. A year later the Securities and Exchange Commission was established to ensure that speculation would be curtailed by rigorous regulation of margin trading and ensuring that corporations disclosed systematic and honest accounts of their financial affairs to investors. And Roosevelt completed his reforms by creating a network of publicly owned financial institutions, ranging from the Home Owners Loan Corporation to the Reconstruction Finance Corporation. Their job was to do what the financial system had proved incapable of doing on its own; providing the twenty-five-year mortgages to home buyers and farmers that the privately owned savings and loan associations had not done of their own accord, and similarly offering long-term bank loans to industry. The financial relief and confidence these measures provided were the single most important contribution the New Deal made to economic recovery.

It was not until the tail end of the New Deal period, in 1950, that the then aging New Dealers turned their attention to creating a framework of company law, passing the Model Business Corporation Act as a template on which individual states were exhorted to model their own incorporation statutes. But even then, with federal government at the zenith of its prestige, having rescued the country from depression and won a world war, the approach was minimalist and cautious. The case for revisiting company law was made not in terms of a need to prescribe how the internal affairs of a company should be constitutionally arranged, but rather in terms of a recognition that increasingly owners of large corporations had to delegate management to professional managers, and there needed to be a legal framework within which this could take place. The company's founding document was moved to center stage, and directors, managers, and officers of a company were required explicitly to accept a fiduciary duty to the company. This had three components: managers were legally obliged to act in accordance with the principles of the founding document, to act loyally in the interests of the corporation, and to accept a duty of care, which was defined as acting in a way that reasonably protects the interests of investors. If shareholders did not like the results of this delegation of duties they could sell their shares, and they could vote on their stock to replace the officers of the company.

The contrast with European and particularly German company law could hardly be more marked. The act made no stipulations about how a company should be governed, which was considered entirely the purview of the management and executives. Thus if a corporation decided that the roles of chairman and chief executive were to be merged and no independent directors required to be on the board, then that was (and is) entirely within its capabilities. Thus, if the chairman were vested with all power, that could not be challenged either. Annual accounts were prepared for shareholders as an account of the management's stewardship of their assets rather than as an account to the world at large, including the government, of what the true performance of the company had been across a wide range of measures. This was and is a world of private-property contracts; the central conception is that, whether decisions are taken by shareholders or directors, private contracts and rights are sacrosanct.

So if managers and directors had become the de facto exercisers of property rights over quoted companies, this was only because they were seen as the only practical place in which to vest those rights. Private ownership was a secret garden into which the state should never pry. It might regulate the outcomes of corporate behavior—but never its internal processes. Indeed, there seemed little need to do so. Managers and directors exploited the latitude open to them and took their obligations to their companies' founding legal document seriously; the divorce between ownership and control meant their first obligation was to their company as an organization. They expanded, husbanded, and invested in their companies as never before. The legacy of the federal government's enormous buildup of defense spending was a vast array of new technologies, ranging from television to jet airplane manufacture, and corporate America fell on them hungrily. Boeing developed the first civilian jet by transferring the technology from the wartime B-47 and B-52

bomber programs; IBM's leadership in computer manufacture hung on
the pathbreaking computers it built for the new computerized air defense
system, SAGE; the semiconductor industry was brought into being by
defense orders, which accounted for 38 percent of all production between
1955 and 1965.[1] The Buy America provisions, directing the U.S. government to purchase strategic goods from U.S. firms, meant that all the
business went to U.S. firms—giving birth to the military-industrial complex of which Eisenhower had warned. Between 1949 and 1973 annual
productivity growth averaged over 3 percent, and one key link in the virtuous circle of growth begetting investment begetting employment and
spending that in turn generated more growth was the high-investment
corporation feeding off government-generated state-of-the-art technologies. Indeed, all corporations shared the same dedication to growing
their companies in the round. The delegation of control to directors
committed to growing the organization as a whole, rather than just serving the interests of the shareholders, was having remarkable results.

As the 1960s gave way to the 1970s the pattern of company ownership
began to change, with consequences that are still unfolding. Stock ownership began to migrate from individuals to large financial institutions, like
mutual funds and pension funds, investing on their behalf. In 1945, 93 percent of shares were held by individuals: by 1997 the proportion had fallen
to 43 percent.[2] A feeling began to grow among the powerful institutional
shareholders that corporate America was interpreting its fiduciary duty
with too little regard for their interests; the 1960s saw the first hostile
takeover. CEOs might be effectively growing corporate America, but in the
process they had become barons of all they surveyed, running companies
as if they were the owners, even though they were only servants of the
founding legal document and the shareholders beyond that. During the
1970s, as company profits reeled in the aftermath of the oil shock and
growth and productivity fell, management theorists and the new powerful
institutional investors began to agitate for a proper restoration of their
property rights—and the running of companies to serve their owners.
The shareholder value revolution was born.

This was disingenuously presented as an exercise in enfranchisement
rather than self-interest, a campaign to restore property rights to those in
whom they should properly be vested—the shareholders. By making man-

agement more responsive to shareholders, ran the argument, American capitalism would become more vibrant—neglecting the important fact that it had been managements' freedom from shareholder interests that had contributed so largely to making American capitalism so dynamic in the years after World War II. The United Shareholders Association, founded in 1986, quickly became a national movement of "shareholder rights activists" (in a self-conscious reference to civil rights activists) and cast itself as the rescuer of American companies from greedy, lazy managements. Dividends should be put first. The mutual funds latched on to the mood, claiming to be the means through which small investors could exercise their property rights more effectively—and get richer quicker.

As the Internet grew in importance over the 1990s, with ten million shareholding accounts held in Internet brokerages, Websites like the Motley Fool kept up the dreambeat of hype that ancient American myths of the individual citizen-owner could be repeated in cyberspace. Suddenly the market had become cool and individual investment anti-elitist. The quest for shareholder value was nothing more than the legitimate desire by every owner—whether a small investor or a gigantic pension fund—to see his or her property managed to deliver the maximum gain that they naturally wanted. Chief executives should be given the incentive to act in the real interests of owners by hooking their own remuneration to the stock price. So, as individual Americans trebled the proportion of their savings held in stock market assets within just fifteen years, CEOs enjoyed a parallel boom in share option plans, which rose in value from $60 billion to $600 billion over the 1990s. Everybody wanted to be an owner, and to share in the spoils of a rising stock market. The powerful and moneyed might benefit most of all—64 percent of American households own less than $5,000 worth of shares[3]—but a stock market that grew on average by 17 percent a year over the decade seemed to offer sufficient gains for everyone. Wall Street had become the new embodiment of the American dream.

In this heady atmosphere the Rooseveltian restraints on American finance seemed like annoying Lilliputian bonds that must be broken as soon as possible to give the financial machine more room to move. Wall Street had its own agenda, which aligned it with the shareholder rights lobby. It was having growing success in lobbying for the dismantling of international controls on the operation of U.S. financial markets, as we will see in chapter 6, thereby increasing the volume of tradable financial assets; the promotion of shareholder value was a means of promoting the role of stocks and stock trading, and thus further swelled the business of Wall Street.

One of the great boons of the American financial system had been the plethora of its banks. For fifty years after the Great Depression the United States enjoyed the services of 14,000 banks, which under the protections afforded by the Rooseveltian legislation had been able to become relationship banks, committed to offering medium- and long-term support to America's small and medium-sized business. The ideology of the American way, of course, continued to cast them in a different light as nothing more than market-driven facilitators of credit; but, protected from competition from banks in other states, their own competitive position entrenched by regulation, and their depositors given confidence by federal deposit insurance, they had created unique franchises—almost along north European and Asian lines—supporting local enterprise. America's great cities had become centers of regional banking, careful to nurture industry in its own backyard. If Germany had its great regional mutual banks and specialist industrial banks, and Japan its own industrial banking system, the Americans had their network of state and city banks that knew their business customer base well and wanted to support local business champions. This was grassroots business banking at its best.

For the shareholder value merchants, the American banking system was a ripe plum ready for the picking. There were too many banks protected by outmoded regulations. Some of the regulations, like the ban on interstate banking, were being made redundant by the explosion in mobility. Businesses were moving beyond their local bases, and businesspeople looked to banks that could offer them a national rather than a regional service. Other regulations, like the ceiling on interest rate payments, were being evaded by the capacity of individual Americans to invest on the New York money markets via mutual funds. As important, the banks and financial institutions themselves were agitating to be freed from controls over what they might do and to whom they might lend. Shouldn't they be able to do what they wanted with their property, like any other American or American business?

The experience of the deregulation of the savings and loan associations (S&Ls), mentioned in the previous chapter, should have been an awesome warning. In 1982 the controls were lifted on what the S&Ls could lend, but the guarantees enjoyed by their savers remained. The S&Ls saw the new structure—rightly—as a one-way bet; they could lend whatever they liked to whichever property developer they wanted—including themselves—confident that if things went well they would make millions, but if the return did not materialize then government deposit insurance would pick up the bill. What followed was one of the greatest orgies of unsound lending in history, including fraud on an epic scale, leading in 1989 to the creation of the Resolution Trust and a bailout conservatively estimated at $200 billion.[4] Thus one industry in the private sector wasted more than the entire government had managed in the postwar period. But the conclusion drawn by conservatives was not that the Rooseveltian framework was sound and should be tampered with only cautiously; rather, it was that deregulation should have gone much further and much faster, removing the protections for savers as well. After all, in the land inhabited by conservatives all government is bad and everything in the private sector good. The clamor for deregulation and for shareholder value continued unabated—and against no very great opposition. This was a nation of wannabe owners, keen to extract value from their assets and ride the gathering stock market boom.

Meanwhile Wall Street and the banks combined to press for more financial deregulation for reasons of self-interest—and Washington, penetrated by financial interests and political lobbyists, and in any case seeing advantages from building up the size of U.S. financial markets in order to finance the budget and trade deficits, was happy to oblige. Already the Federal Reserve had been allowing banks to offer a growing range of financial services; over the 1990s the pace of deregulation quickened. In 1994 the ban on interstate banking was lifted; in 1996 the rule (Regulation Y) limiting the pace and scale of bank mergers by stipulating that a bank could acquire another bank only if it was 35 percent of its own size was abolished; and in 1998 the Glass-Steagall Act was finally rescinded after a lobbying campaign of more than a decade.[5]

Through the 1990s the pace of bank mergers accelerated at a bewildering rate; as Gary Dymski reports, by the end of the decade, the number of

U.S. banks had halved in twenty years.[6] The justification put forward is that larger banks are more "efficient"—but, as Dymski argues, efficiency is identified in narrowly economic terms as closing bank branches and concentrating bank operations. The value of the banks' relationships and their capacity to support local business is ignored. Closures create a one-time boost in profits through a one-time reduction in fixed costs, and raise the merged banks' share price, usually enriching the bank CEOs and the investment houses that brokered the merger. But the price is the destruction of America's banking infrastructure that allowed the gathering of local knowledge essential to judging the true creditworthiness of borrowers, especially important if they are local businesses. Instead, loan applications are judged according to formal criteria by loan officers not rooted in local communities and who must necessarily ensure that business lending is backed by property collateral rather than the true strength of the business. The powerful results of local banks working with local businesses in local clusters exploiting informal networks and with strong incentives to develop the local economy are lost, and with them a major prop of local enterprise and American business dynamism. The beneficial wider social impacts are reduced and the public good of local banking diminished. But the value so extracted benefits profits and the share price, now more important than any other consideration to the United States's business community— whose priorities seamlessly translate into Washington's political priorities.

Even the mounting evidence that bank mergers have tended to destroy shareholder value has been insufficient to halt the Gadarene rush.[7] With Wall Street reaching new highs as the new century began, the conservative position seemed amply justified. The paradox was that beneath the surface the underlying innovativeness and competitiveness of the United States were being undermined. The infrastructure of supportive banking was being removed, and the new focus on boosting the share price at all costs would further hollow out American business. The triumph of the market had created a stock market bubble that would enfeeble the new economy it had helped to bring into being—an ominous echo of the 1920s. At its apparent zenith, conservatism has failed to meet its boastful promise.

The Story of Boeing

The jumbo jet and the B-52 are two of the most visible expressions of American technological and military superiority—and Boeing, the company that made them, is a corporate name to rank alongside Microsoft, Coca-Cola, and Ford as a global brand. But Boeing, like so many of the top American companies, is itself a victim of the collapse of American liberalism and the rise of the conservative right. Within a generation its capacity to take technological risks and to put building planes as its number one corporate purpose has been undermined by the extraordinary pressure of Wall Street for American companies to deliver immediate high financial returns as their overriding objective. When the new superjumbo, carrying 555 passengers, enters service in 2006, it will have been built by Europe's Airbus consortium. Boeing is fading as a leading aircraft manufacturer. It will look less to innovative leaps to fuel its growth, as it did when building the jumbo: rather it will hope to grow its less risky aircraft service business, building avionic and air-traffic management systems.

The ascendancy of conservatism and its accompanying economic maxims has found expression in a new corporate doctrine in which investment, husbanding human capital, and organic growth are seen as secondary to the real business of corporations: enriching their directors and owners in the name of shareholder value. The entire U.S. economic structure and the society built upon it is now wedded as never before to the interests and needs of high finance and the financial markets. Four thousand executives on Wall Street earn more than a million dollars a year each,[8] and the chief executives of the 362 largest U.S. companies in 1999 received an annual average remuneration of $12.4 million—six times that of 1990.[9] No economy and society anywhere have so interlinked their fate with the appetite of the stock market for short-term profits, or structured their financial system with such close attention to the interests of markets and short-term profit maximization.

The story of Boeing offers a salutary lesson. In the mid-1960s this was a company dedicated to technological excellence and the development of its highly skilled, loyal workforce—and whose close relationship with government, rather than the hindrance painted by conservative ideologists, was a source of competitive advantage worldwide. Its managers were loyal to the company's founding document; this was an organization dedicated to building the best planes in the world—and it did. Bill Allen, chief executive from 1945 to 1968, captured the company's intent when he wrote that "Boeing is always reaching out for tomorrow!" It had developed the first generation of civilian jet airliners from the technical advances and strong financial position it had developed as a leading defense contractor during World War II and the early years of the Cold War; and it retained a healthily profitable military division. At this juncture, with the bulk of its stock held by patient individual investors and supported by a network of local state banks with a close interest in the company's growth, it embarked on the then vastly ambitious project to build the 747, the jumbo jet. This was what Boeing should be doing.

Part of the financial risk was underwritten by its own financial structure, with a multiplicity of small and loyal shareholders, and part by a large order from Pan Am, whose own ability to order aircraft was in turn underwritten by its own sheer scale and financial structure—and an airline environment regulated by the U.S. government through the Civil Aeronautics Board (CAB), which kept airlines profitable by closely regulating ticket prices and boosted technological innovation. The project was plagued by technical difficulties and foreign cancellations of orders, but $2 billion ($6 billion in 2002 dollars) later, in 1970, the first jumbo was delivered to Pan Am. Twelve and a half thousand engineers had worked exclusively on the project. The next five years were extraordinarily hazardous, with Boeing laying off 60 percent of its 142,000 workers and actively considering abandoning the aviation business as sales of the jumbo remained stubbornly depressed; the company was found guilty of bribing foreign airlines to win orders. But by 1978 the colossal gamble had paid off. In that year a booming airline business placed orders for eighty-three 747s, and Boeing's financial returns climbed to the highest in the Fortune 500.

Over the next decade Boeing reaped the rewards for the risk it had taken, ultimately making $20 billion in profits from its $2 billion investment; with no competitors, it was able to insist on airlines paying full price for the 747, and despite the launch of the airbus by its European challenger, Airbus, it consolidated its position as the dominant actor in the world aircraft industry.

But Wall Street was leery. This was a cyclical business that required high research and development costs together with sustained investment in people to stay ahead; it did not lend itself to quick dollars. Moreover, the new conservative economic thinking was undermining one of its chief supports—a domestic airline industry rich enough to pay good prices and provide forward order books for aircraft. Deregulation of tickets and routes, beginning with the abolition of the CAB in 1978, along with a wave of mergers and acquisitions aimed at boosting short-term profits, made U.S. airlines more hawkish in their purchasing policy. The world in which a company like Boeing could in effect bet itself on a vast project embodying state-of-the-art technology was disappearing.

The pivotal year was 1987. T. Boone Pickens of Texas, apostle of southern raw capitalism, supporter of Reagan and founder of the United Shareholders Association, had already established a reputation for himself as one of the leaders of the new generation of "corporate raiders." Now he dared to try to buy a stake in Boeing as the first step to a full-blooded bid. The romanticism of their "raiding" image belied the raiders' real aim; these were not swashbuckling adventurers so much as corporate vultures whose objective was to dismantle large organizations, stripping them of cash and assets in order to unlock "value"; so long as the disposal proceeds were greater than the purchase price, they would make their profit. Pickens dismissed the charge that he was short-termist, saying it was no more than a "theory that freed executives to scorn any shareholders they choose to identify as short-termers."[10]

The raiders' operations had been made feasible by the new dominance of institutional investors—pension and mutual funds—that now owned the majority of any corporation's shares; instead of trying to persuade tens of thousands of individual investors of the merits of their case, as they would have had to do in the 1960s, raiders like Pickens had to convince only a dozen or so major institutional fund managers—who themselves were anxious for short-term performance to boost the sale of their units and pension plans—that they should be backed. Boeing's share price at this time—$7, compared with an estimated net worth of $75 a share—reflected the degree to which Wall Street shunned America's national champion in aircraft manufacture.

Pickens was sent packing, but Boeing was never to be the same company again. Plans for new planes were frozen, R&D spending was slashed, and close to 50,000 workers were laid off in an attempt to boost the bottom line. In taking this approach Boeing was following the lead of the high priest of shareholder value, Jack Welch, chief executive of GE. Welch had not needed the attentions of a corporate raider to persuade him that the interests of shareholders must come first; he saw the quest for "value" as focusing a management's objectives and ideologically the proper and only true purpose of a capitalist enterprise. This was the model that Boeing now set out to copy, fearing that if it did not it would suffer from the attentions of another corporate raider or the takeover ambitions of another large corporation seeking to sustain its profits growth by milking Boeing. Indeed, one of the companies eyeing Boeing was GE itself.

Throughout the 1990s Boeing's objective has been building rapid earnings growth rather than developing new planes; in 1997 it bought its great rival McDonnell Douglas in order to boost the steadier income from military contracts. McDonnell Douglas's boss, Harry Stonecipher, had spent twenty-seven years with GE; this disciple of Welch's and apostle of shareholder value became Boeing's new president. When, that same year, Boeing declared that it had no intention of trying to build a superjumbo, the share price climbed to an all-time high of $60. Philip Condit, the then CEO, acknowledged the new order of priorities when he told *Business Week* that "a very fundamental thing was going on." In the old days the preoccupation had been meeting "technological challenges of supreme magnitude" like building "an airplane that went further than somebody else's." "Now," he declared, "we are going into a value based environment where unit cost, return on investment, shareholder return are the measures by which you'll be judged. That's a big shift."[11]

But while a value-based environment may enrich executives and Wall Street, it is proving a pernicious context in which to develop and build aircraft. The nadir was reached in October 1997, when a combination of staff shortages incurred from too many layoffs and an overstrained supply chain organized around minimalist "just-in-time" delivery principles to boost operating margins forced a seizure in production; Boeing literally stopped building airplanes for some weeks, for want of parts and people, at a cost of $2.6 billion. Productivity per worker had been raised, but the production process had become so hollowed out that continuous production was endangered. More seriously, it is simply unable to compete with Airbus, now attracting half of all commercial aircraft orders even before the launch of its new superjumbo, the A380—a market that Airbus has to itself, for Boeing today has not the skills, the engineering capacity, the financial stability, or the access to long-term support. In short, it is surrendering technological leadership to the European consortium, whose stabler ownership structure and long-term financing environment leaves open possibilities for Airbus that no longer exist for Boeing.

The development costs for the A380 will exceed $12 billion, a challenge Boeing might have considered in the mid-1960s but can no longer entertain today. As Matthew Lynn has written, "Where once Boeing had led the industry, breaking new ground, inspiring new departures, it was now content to leave the ground-breaking to others and give chase where necessary."[12] Each model it developed over the 1990s was a reaction to a prior move by Airbus. Boeing concedes this, claiming it sees it as an advantage in the short term. But in the long run Boeing's reputation as a producer of quality innovative aircraft is suffering. In February 2002 it had a smaller production backlog than Airbus. The United States may protest that Airbus enjoys government subsidy, forgetting that juicy defense contracts have been essential to U.S. success (the arguments are examined in more detail in chapter 9)—but that is not the point. Even if Airbus did not exist, Boeing would be in trouble.

Conservative America has constructed a financial environment where technology and manufacturing prowess take a back seat to the financial criteria set by a Wall Street crazed by greed and rendered irrational by the dictates of its own competitive dynamics. Senior executives in investment banks can earn their $10 million remuneration packages only by engineering megadeals—and Boeing knows that if it bets $12 billion on a new generation of planes, the result will be a plummeting share price and a shotgun merger. To preserve its independence its strategy has been to milk its existing range of planes for cash and profitability—for example, planning only to build a stretched version of the 747,the 747X, to rival the A380 rather than developing a new superjumbo—and to move into the aviation service business. Yet to maintain the stock price, the 747X has been shelved due to lack of customers. This judgment would have killed the 747 at the same stage. Even the radical Sonic Cruiser, a smaller 200–300 passenger craft, is in doubt. In a talismanic retreat of this once great company, it has moved its headquarters out of Seattle to Chicago. As the airline industry retrenches before the fall in demand prompted by the aftermath of the terrorist attacks of September 2001 and orders to aircraft manufacturers fall, Boeing's lack of financial solidity and new priorities are even more exposed. An industry that the United States once dominated is being ceded to the Europeans.

The Destruction of Value

Corporate America now no longer principally seeks to innovate, build, and marshal resources over time to create value; it tries to extract value by financial engineering. Wall Street, always an uneasy ally of U.S. business, has become its master. In the 1960s 44 cents of every posttax dollar of profit was distributed as dividends; by the 1990s the proportion had nearly doubled to 85 cents as companies sought to please the hawkish financial markets and support their share prices, to which CEOs' remuneration, via stock option packages, was so tightly linked.[13] Around half of CEOs' total earnings now comes from stock options.[14]

The institutional investors who own more than half the stocks traded on the market are restless in their search for higher performance to please their own demanding customers; on average they turn over 40 percent of their portfolio in a year looking for higher returns. By contrast, in 1960 Wall Street turned over only 12 percent of its entire capitalization. Every corporation does everything in its power to keep the fund managers happy, promising to deliver ever higher profits every quarter, topping up their efforts with stock buybacks and financing investment by asking the markets for as little new cash as possible. Ninety percent of business investment is self-financed; between 1985 and 1995 over $500 billion was spent by companies buying back their own shares to support the price.

The story, from the commanding heights of the Harvard Business School and the *Wall Street Journal*—aided and abetted by the all pervasive free-market American economists—to every statement by a CEO, is that this new environment is the principal explanation for the recovery in American productivity and growth. The Business Roundtable in 1997 declared that "the principal objective of a business enterprise is to generate economic returns to its owners. . . . [I]f the CEO and the directors are not focused on shareholder value, it may be less likely the corporation will yield that value."[15] For George Baker of the Harvard Business School it was this change in attitudes and in the behavior of owners and managers alike that had produced rising productivity and profits.[16] Michael Jensen used his presidential address to the American Finance Association in 1993 to insist that it was only because of pressure from the stock market that American corporations were likely to adjust quickly and efficiently to the realities of globalization.[17] And all this is supported by a daily drumbeat from the American financial press and media.

The thesis is simple. Companies are driven wholly by price signals and the desire to maximize profits. They combine labor and capital as prices dictate in a network of contracts, for example labor or supply contracts, that can and must be dissolved the instant a better contract is available elsewhere. If those who manage these assets—the company directors—have their remuneration closely linked to the company share price, they will be brave and rigorous in trimming out fat and squeezing as much as possible from the assets. A second pressure to maximize profits comes from the stock market, because if the directors are inefficient the company's share price will sink and they will lose control, being taken over by a company and directors better able to do the job. Financial markets are so efficient that they consistently put an accurate price on a company's worth, lifting the prices of efficient companies and lowering those of inefficient companies—so takeover is an ever-present threat and the "market for corporate control" is an essential instrument for efficiency.

But the whole narrative is shot through with intellectual and empirical inadequacies. In the first place this is an entirely economistic view of the organization. If all contracts can be unwound at a moment's notice and reorganized around a better set of prices, this is only another way of saying that organizations have no history. In this conception, companies should be visualized as simply a peripatetic, permanently shifting network of deals between workers, suppliers, creditors, and shareholders. Loyalty, trust, the organization's social capabilities, and the capacity to learn over time count for nothing. The truth is that they count a lot, as argued in the chapters ahead.

It is an open question whether the shareholder-value, free-market thesis even works on its own terms. One intriguing study demonstrates that high CEO pay tends to be followed by weak rather than strong share price performance; between 1993 and 2000 the majority of companies headed by the ten highest-paid CEOs underperformed the stock market average over both one year and three years afterward.[18] As for the efficient-market hypothesis, this is the most fiercely contested theorem in economics. Despite enormous intellectual effort, nobody can prove that stock market prices accurately reflect all the information available—a vital component of the conservative theory. In fact, the evidence points the other way. Mary O'Sullivan, reviewing the evidence, insists that it is more a matter of faith than proof, and that "anomalous evidence on the behaviour of returns is rife."[19] Indeed, Michael Jensen, one of the high priests of the hypothesis, found no fewer than six studies showing that after a takeover share prices fell by an average of 6.56 percent, rather than rising as they should. "These negative abnormal returns are unsettling because they are inconsistent with market efficiency and suggest that changes in stock prices during takeovers overestimate the future efficiency gains from mergers," he conceded.[20] Quite so.

There is a vast literature proving that, far from creating value, takeovers and mergers destroy it. McKinsey, for example, reviewing 160 mergers between 1992 and 1999, discovered that only 12 of the merged groups succeeded in lifting organic growth above the trends before the merger; the other 148 failed.[21] Another management consultant, KPMG, found in a survey of over 700 cross-border mergers between 1996 and 1998 that only 17 percent added value, while as many as 53 percent actually destroyed shareholder value, with the remaining 30 percent of deals making no difference.[22] Mergers and takeovers, in short, do not work. The marrying of two different organizations with disparate cultures and people systems cannot be performed as the by-product of a shotgun wedding to appease the financial markets; companies are more complex than the doctrine of shareholder value ever comprehends.

That has not stopped the tidal wave of takeovers and mergers, which since 1994 has seen a cool $5 trillion change hands. There were 5,000 mergers in 2000, double the level of a decade earlier. They may destroy value and lower growth, but each CEO believes that he or she will be different—and investment banks, chasing the fees, do nothing to disabuse them.

The authors of the McKinsey and KPMG reports do not conclude that there is something structural about mergers that makes them very unlikely to work; for the consultancies see the opportunity for fees in trying to facilitate the impossible. The whole culture produces deeper economic weakness. Success in a takeover demands that the predator be in favor with Wall Street; the predator's market valuation must be higher for every dollar of profit than the potential victim's, so allowing the predator to pay for the bid by the market accepting more of its shares. AOL could never have succeeded in its bid for Time Warner, for example, had Wall Street not valued its shares at absurd levels, with the price more than a thousand times the annual earnings apportioned to each share. Today, after a record $54 billion write-down and accusations of rigging its accounts—and without the promised synergy—the stupidity of this merger price is obvious to all.

This pressure to keep up the share price, to be the predator, intensifies the already acute competition to maximize shareholder value, so that economies in research, investment, or the workforce are immediately rewarded in higher short-term profits and a higher share price. It also implies a worrying trend to manipulate financial accounts so that they show a consistently rising upward movement of profits—a concern originally voiced by no less an authority than the chairman of the New York Stock Exchange.[23] In the wake of a series of unparalleled corporate scandals, this behavior has now become accepted as a widespread and fraudulent aspect of American capitalism that must be remedied. But the collapse of Enron in November 2001 truly signaled the extensive rot. At the time America's largest-ever corporate meltdown, it transpired through a series of chronically loss-making and imprudent off-balance-sheet deals not disclosed to either the authorities or investors—and apparently undetected by the auditors. The chief executive behind Enron's growth, who had resumed his position as CEO just months before the company's collapse, was Ken Lay. He had been a passionate advocate of deregulation, shareholder value, and the uselessness of all forms of public intervention—a posture from which Enron directly benefited as it expanded into areas hitherto the preserve of publicly owned or regulated utilities, lubricated by well-targeted contributions to both parties, but especially to Republicans. Now the subjects of federal and congressional investigations into their conduct, including potential fraud, he and his company are emerging as one of the very best examples of why the philosophy he championed is so suspect—and why, despite the pleas of business, there remains a case for regulation. Enron proved not to be alone. In January 2002, Global Crossing collapsed amid overinflated profits and bogus revenue. Shocking at it was, Global Crossing's fall was a mere prelude to the biggest bankruptcy of all—WorldCom—America's second-largest long-distance telephone company, with assets of $107 billion.

Run by another charismatic CEO, Bernie Ebbers, WorldCom was a classic product of the conservative revolution—a company whose growth was only made possible by the mania for deregulation along with an accommodative approach to deal making and accounting. Ebbers completely understood that the new object of corporate America was to make the stock price grow and to use stock to take over rivals. American accounting would go along, with generous interpretations of profitability after each deal. So, WorldCom kept swallowing companies to pump up its profits, not worrying much about integrating all these businesses or controlling costs. Each new deal would keep Wall Street at bay. But when World-Com's $129 billion merger with Sprint was blocked in 2000, Ebbers and his cronies had to resort to voodoo accounting, to the tune of $7.2 billion. Profits must continue to grow. Exposure was inevitable.

All of these scandals are linked by the same golden thread. Under acute pressure to meet Wall Street's profit targets quarter by quarter, firms manipulated and often faked profit-and-loss accounts. Even the great GE has come under skeptical appraisal for strategies used to portray the smooth rise in profits so dear to Wall Street. The growing concern that much of corporate America's balance sheets and profit statements cannot be trusted prompted a massive sell-off on Wall Street in summer 2002 and may yet cause further weakness.

And yet such scandals are only the beginning of the problem. They dramatize that the new emphasis is not conducive to innovation achieved by research and development; corporate spending on research fell consistently by some 1 percent a year in constant dollars over the 1990s. Instead, as the leading authority on U.S. industry outlines, companies look to short-term, low-cost adaptions and accommodations, exploiting partnerships with government-funded research at universities or ideas generated by alliances with foreign companies.[24] U.S. companies, in short, have invested in tactical product development—spending more and more on this over the 1990s in the attempt to shore up market share—or tried to take over other companies to achieve market leadership and with it the power to set prices and operating margins. The number one in a sector consistently makes higher returns than the number two, and the number two more than the number three. Hence the struggle, by fair means or foul, to be number one.

So it is, with U.S. companies looking for higher returns over shorter periods than their competitors,[25] that the United States has less invested capital for every hour an employee works than Germany (around 75 percent) and France (85 percent)—despite a decade of rising investment. American companies compensate, however, by insisting that their workers work longer hours (28 percent more than German workers and 41 percent more than French workers)[26] to maintain comparable levels of productivity. The quest for economies is relentless; the National Bureau of Economic Research has found that half of all firms each year have gone through a wave of downsizing with results we will explore in the following chapter. But the lack of invested capital means that, despite all this effort, the output per hour worked is not only lower than the United States's main competitors but until the mid-1990s was consistently growing less rapidly. Even since 1995, properly measured, U.S. productivity growth has been only marginally higher than in Europe, even falling back below it in 2000[27] —and, as we will see in the next section, it is disputed how much of this increase is attributable to the improvements generated by ICT, and how much to the long American boom. Between 1991 and 1998 European productivity growth actually exceeded that in the United States. Further, Britain's Professor John Kay may be right in saying that American statisticians overestimate the productivity impact of information and communication technology (ICT) investments (see www.johnkay.com). If so, then the European lead is even greater.

The United States did enjoy a remarkable decade over the 1990s—but it was not driven by the rise of shareholder value and the alleged disciplines of Wall Street, as the conservative consensus insists. The sustainability of the recovery, given its extraordinary imbalances, has been discussed earlier, as have its sources in financial deregulation, the credit explosion, cheap money, and cheap oil. It was within this extraordinarily benign environment that corporate America prospered, helped by the problems of the opposition. Japanese competitors were flattened by the decade-long stagnation of the Japanese economy, while European rivals were hindered by the restrictive economic policies operating in the EU as member countries prepared to meet the demanding criteria for European monetary union.

Moreover, American companies enjoy one great advantage over any of their competitors. They operate in the world's largest single market; the United States is the highest-income region that has such deeply unified markets for goods, technology, capital, and labor. It is inevitably a testbed for new innovation, allowing scope for experimentation and failure that no other national market can offer. This combination of exceptional natural resources and a continental market has been identified by economic historians as the core of U.S. competitive advantage[28]—despite the impediment of the stock market–based financial system. The 1990s thus saw the world's largest market growing consistently for close to ten years—its longest-ever sustained period of expansion. Against this background the surprise would have been if American companies had not performed relatively well. Indeed, from the rest of the world's point of view, it is just as well that the United States has disabled itself with its financial and corporate structures and their accompanying culture.

And there is a third, unsung advantage that U.S. companies enjoy: the powerful role of federal spending, especially on research, through the massive university system, and the competitive advantage that accrues through U.S. regulatory agencies. David Mowery reports that by 1995 universities accounted for 61 percent of all basic research, which was largely paid for by federal funds.[29] The research has a remarkable pro-business bias, too, with the universities having set up over 500 research institutes seeking to support business interests. This is a mobilization of free research effort for business no other country can match. American economists have demonstrated that the returns on such pure university research are phenomenal, much higher than for private research, because they are freely available to the business community—and that every dollar spent on public research provokes another four dollars of private research.[30] This U.S. research network, as we have seen, is one of the country's formidable competitive advantages; in the past it has created world leadership in a number of key sectors and it is one of the drivers of the new "ideopolises." Yet for conservative theorists this is the truth that dares not speak its name. For it is work performed by the public sector.

Seventy-three percent of U.S. patents cite publicly funded science as the basis for the invention; yet in a national discourse dominated by conservatives, federally funded frontier research has declined. To turn this situation around, said the U.S. Competitiveness Council in its report for 2001, the United States must increase national investment in frontier research, strengthen support for fundamental disciplines that have been neglected, expand the pool of U.S. scientists and engineers, and modernize the nation's research infrastructure.[31] The federal share of national R&D dropped from 46 percent in 1985 to 27 percent in 1999. U.S. research facilities are falling into disrepair. In 1998, a majority of research institutions claimed that they had had to defer necessary construction or repair programs because of a shortage of funds. As matters stand, the report continued, the United States will be unable to meet the demand for scientists and engineers in coming years. By 2008 there should be jobs for six million scientists and engineers in the United States, but it looks unlikely to be able to supply them. Forty-one percent of Ph.D.s in science and engineering awarded in the United States go to foreign students, many of whom return home afterward. While conservative economists try to prove the efficient-market hypothesis—really trying to justify what we already know to be the irrationalities of Wall Street—the United States is allowing the true source of its economic strength to rot on the vine.

Unsung public support for the economy does not stop with R&D. America's regulatory agencies are gatekeepers for the world's largest market, and their approval is essential not just for new products in the United States, but for producers seeking access to the rest of the world. The Food and Drug Administration's tough tests for new drugs, for example, have become a world gold standard, forcing every pharmaceutical company to have a strong research presence in the United States—witness GlaxoSmithKline's decision to move its research headquarters to America. The flow of foreign companies wanting to undertake R&D in the United States has become a tidal wave, and most seek U.S. partners—so that U.S. companies wanting to limit R&D costs to boost short-term profits have a ready supply of collaborators.

These advantages have only partially offset the new Wall Street–inspired priority accorded in corporate strategy to financial considerations, which has hastened the dumbing down and hollowing out that began in the 1980s and continued over the 1990s, even if its worst effects were masked by the boom and the impact of ICT. As the painstaking work of Michael Porter at Harvard University has demonstrated, the United States has surrendered technological leadership in a wide range of sectors—and the key driver in the process has been the priorities and business objectives set by Wall Street. Even the much-vaunted productivity miracle, discussed later in this chapter, is of much less dramatic proportions than claimed. The United States has enjoyed a boom that its conservative ideologists have wholly misinterpreted; and by doing so they have undervalued and further undermined the country's sources of real advantage. As the economy enters more uncertain waters and the stock market bubble deflates, the tenuousness and fragility of America's economic success are becoming more obvious, extending even to the jewel in the 1990s crown—information technology and the New Economy. This was supposedly the ultimate proof that conservative economics worked. Now we are learning otherwise.

So What about U.S. Leadership in the New Economy?

Such a critique will surprise many readers. Surely America's powerful stock market and accompanying "equity culture" are meant to lie behind its recently established leadership in the New Economy, which is now lifting productivity growth back to the rates of thirty years ago? Critics may moan about short-termism and the rest, but surely America's highly developed and liquid stock markets are fundamental to its success? They make it easy to buy and sell shares in quoted companies and encourage savers to part with their cash because they know they can quickly realize their investment whenever they want. Without this structure, along with the preoccupation with shareholder value and a willingness to take risks to get above-average profits, the flow of venture capital—$90 billion a year at its peak—to high-tech start-ups and dot-com companies would never have taken place. The New Economy would never have happened.

The stock market permitted the development of the market in young, unproven companies that became an indispensable part of the dot-com revolution, allowing venture capitalists to release their initial investment in high-tech start-ups as the companies were floated on the stock market as Initial Public Offerings (IPOs). Even the sour taste left by the recent stock market collapse can never obliterate the scale of the achievement over the 1990s, which left the world with one of the great waves of innovation and reestablished America's technological leadership. As Michael Mandel, economics editor of *Business Week*, has written, "The stock market is not simply an innocent by-stander in the New Economy. Rather, with the rise in risk capital, the market has become the critical nexus of economic growth and innovation."[32]

Mandel is right; but as even he concedes in his prescient book *The Coming Internet Depression*, the intimate connection between the stock market and the New Economy can be as much destructive as creative. The argument goes further. It is obviously true that the boom in high-tech stocks helped foster new start-ups and greatly accelerated the pace and penetration of ICT development—but it did so at staggering cost. The whirlwind of hype that surrounded the New Economy was created by a vicious feedback loop in which the stock market was an essential transmission mechanism. It delivered extraordinary gains and, by boasting about them, helped to spread the fevered message that something very extraordinary was going on, so that not only the United States but soon every Western and Asian stock market suffered a collective suspension of rational judgment. Wall Street's appetite for short-term gains in share price that had proved so counterproductive for companies like Boeing, undervaluing the patient commitment to business building that is at the heart of any successful enterprise, had now been magnified hugely into an epic stock market bubble. Its implosion is not only having calamitous effects on the American economy but has exposed the weakness in the way the New Economy was constructed.

Information and communication technology and the Internet are important, but in any ranking of the great technological developments of the twentieth century they still rank below the impact of, say, electrification or the car—although as ICT becomes used more pervasively the chances are that it will rank alongside them. Thus, although American productivity growth did improve modestly between 1995 and 2000, it is probably still too early to explain this entirely in terms of New Economy effects. Professor Robert Gordon of Northwestern University, the United States's leading guru on productivity, argues that two-fifths of the productivity spurt is wholly explicable in terms of the usual upturn that comes at the end of an economic recovery, and the rest of the growth has been focused on the 12 percent of the economy engaged in the manufacture of ICT and ICT-related durables that benefited from the doubling of computer investment after 1995, which is unsustainable.[33] Beyond that there has been little or no increase in underlying rates of productivity growth. Half of U.S. investment spending in 2000 was on high-technology goods, up from 15 percent in 1992—a position that will plainly fall, especially as much of the investment has failed to produce a return, according to an important report by the management consultants McKinsey & Company.[34] The authors show, in confirmation of Gordon's findings, that most of the increase in U.S. productivity growth after 1995—such as it is—was focused on only six sectors (three of which were semi-conductors, computer manufacturing, and telecommunications) and that the other 70 percent of the economy recorded little or no increase. The evidence for a transformational increase in U.S. productivity that is sustainable as high-tech investment falls back to normal levels is scant.

Gordon sees little prospect of ICT making the same impact on productivity as the great clusters of inventions ranging from chemicals and oil to water sanitation, but on this the jury is still out. My own view is that ICT will ultimately make all organizations more porous, permeable, and thus networked—opening up a potential for cost reduction and change in organizational structure the scale of which we can only guess at. But that is for the future. For the purpose of the present argument, all we need to note is that the idea that any transformation was happening of the scale and speed that the stock market was explicitly indicating during the late 1990s, given the prices ICT shares achieved, was for the birds.

Here the new conservative ideology reinforced the market's inherent desire to believe fanciful stories to justify incredible short-term profits. In the past, technological innovation had always been driven by large corporations and government; now the media, new ICT moguls, and stock market hucksters all agreed that, as it was being propelled by hungry venture capitalists and fast-moving ICT-created networks, it had to be faster and better done. After victory in the Cold War there was a new triumphalism in the air—"We're bullish on America," screamed Merrill Lynch—and the death of inflation together with the benefits the ICT revolution brought in due time seemed to justify claims that America had entered a new era.

Wall Street's own enthusiasm thus created a self-fulfilling prophecy and apparent virtuous circle. Because the markets believed in the privately led, entrepreneurial economic transformation, they were prepared to deploy vast sums of private risk finance in the service of technological innovation—and this very enthusiasm created and sustained the buoyant markets in which the start-up dot-coms could be sold for a fortune, thereby justifying the initial support. As venture capitalists found themselves habitually making returns on average 7–10 percent higher than the rest of the equity market, that became further evidence that the New Economy was something special—and inflated the bubble further. So, however out of control and absurdly valued it became, the stock market was essential to the high-tech revolution—and the high-tech revolution was equally essential to the bubble. We now know, via inquiries by New York State Attorney General Eliot Spitzer, that investment banks knew many of these offerings to be worthless. In some cases, their advice to the investing public was wholly self-interested. Merrill Lynch has paid a $100 million fine for the way its analysts privately trashed some IPOs as "a piece of crap," "piece of shit," "dog," and "piece of junk" while recommending them to buyers. Clearly, gutting the Glass-Steagall Act turned Wall Street's clock back seventy years.

These conflicts of interest only serve to underline the American financial system's greater frailty: its short-term time horizons.

There is a tension inherent in any stock market between the financial community's desire for liquidity, so that it can keep its options open, move money from underperforming to potentially higher performing assets, and take profits at will, and businesses' desire for commitment over time and their need for investors to stick by them in tough times and not get too excited in good times. All stock markets tend to value short-term profits more highly than long-term profits,[35] with some estimates suggesting that cash flows more than five years in the future are discounted at twice the rate of shorter-term flows. Economies can live with this irrationality as long they have some countervailing capacity, either through some part of the shareholder base being committed to them whatever the stock price (family owners, employee owners, or cross-shareholdings, in which friendly companies hold stock shares in each other, for example) or through a system of corporate governance that protects them from the markets' worst excesses. The U.S. system offers little such countervailing power; indeed, the stock market is at the heart of the financial system. So when the market lost its head with enthusiasm for the New Economy—rather as seventeenth-century Dutch investors were seized with enthusiasm for tulips, or nineteenth-century British investors with zeal for railway companies—not only did it simply run away in a classic asset price bubble that represented a collective madness, but the consequences poisoned the heart of corporate and investment decision making and ultimately threatened the sustainability of the New Economy itself.

The old dictum of John Maynard Keynes, the greatest British economist, is that the object of much stock market investment is to buy, hope the upward momentum lasts, and then sell—an exercise in guessing the state of average opinion about affairs rather than what the affairs actually are. Or, as foreign-exchange dealers put it more succinctly, the trend is my friend. In the United States of the late 1990s this principle was taken to extremes. The markets' permanent short-termist tendency was exaggerated by a matrix of cultural and psychological factors into the most colossal irrational feedback loop of modern times, brilliantly described by the Yale economist Robert Schiller in *Irrational Exuberance*. Keynes said that the best way of conceptualizing much stock market investment was as a classic game of musical chairs with the players circulating around the chairs at ever greater speed, hoping that when the music stopped they would find security in the form of a safe chair by selling—and another player would be left holding the losses. In the first few months of 2000 it seemed that the entire United States—from 37,000 investment clubs and tens of thousands of day traders to ordinary Americans sharing the belief that markets naturally produced amazing returns—was playing musical chairs in the hope that someone else would be left holding the losses when the bubble burst. It proved a delusion.

For, as the bubble approaches bursting point, the only assessment that counts is whether it will last long enough to make a turn in the few trading hours ahead and pass the vastly overpriced security to a fool greater than you. Prices reach stratospheric levels. Cisco Systems, for example, was valued by the stock market at $160 billion in 1998, more than thirty times its sales; put another way, even though its sales and profits grew by 150 and 120 percent, respectively, throughout the 1990s, its share price rose at an annual rate of 2,000 percent over the same period. Its fall to earth, along with the rest of the high-tech sector, was inevitable. The apologists argue that this willingness to support companies at such high prices was a tribute to the stock market's long-termism; the lie to that was the average length of time high-tech shares were held. At one point at the peak of the boom Yahoo! shares were held on average for no more than eight days and Amazon shares for seven days. By contrast, shares in Coca-Cola are held on average for twenty-six months and GE for around thirty months—hardly a statement of commitment by the standards of serious technological development, which can take up to a decade, but an age compared with dot-com norms. The markets had become hypermyopic, with the consequence that the real prospects for high-tech companies were irrelevant.

Rationality ceased to play any role. Companies that offered little more than on-line specialist retailing, following the apparently successful example of Amazon and its selling of books and CDs, were valued at levels that were simply crazy. Thousands have simply folded. Even Amazon itself, enjoying all the advantages of early entry and a global brand, has proved to be founded on an economic model that delivers little profitability. The discounts at which it buys have to be passed on to customers, leaving it with woefully thin margins to cover its overhead; it makes just 2 percent on every book sold, compared to 30 percent for Barnes & Noble, the United States's leading bookseller. It has relied on a mad share price both to raise cash and to offer incentives to its workers; but stock options are worth less as stocks plunge. Workers have found that, rather than enjoying a position as flexible "owners" at the cutting edge of a technological revolution— which is how they were instructed to think of themselves at the peak of the boom with their stock options—they are now working up to seventy hours a week at low hourly wage rates. And even those terms are under threat from competition in the low-wage parts of the United States or Asia to which Amazon is moving as unhesitatingly as any other U.S. company under pressure to deliver stock-price performance. Motivation has plunged. Amazon's stock price lost as much as 90 percent of its peak value, and the company has aggressively laid off workers; both factors should make it easier to show a profit and yet the struggle goes on. Ravi Suria, a leading ICT analyst at Lehman Brothers, doubts its position is sustainable.[36]

To point this out is not to decry the inventiveness or importance of the companies at the heart of the ICT revolution; rather, it is to observe that the stock market that once succored and nurtured them is now their enemy. The search engine and Internet portal Yahoo! is a remarkable company by any standards, even if it was never worth the $150 billion or more at which it was once valued. And the essential role of Microsoft in developing user-friendly software to exploit the Net cannot be overestimated. But even these companies have been caught out by the reversal of the extravagant valuations of the market and the greed it fostered. Not only executives but many core staff insisted on being paid in stock options, so their loyalty and commitment lasted only as long as the high-tech bubble. As the bubble has deflated and the stock options become worthless, the dot-com and ICT companies have found it impossible to hold on to their staff, with turnover rates of 50 percent or more in a year commonplace. Yahoo! lost three chief executives of its regional operations; and when the chairman relinquished the overall chief executive role in February 2001 as advertising revenue plunged, it was almost impossible to recruit a successor. Eighteen months later, like Amazon it is building a fragile profitability that is scarcely sufficient to justify the former hype. Venture capitalists have found that the organizations they created to float on the stock market disintegrate no less quickly; directors and key staff simply walk away from companies whose sole objective was to make their backers overnight fortunes. Even the mighty Microsoft, which privileged its early joiners with generous stock options, has found it necessary to hire successive rounds of new employees on a temporary basis with none of the rights of the core staff in order to keep costs low and profits growth high—thus dividing the workforce against itself.

Much of the real performance of the ICT sector was itself dependent on the capacity of other ICT companies to raise cash on the bubble market. Yahoo!'s revenue came from other dot-coms advertising on its Web pages; as they imploded with the collapse in stock market values, so they cut their spending. The business model of much of the ICT sector was itself part of the bubble What the stock market had given, so it took away.

Indeed, the collapse of the stock market forces the mirror image process of severe contraction upon companies as aggressively as it once permitted growth. All companies in a market economy suffer retrenchment when sales and profit growth falter—but when a stock price falls to a tiny fraction of what it once stood at, retrenchment turns into rout. Marchfirst, an Internet consultancy with a turnover of $1 billion, saw its stock price dive by 92 percent; 2,000 layoffs, a third of its U.S. labor force, followed within three months in November 2000 as it struggled with the financial consequences of being unable to raise further stock market cash. By April 2001 it had filed for bankruptcy. The telecommunications manufacturer Lucent was tempted by the prospect of ephemeral stock market gold to try to turn itself into a digital, Web-based provider of Internet access equipment and software, using its own ludicrously high stock price to acquire a succession of Internet companies. But it could not make the transition, and it has decimated its workforce in the struggle to recapture profitability—its own sales having been sharply affected by the rash of bankruptcies among dot-com companies themselves. Lucent was not alone: high-quality companies like Xerox and Kodak felt the compulsion to digitize their operations quickly and rashly, and have incurred massive losses as a result. Xerox, yielding to the temptation to disguise its problem, overstated earnings by $1.4 billion. The whole bubble has led to a massive misallocation of resources and managerial effort in the quest for instant riches.

The cutbacks that follow from these mistakes become self-perpetuating. Bankrupt and ailing ICT companies themselves cut back on demand, and that causes a fresh round of retrenchment and loss of confidence—and contingent, temporary workers are the first to be laid off. Traditional companies tempted into the morass find themselves having to unravel their mistakes. The hope is that the current recession will be short-lived, but the structural weaknesses of the ICT sector do not permit a rapid recovery. The dot-com boom has proved, in the words of Mark Anderson, technology consultant and editor of the Strategic News Service,[37] to be little more than a scam—but one in which the pension funds who were the ultimate providers of risk capital to the venture capitalists have lost billions. The

United States may have launched the ICT revolution, but its financial system is disabling it from maintaining its leadership. A casino is not the best platform on which to grow long-term investment and innovation.

The bursting of the dot-com bubble and the repercussions of the closely associated frenzy in telecommunications (explored in chapter 6) have left the American financial system facing the most extensive losses since the 1920s stock market crash. No less a Wall Street grandee than Henry Paulson, CEO of Goldman Sachs, observed that "In my life, American business has never been under such scrutiny. To be blunt, much of it is deserved."[38] As American consumers retrench and the financial system tries to stitch back together its tattered balance sheet, the U.S. economy looks floored, facing years of depressed growth, however shortlived the 2001-2 recession may be. The productivity miracle has proved a mirage. Great economic assets, from the American banking structure supportive of small and medium-sized enterprises to its infrastructure of R&D investment, have been neglected and run down. Nor are the costs only economic. This episode has been the backdrop for a massive social experiment—the tolerance, indeed promotion, of extraordinary inequality along with the privatization of the public domain—whose social implications are only just becoming apparent. The worst of it is that the rest of the world is willy-nilly drawn in. American conservatives have a lot to answer for.

5

To Those Who Have Shall Be Given

America is the most unequal society in the industrialized West. The richest 20 percent of Americans earn nine times more than the poorest 20 percent, a scale of inequality half as great again as in Japan, Germany, and France. The United States has more of its population living in poverty—19.1 percent—than any other Western industrialized country;[1] worse, the bottom 10 percent of Americans, even though they live in a richer society, are poorer than their counterparts in Europe, Canada, and Japan[2]—only the poorest British rank below the poorest Americans. And at the very top of American society, incomes and wealth have reached stupendous proportions. The country boasts over three million millionaires, and the richest 1 percent of the population holds 38 percent of its wealth—again, a concentration more marked than in any comparable country.

Ever since the early 1980s this already unequal society has been growing more unequal. Average household incomes have fallen as blue-collar wages in real terms have fallen, a trend particularly marked in the bottom fifth of the population. Salaries for those at the top, meanwhile, have exploded—a trend that has if anything accelerated over the last twenty years and which in terms of disposable income has been powerfully reinforced by the structure of first Reagan's and now Bush's tax cuts. It is true that as unemployment fell in the later stages of the economic recovery after the mid-1990s the wages of blue-collar workers began to rise in real terms for the first time since the late 1970s; but elsewhere middle Americans' incomes were held back by waves of corporate downsizing. The rate of growth of inequality between the top and bottom may have slowed down, but the gap between the middle and the top has widened further.

This inequality is the most brutal fact of American life, a standing offense to the American expectation that everyone shall have the opportunity for life, liberty, and the pursuit of happiness. Plainly those at the top have very much more liberty and material grounds for happiness than those at the bottom. But equally, while this may be a rampantly commercial society, it genuinely subscribes to the view that everyone must have opportunity. Birth, race, and gender should not obstruct the chance for upward mobility. There are no titles in America; it was the founding fathers' profound belief that the United States should escape the flummeries and nuances of class evinced by the aristocratic hierarchy of titles. The republic even banned the aristocratic idea of primogeniture: land should not be handed down through the first-born, but repeatedly split up so that the individualism of every American would be supported by access to property, whether they were born first or last.

Every immigrant who became and becomes a citizen should be able to bootstrap themselves up by their own hard work, and the country's most repeated story is of how those who have made it have done so by individual merit and effort. To support this morally correct and socially imperative urge, education should be universally available, and a commitment to this principle seemed to be borne out in practice: a university was one of the first institutions each new state established as the West was opened up. Even in 1800 the United States had more universities than England. The United States invented the scholastic aptitude test (SAT), purporting to give the most objective view of every American student's intelligence, so that advancement in the education system would be—and would be seen to be—by merit. The interwoven conception is that all Americans have equal chances of advancement, as befits the citizenship the constitution confers, and that social mobility is the reward to all who work. The founding fathers and John Locke cast a long shadow.

However, the reality of extraordinary inequality makes a mockery of this account of American life, an account which is integral and essential to the conservative story. It discredits the entire conservative belief system: in the face of this reality, a just society cannot be conceived as an aggregation of morally pure individuals pursuing their own liberty with minimal taxation, minimal government, and minimal welfare. It suggests, at the very least, that John Rawls's argument for an infrastructure of justice to facilitate the access of everyone to opportunity and provide some minimum underwriting of basic needs is more than justified. There is a role for government. Individualism alone does not suffice to deliver the outcomes that the framers of the constitution intended and American culture seeks.

This is why conservatives expend so much effort in attempting to explain away inequality, dispute the figures, and redefine the argument. If the American way has only the insecure understanding of what drives wealth generation outlined in chapter 4, and produces the unfair social outcomes suggested by the existing degree of inequality, then the whole conservative intellectual and political edifice is exposed as a mere sham to justify the position of the rich—and a fundamental betrayal of the idea of America. It also means that the Europeans who want to copy the United States need to think again; a more self-critical America might find that after all it has something to learn from the Europe it spends so much time decrying and mocking.

The key element in the conservative retort to protests at inequality is that the pattern of rewards is essential to keep the American economy dynamic, and that the same dynamism is socially expressed but hidden in the static inequality figures. It may be that at first sight America appears unequal, but what is disguised is that there is an enormous rotation upward and downward, so that individuals are swapping places in the income hierarchy both from year to year, and over their lifetime. They may begin their career on a low income, but they finish it on a high income; they may be born to poor parents, but they end up rich. Here is Milton Friedman joining battle to defend inequality in the early 1960s:

> Consider two societies that have the same distribution of annual income. In one there is a great mobility and change so that the position of particular families in the income hierarchy varies widely from year to year. In the other, there is great rigidity so that each family stays in the same position. Clearly, in any meaningful sense, the second would be the more unequal society. The one kind of inequal-

ity is a sign of dynamic change, social mobility, equality of opportunity; the other of a status society. The confusion behind these two kinds of inequality is particularly important, precisely because competitive free-enterprise capitalism tends to substitute the one for the other.[3]

The difficulty for Friedman, and the many conservatives who repeat this argument, is that, as we will see, while they need this argument to be true, it is false. America's social rigidities are as embedded as—and sometimes worse than—those in Europe.

The Polarized Society . . .

U.S. society is polarizing and its social arteries hardening. Inequality is producing an ever more pronounced social stratification. Uppermost are the privileged top 20 percent: an educated, propertied class whose incomes and wealth are steadily rising and whose grip on the great institutions of upward mobility—the elite universities, the law and business schools—is growing more secure by the year. Then there is the middle 60 percent of the population, whose household incomes are stagnating, who had a surprisingly small stake in the share price boom, who are now severely indebted and whose working lives are increasingly at risk with little to compensate. And then there are the bottom 20 percent, who are locked into low-wage, low-skill jobs, are served by chronically indifferent schools, have scant access to health insurance, and are trapped in their circumstances, with fewer avenues out of poverty than the poor in other industrialized countries. *The State of Working America*, described by the *Financial Times* as the most comprehensive independent analysis of the American labor market, reports, for example, that the poor in the United States are less likely to exit poverty in any one year than the poor in Canada, Germany, the Netherlands, Sweden, and the UK—and if they do are more likely to have reentered poverty after five years.[4] Whatever else this picture suggests, it hardly corresponds to the conservative vision of a country whose social mobility is so much higher than other countries that it can justify having the highest inequality.

The polarization is taken to the extreme at the top and bottom. At the very top an overclass is emerging that increasingly is opting out of American life, using the conservative, antistatist political philosophy to justify its detachment. At the very bottom there is an underclass that is also developing its own culture, one of resignation, disaffection, and alienation, locked in a desperate struggle for survival and bitterly familiar with the gun violence that disfigures American life. The respective sumptuousness and bleakness of the two lifestyles represent a scale of difference in opportunity and wealth that is almost medieval in its scope.

This unease is captured by the decision of 120 billionaires, including the legendary investor Warren Buffett, America's fourth richest man, to found the campaigning organization and pressure group, the Campaign for Responsible Taxation. Launched in the wake of the capital gains tax reduction awarded in 1997 as part of the budget deal between President Clinton and a Republican-controlled Congress, the group promised to use its tax savings to finance the pressure group's case for fairer taxation and oppose the new Bush administration's plans for eventual elimination of both capital gains and inheritance tax. Buffett's argument is that the United States is in danger of developing an aristocracy of the wealthy. Just as it would be absurd to select the U.S. Olympics team for 2020 from the children of the winners of the Olympics in 2000, he says, so it is wrong to construct a society whose likely leaders tomorrow—given the advantages that wealth confers—will be the children of today's wealthy. This does not just offend the values of democracy and equality of opportunity on which the United States is constructed; it will be economically disastrous. Buffett and his fellow campaigners are right—even if they have been unsuccessful in making their case; but the pass has long been sold.

The chief means by which contemporary Western societies offer their citizens a chance to reach reasonable living standards and move up the socioeconomic hierarchy is education. At first sight the United States does well. In its schooling system, fourth-grade students do better than their international counterparts, and 37 percent of its 18–21-year-olds go through higher education—one of the highest proportions in the industrialized West. Moreover, the United States's university standards, especially in the top fifty universities, are on average the best in the world. Salaries are high and the research record is excellent. So they should be: the

United States allocates 1.4 percent of GDP to tertiary education, twice the proportion of Britain and significantly higher than the 1.0 percent spent by Germany and France.

But take a closer look, using more stringent criteria. As a system that offers every young person a chance for educational achievement and the acquisition of formal academic or vocational qualifications—the key instrument for social mobility—the U.S. structure fails. By twelfth grade American students are falling behind their international peers, especially in mathematics and science. And while in Germany, for example, 80 percent of dropouts go on to receive either vocational training or a degree, and all except 1 percent receive formal postsecondary education or training, in the United States 46 percent of dropouts gain no certificate or degree—and an extraordinary 31 percent receive no formal training or education after leaving school.[5] The message is stark. Those Americans who do not go to college are pushed into the labor market with a severe lack of skills, education, and vocational training.

And those who do go to college are overwhelmingly students from the higher socioeconomic backgrounds—just as they always have been. A key study in 1965 found that two-thirds of the explanation for educational achievement was accounted for by family income, and another study thirty years later arrived at exactly the same figure.[6] The SAT, which is the key measure of intellectual ability offering entry into the best colleges and universities, is—as Nicholas Lemann exposes in his monumental study *The Big Test*—not so much a measure of innate mental abilities as a measure of middle-class mental abilities. What the U.S. testing system is doing is validating the middle-class grip on the university system; private coaching to help pass the test is extensive, with fees in New York ranging up to $29,000. It is thus hardly surprising that the most exhaustive study of upward mobility for white men since 1950 finds that there has been no net change.[7]

These historical numbers are worrying enough; but, as inequality has risen over the last twenty years, it is becoming more and more obvious that surveys of mobility in the future will more than warrant Buffett's concern about the emergence of an aristocracy of the wealthy. For the cost of higher education over the last twenty-five years has exploded. The average cost of tuition, fees, and room and board has risen fourfold since 1977 to an average

$10,315 today; the overall average masks a stark contrast between the average cost of study at private universities ($17,613) and public universities ($7,013).[8] Yet as costs have risen, federal and state support to help fund students' costs has both declined and been refocused on the middle class. In 1965 the Pell Grant, the largest federal program for poor students, covered 85 percent of the cost of four years at a public university; in 2000 it covered just 39 percent of the bill.[9] The Hope Scholarship, introduced by President Clinton, provides up to $3,000 in tax credits to fund university education—but it goes mainly to families earning between $30,000 and $90,000, whose children would have gone to college anyway. States have cut their support for college students on average by 32 percent since 1979.

The result of this vicious scissor movement—rising costs cutting against falling state and federal support—is a calamitous drop in the chances of a poor student acquiring a university or college degree; and this in an environment where there are negligible alternative forms of vocational and formal education. Borrowing money on the scale now needed to finance college is easier for students from better-off families and expectations of reasonable earnings than for students from low-income families. As Gaston Caperton, president of the College Board, admits, the United States "is not doing a good job helping low-income students succeed."[10] In 1979 a student aged eighteen to twenty-four from the top income quartile was four times more likely to obtain a degree by age twenty-four than a student from the bottom quartile. By 1994, the latest year for which we have figures, the figure was ten times more likely. Given current trends in inequality, college costs and falling state support, this already disastrous ratio can only have gotten worse over the last eight years. We can thus be certain that American social mobility over the decades ahead will deteriorate below its already modest level.

As if all this were not enough, there is also a widening gulf between public and private universities. The poorer public universities are finding it harder to recruit and retain the best staff, and are locked in a vicious circle of a weakening reputation, falling funding, and high student drop-out rates; only 67 percent of students at public colleges and universities complete their degrees, compared to 83 percent of students at private universities. To British eyes, the inequality of the American system is startling. If 7 percent of British schoolchildren are educated privately at schools that dominate the academic league tables (98 of the top 100 schools in the *Financial Times* 2001 league table ranking A-level [similar to SAT] results are private), 11 percent of American schoolchildren are educated privately at similarly top-performing schools. Moreover, 22 percent of American students attend private colleges and universities, for which the average fee, as noted above, is $17,613—an outlay that requires, for all but the very wealthy, a willingness to take out enormous loans. The British university system, by contrast, is almost entirely publicly funded and, for all its weaknesses, has a much more equitable system of grant assistance for poorer students.

America's private universities represent the pinnacle of the U.S. system. Ninety-two percent of the 1.4 percent of GDP that the United States spends on tertiary education is spent on private universities and colleges.[11] The network of private Ivy League universities in the east is world famous, including the elite names of Harvard, Yale, Cornell, and Princeton; but there are private universities of equal rank in the West (Stanford in California), Southwest (Rice in Houston, Texas), Midwest (Chicago and Northwestern) and Southeast (Emory in Atlanta, Duke in North Carolina). The United States's two leading technological universities, MIT and Caltech, are also private. Together these institutions enjoy privileged access to the top positions in American life. The total annual costs of attendance at these elite private universities can reach $35,000, although they are well-endowed enough to offer need-blind admissions (i.e., so that income level should not dictate the offer or acceptance of a place), providing grants from their own funds to help support poorer students. However, the growth of endowment income, except in the richest institutions, is not keeping pace with fees, so that even this support for poorer students is weakening—and even rich universities are not indifferent to the advantage of admitting the children of rich families and the subsequent contribution they will make to the endowment fund. The way Britain's leading private schools, like Westminster and St. Paul's, still manage to produce a disproportionate supply of students to Oxford and Cambridge is reproduced in the United States in the way private schools like Andover and Exeter still manage to get above-average representation at Harvard and Yale. Money talks, and the well-funded private schools and private universities are locked in an exclusive and privileged embrace.

Despite America's public attachment to the idea of meritocracy, the wealthy—just as Warren Buffett argues—ensure that their children get privileged access to the best schools, the best universities, and the most influential networks. They can pay the fees. The Bush, Gore, and Kennedy families are only three of the more famous political examples of how wealth begets both more wealth and influence. Five generations of Bushes, for example, have been "tapped" to become members of the Skull and Bones Club at Yale, whose initiates retain a commitment to the lifelong scratching of each others' backs, while never acknowledging they were members; other alumni include a roll call of American presidents and statesmen. In itself there is nothing remarkable about private clubs of privileged insiders in private universities; it is just that the country that boasts them should be more guarded about its pretensions to meritocracy. Behind most of the Fortune 500 companies lies a rich, self-reproducing family network based on the fortunes made by the founder.

In one sense, membership of this super-elite *is* democratic; for money buys entry to the club, and new money is as valid as old money. The precondition for the rich tightening their offsprings' grip on the upper echelons of American society in new dynasties, via education, is the fact of being rich and growing richer. Over the last decade the new fortunes made in the United States have been spectacular, with CEO remuneration packages topping $12 million (see chapter 4). The story, of course, is that the fortunes and the incomes are essential to make American capitalism work so well; but, again as observed in chapter 4, high executive pay is closely followed by poor corporate and share price performance. Performance has little to do with reward. Rather, as Cornell University's Professor Robert Frank argues, incomes at the top are rigged by winner-takes-all effects, which the better-off are only too willing to exploit even as they attempt to justify them as the returns for risk and effort.[12]

News of a winning formula or individual, for example, in any industry or sector, is more quickly disseminated in an era of information and communication technology; and because the new drive for shareholder value makes winning more valuable, the competition to get the exclusive services of "winners" has grown more intense. Thus from publishing to investment banking, executives with a track record of success are in a unique position of market power, which they have exploited with increasing ruthlessness to achieve staggering salary and share option deals. Robert Reich in *The Future of Success* shows how individuals in every walk of life exploit the new culture of "putting yourself in play" to get the market to bid up the price of one's personal brand to stunning levels.[13]

And although these rewards are objectively irrational and absurd, they become a self-fulfilling need. If social standing depends on the possession of ever larger "trophy" homes or yachts, then, as Robert Frank argues, executives need the wherewithal to buy them in order to compete with their peers.[14] Thus what drives incomes ever higher is not scarcity of talent or outstanding performance; rather, it is the market price of the luxury goods that executives need to own to show that they are part of the same executive community. This is a world in which membership fees at the right golf club can run over $30,000, the right Patek Philippe wristwatch up to $17,500; to compete, executives have to be earning $1 million or more a year.

Spending on luxuries—from premium cigars and wines to vacation homes—has risen dramatically faster than overall spending; between 1995 and 1996, for example, it rose at four times the rate.[15] As argued in the previous chapter, there are no rules for the determination of executive incomes built into company law, despite the best efforts of the SEC, which has no powers to interfere in corporate governance; companies are the private property of shareholders and their directors, and if they feel the need to pay themselves extraordinarily there is no effective obstacle to their doing so. In this climate, luxury goods become disposable commodities; trophy homes are built, discarded, and destroyed once their function as emblems of luxury display has been fulfilled—rather as trophy wives are divorced as their looks fade.

Yet this irrationality cannot be openly acknowledged. The elite must necessarily tell the story that wealth creation and business success require incentives on this scale. Most elite members are fierce advocates of free-market economics and equally fierce critics of any form of public intervention as inevitably ineffective and self-defeating. Their incomes are to them the proof that free-market economics works. Moreover, their wealth and spending power allow them to live independently of any form of state initiative, without using any facility or function delivered by the state. They can live in their own privately defended villas, mansions, or ranches, insure themselves privately for private health care, educate their children privately, and travel by private plane and car. In short, they can secede from the civic realm and be materially better off—proof positive that there is no need for the state and that the universe of the private is morally superior. They are simply ignorant of the condition of their fellow citizens.

In this sense the super-elite are in the vanguard of a civic secession that is spreading throughout the privileged top 20 percent of American society. There are now some three million Americans living in over twenty thousand gated communities offering the same privatized lifestyle to better-off Americans as the super-rich can claim.[16] The gated community achieves its most extreme form yet in the new fully independent incorporated cities, like California's Hidden Hills and Rolling Hills, where residents declare political independence; exempt from state (but not federal) taxes, they collect their own taxes and provide their own benefits. These cities are getting bigger; Green Valley in Las Vegas, to be completed in 2005, will have a population of sixty thousand. Formally known as "homeowners' associations" (HOAs), they are the most complete expression of opting out and detachment; their members need never come near public institutions or participate in wider civic life. But they are not nonpolitical; in California, HOAs were the organized base for campaigns against school busing and in favor of lower taxes (like Proposition 13). Their justification is not just the political and cultural need to opt out; they represent Americans' search for the ideal community and an escape from the haphazard violence of much American street life. For, as Edward Blakely and Mary Gail Snyder write, gated communities and HOAs are "more than walled-off areas and refuges from urban violence and a rapidly changing society. They are also a search for socio-spatial community—the ideal community that Americans have sought since the landing of the Pilgrims."[17] But in expressing that quest by founding a community from which others are kept out—the terms for admission to an HOA can include a minimum age for children and weight for dogs; intruders can be shot—and which exists as a civic bubble insulated from other citizens, the instigators and owner–members are mounting nothing less than a civil revolt that paradoxically reinforces the trends from which they are fleeing.

For the new inequality is eating at the bone marrow of American civilization, helping to create a culture in which impersonal contract, hawkishly policed through a mountain of ever more aggressive litigation, is succeeding trust, community, and assimilation as the principal form of social exchange. Patrick M. Garry, in *A Nation of Adversaries*, argues that civic secession is helping to create a litigation culture, which in turn accelerates the breakdown of American communities. Between 1960 and 1997 the number of lawsuits brought annually has quadrupled, so that litigation is increasing at seven times the rate of the population. Litigation, of course, is not all to be deplored; it remains one of the great instruments ordinary Americans have with which to fight back against corporate power or abuse of political power. The difficulty lies in its intrusion into large areas of private life, so that in matters where norms, traditions, and expectations of reciprocal behavior used to define accepted practice—bringing up children, responses to death, relationships between the sexes—litigation has come to occupy a decisive role. The law has become one of the United States's fastest-growing professions—since 1970 growing three times faster than the economy[18]—to the point where the United States now has the highest number of lawyers per 1,000 inhabitants in the industrialized world. Cooperation is giving way to a pervasive adversarialism in which confrontation and litigation, rather than community endeavor or political action, are seen as the principal means of achieving one's goals. Even to say "sorry" after a road accident has become culturally difficult because it might mean acknowledging some liability in a subsequent court action.[19]

The Americans, as noted earlier, and as explored at length by Robert Putnam in *Bowling Alone*, are ceasing to be a nation of participators; instead, they are turning into individualist, suspicious litigators. In Putnam's formulation, a long civic generation born between 1920 and 1940, that voted more, joined more, and trusted more, is giving way to new generations that have become progressively disengaged from all forms of civic life. There is no one index of social capital, but Putnam identifies the same phenomenon across the gamut of American life. Membership in unions and political parties is down; readership of newspapers and audiences for mainstream television network news are down; attendance at parent-teacher associations is down. Indeed, between 1973 and 1994 attendance at a public meeting of any local club or organization fell by 40 percent.[20] In 1965, 7 percent of an individual's time was spent in community organizations; by 1995 this was down to 3 percent.

Putnam's work must nevertheless be treated with caution. The better

American values have shown remarkable stability, as argued in chapter 2, and there are new forms of association—for example, Internet chat rooms and teenage clubbing habits—that even his exhaustive work has undervalued or neglected. And while on international comparisons of trust the United States may be well below the Scandinavian countries, it still scores significantly higher than France, Germany, and Italy.[21] If American social capital is declining, it is from a relatively high base. On the other hand, mainland European countries, as argued in chapters 8 and 9, have much more vigorous public systems for underwriting and expressing community, and rely less on the informal private systems of self-help and association that traditionally have been important in the United States. They have mechanisms for compensating for the deficiency of social capital that the United States does not.

Even allowing for some overstatement on Putnam's part, the evidence points in the same direction across the board. The growth of gated communities and the explosion of litigation are parts of the same pattern as the decline in joining and participating. American civilization is becoming more fragmented, polarized, and dissociated as the shockwaves of the conservative revolution radiate through the system. Students from higher-income families are increasingly more likely to win degrees; social mobility is only modest and set to decline. These trends have causes deep within conservative attitudes and policies; and the extension of the same principles into the American labor market and into the country's culture and public realm are intensifying the polarizing processes.

. . . Exacerbated by the Flexible Labor Market

The magical, iconic quality in a market economy in thrall to the maximization of shareholder value is flexibility. Indeed, the concept has come to have an almost noble connotation: flexibility implies agility, adaptability, intelligence, and responsiveness. There is scarcely another word in the American lexicon that embodies so many virtues. Flexibility is what makes a market economy work. Financial capital, for example, is mobile and flexible; it has no loyalties, nor does it expect any. Its job is to chase the highest returns. Over the last thirty years, corporations have increasingly looked for the same quality from their workforces. If a company chooses to run down a branch of production, then it needs the flexibility to extract itself as quickly and cheaply as possible. When it increases output, it needs to do so in such a way that, if market conditions change, it can disinvest as quickly as the financial markets may choose to disinvest from its shares. Hiring a worker is not so much a contract with reciprocal obligations as a cash deal—one that the employer should be able—flexibly—to cancel at will.

American employment law has always been aggressive in its insistence that companies are, in the words of the precedent-setting 1884 judgment by the Tennessee Supreme Court, free "to discharge or retain employees at will for good cause or for no cause, or even for bad cause without thereby being guilty of an unlawful act per se."[22] The doctrine of employment at will has long been fiercely contested as Dickensian, and over the last twenty-five years most state courts have recognized exceptions to the general principle. But as the courts have decided in favor of workers' rights, employers have gone to ever greater lengths to preserve the original doctrine, both in custom and in practice. More than three-fifths of employers report that they sometimes offer no form of employment contract; over half concede that they sometimes include wording in their contract specifying that the employment can be terminated summarily for any reason.[23]

The upshot is that the American labor market is characterized by impermanence, from which not even the professional and managerial classes are immune; in 1993, for the first time ever, more white-collar workers than blue-collar workers were unemployed. As the labor market tightened in the second half of the 1990s, impermanence worked to the advantage of those workers with scarce skills, who were able to bid up their wages in the "talent war." Even the poorest have managed to work more—though their wage rates have scarcely risen.

However, this cyclical effect does not disguise the underlying trends. Over time the story is one of rising turnover rates, more contingent work, an explosion of the use of agencies supplying temporary workers, and longer hours. The average American now has nine jobs in a lifetime, and nearly three in ten Americans work in jobs on nonstandard terms—part-time, temping, on call, or day labor. In a strong labor market the essential riskiness of being permanently disposable is not so apparent, for another job can be won quickly; and in any event, in the strong labor market of the late 1990s standard employment grew as employers bowed to the inevitable and accepted more contractual arrangements and accompanying workers' rights. Nevertheless, this trend cannot be expected to continue. Nonstandard jobs are advantageous to employers because they lack basic entitlements. Only 60 percent of contingent workers, for example, and a bare 40 percent of temp agency staff, have health insurance coverage.

It should be no surprise that the most dynamic growth in the U.S. labor market has been in temping. Growing at 11 percent per annum over the 1990s, the sector now employs nearly 2.5 million workers; 10 percent of all vacancies in the United States over the 1990s were filled by temporary employment agencies. Manpower, with 600,000 staff, is the largest employer in the United States. The employee's relationship with a temp agency is the purest, most flexible cash deal there can be, with no attendant workers' rights. The risk of changing market conditions is displaced onto such workers, notwithstanding that they are the least well equipped to bear such risk. The same drive to minimize obligations to the workforce lies behind the desire to employ part-time, defined as any job that requires less than forty hours a week. Part-time workers do not qualify for overtime rates, for example, and their hourly wage rate is typically two-thirds of the rate for the same full-time job.

The American workforce is keenly aware that these trends are but more evidence that every employer is under growing pressure to be hawkish. What was conspicuous about the 1990s was that the pace of corporate reengineering was sustained without letup over the economic recovery, so that in 1995, the last year for which figures are available, 15 percent of male American workers had lost their job in the previous three years. Between 1993 and 1995 (again, the most recent years for which data are available) nearly as many jobs were lost as during the 1981–83 recession. Between 1980 and 1995, thirty-nine million Americans were caught up in one or another corporate downsizing program.[24]

In these conditions, even in a tight labor market workers have been wary about pushing for higher wages; the reality of downsizing, the growth of contingent work, and the threat to move jobs to low-cost parts of North America or abroad (General Motors has moved over forty plants to Mexico, for example) are all parts of a picture in which work is at risk. As a result, average wages steadily fell in real terms for more than twenty years up until 1995 for all but the top 20 percent of the workforce. It was only the boom of the late 1990s—now looking unsustainable—that reversed the trend. To compensate, those four-fifths of Americans who faced falling real wages worked longer hours over the same period and continued to do so into the second half of the 1990s, even as wage rates in real terms began to harden. On average, Americans now work around fifty hours a week, up from about forty in 1973—more than any other industrialized country except Portugal; they also have the fewest paid holidays.[25]

If working life is hard for the majority of Americans, for around a fifth of the working population at the bottom, who on average have incomes of no more than half the median income (the European definition of poverty), life has become increasingly desperate. (The overall figure for this proportion of the population masks the disastrous condition of blacks and Hispanics, among whom poverty is twice as common as for whites.) Eligibility for income support and public assistance is being steadily withdrawn; cumulatively, it had halved by 1998–99 from the levels of twenty years ago.[26] Poorly educated and with negligible access to training programs, the poor are locked into their status. Fifty-four percent of those in the bottom 20 percent in the 1960s were still there in the 1990s; only 1 percent had migrated to the top 20 percent.[27]

The journalist Barbara Ehrenreich conducted her own social experiment, spending 1998 working in a series of low-wage jobs as a waitress, hotel maid, cleaning woman, health care worker, and Wal-Mart sales clerk. The result of her year, documented in *Nickel and Dimed*, is an extraordinary, Orwellian testimony to how tough American working life is for the bottom 20 percent. She had absolutely no financial margin beyond paying the rent and what she needed to survive; saving or finding the time for any training to upgrade her status was beyond her. "Most civilized nations compensate for the inadequacy of wages by providing relatively generous public services such as health insurance, free or subsidized child care, subsidized housing, and effective public transportation," she writes. "But the United States, for all its wealth, leaves its citizens to fend for themselves—facing market-based rents, for example, on their wages alone. For millions of Americans, that $10—or even $8 or $6—hourly wage is all there is."[28]

For the advocates of welfare "reform" the absence of these supports, along with the new five-year time limit for receiving welfare, has produced the social success of lowering the number of families on welfare from 4.4 million, when the Welfare Reform Act was signed in 1996, to some two million in 2001. Many states chose to shorten the time limit even further, with Virginia, for example, offering only ninety days to find work before benefits cease. Overall, four and a half million fewer people received welfare benefits following the passage of the act.[29] The incentive, for the states who administer welfare and the recipients alike, is to do everything to find benefit claimants work; even the unemployment rate for single mothers fell from around 40 percent to under 30 percent in 2001, although as recession bites numbers are beginning to rise again. In 2001, too, child poverty fell to its lowest level for twenty-one years.[30]

How much these outcomes are attributable to the simple operation of a booming economy and the investment many states made in child support, thus making it easier for many poor mothers to work, and how much to the threat of losing benefits (the object of welfare reform) is an open question. Nor is it clear, as jobs continue to disappear, how sustainable the improvement will be—or whether the American public will be prepared to accept destitution for those whose five-year welfare entitlement has expired, beginning for women in 2002. Only 39 percent of unemployed Americans have access to unemployment benefits, compared to as many as 70 percent fifteen years ago; if America's slowdown is prolonged, Harvard University's Richard Freeman believes the poverty rate could climb above the 12 percent rate of the last two recessions.[31] But even if welfare reform had worked as the conservatives preached—which it has not, at least not as satisfactorily as they claim—it still leaves the Rawlsian question unanswered. If, behind a veil of ignorance, we did not know whether we would be in the circumstances of America's bottom 20 percent, none of us would willingly deem their condition acceptable. They are not equipped with skills; their basic needs are neglected; they are trapped in their low-wage jobs; they have no ladder upward; they are not offered health insurance; they are not provided with schools that will give their children even the semblance of equality of opportunity; if their children do win places at a college or university, the costs of attendance are beyond them and state assistance is negligible and declining. The infrastructure of justice, in short, is close to nonexistent. What has been put in its place is a system that relieves the middle class of paying the tax that might support such an infrastructure, in the name of a social mobility that equally does not exist. This is self-interested callousness masquerading as morality and economic efficiency.

For these conditions could partly be excused if income and social mobility in the United States were high. It is not. Lawrence Mishel, Jared Bernstein, and John Schmitt, the three authors of *The State of Working America*, compare the mobility of workers in America with the four biggest European economies and three Scandinavian economies. They find that the United States has the lowest share of workers moving from the bottom fifth of workers into the second fifth, the lowest share moving into the top 60 percent and the highest share of workers unable to sustain full-time employment.[32] The most exhaustive study by the Organization for Economic Cooperation and Development (OECD) confirms the poor rates of relative upward mobility for very-low-paid American workers; it also found that full-time workers in Britain, Italy, and Germany enjoy much more rapid growth in their earnings than those in the United States, which in this respect ranks roughly equal with France.[33] However, downward mobility was more marked in the United States; American workers are more likely to suffer a reduction in their real earnings than workers in Europe. Even the OECD, high priest of deregulation, finds itself forced to conclude that countries with more deregulated labor and product markets (preeminently the United States) do not appear to have higher relative mobility, nor do low-paid workers in these economies experience more upward mobility. The OECD is pulling its punches. The U.S. experience is worse than Europe's.

These results are not unexpected; the surveys repeat the evidence accumulated since the war that the United States, despite all the propaganda in its favor, has shown little or no difference in measured mobility compared to Europe. Lipset and Bendix, in their pathbreaking study *Social Mobility in Industrial Society*, could find no evidence in the 1950s that American men were moving any more rapidly from manual to nonmanual labor than men in other industrial societies. Later studies comparing the income mobility of the United States with the Scandinavian countries and Germany find either that there is no difference, or that there is less mobility in the United States.[34] The leading sociologists Robert Erikson and John Goldthorpe found precisely the same result in a more detailed breakdown of mobility, measuring both what happens intergenerationally and what happens over one individual's lifetime.[35] Indeed, they argued, it is probable that American social mobility is overstated because the category used to define the top class—"professional, technical, and kindred workers"—is so broad that it includes workers who would be categorized further down the class hierarchy in the more tightly drawn European classifications. The mystery, as Erikson and Goldthorpe write, is why, given that there is no evidence of American exceptionalism or higher social mobility, the myth persists.

The answer is that nobody in the highly introverted society that the United States has become can believe that foreigners might do it as well as or better than Americans—and the conservative intellectual ascendancy is not going to disabuse them. The point made earlier needs emphasizing. The historical data already show that mid-twentieth-century America had only modest rates of income and social mobility by international standards, and that these showed no signs of improving over the postwar period. The combination in the contemporary United States of flexible labor markets and reduced educational opportunity for low-income students—the great achievements of conservatism—can have only one result: in the future, mobility, disgracefully, is set to fall.

America is developing an aristocracy of the rich and a concomitant serfdom of the poor—and in so doing is laying its own economic vitality open to threat. Not only is it deluding itself, it is deluding the entire globe before which it holds itself up as the economic and social model to emulate.

The Unfair Bargain

However unfair the "flexible labor market" might be in its distribution of rewards and risk, its freezing of the bottom 20 percent into poverty, and its baleful influence on income and social mobility, it is widely regarded—certainly by American conservatives—as the key to American economic success. The American rate of job creation has compared favorably with that in Europe; dig deeper, however, and the story is very different from the explanation offered by conservatives.

If flexibility is defined as the degree to which a wage is a contract that can be unraveled when employers wish, uncontaminated as far as possible by regulations, collective bargaining, or employment protection, and if it is the panacea the conservatives claim, then the United States should have succeeded in lowering unemployment rates across the board over the 1990s. Unemployment among poorly educated, low-skilled workers would be broadly similar to that among better-educated, higher-skilled peers, because their wages would be driven down. But the opposite is the case. The unemployment rate of the poorly skilled in the United States is 4.5 times higher than that of college-educated workers, the highest ratio of all industrialized countries.[36] The American labor market, for all its vaunted flexibility, turns out to be the *least* efficient at pricing poorly skilled workers into work—despite its punitive welfare policies toward the unemployed. It is, however, very efficient at ensuring that top people's pay grows explosively.

The secret of the American job story is less its flexible labor market than what has happened to the structure of its economy as a result of a twenty-five-year credit boom that has fueled a sustained consumer boom, coupled, on the supply side, with the evolution of the sexual revolution and thus women's appetite and ability to join the world of work. On top of this, a consistent supply of immigrants has helped keep wage rates at minimum levels however tight the labor market has become; the United States's long border with Mexico, ensuring a steady supply of cheap labor, in this respect has as much to do with labor market flexibility as lack of employment regulation. In any case, to present the U.S. labor market as wholly unregulated is again to comprehend the world through conservative eyes: American employers have to comply with a raft of stringent rules over health and safety, along with racial and sexual discrimination. All societies, even the United States, have to set limits to the degree work can be treated as a commodity and employers have a free hand.

Over the last two decades America has created the world's largest service sector, driven by astonishing consumption growth, and in turn has created forty million jobs. As Americans turned into a nation of credit-financed shoppers preoccupied with their health, they created over fourteen million jobs just in the nation's shopping malls, hospitals, and health care centers—most of which were "nonstandard" jobs filled by women. A female army of cashiers, sales clerks, nurses, cleaners, and waitresses has fanned out across America, picking up temporary work in the low-productivity service sector, their experiences so ably documented by

Barbara Ehrenreich. What has driven their willingness to work is not just a new readiness to join the labor market; it has been need. The Employment Policy Institute in Washington computes that 29 percent of families have incomes that fall below a reasonable estimate of their budgetary need; mothers simply have had to work, especially over a period in which male wages have been stagnating in real terms.[37] Americans, in short, have created a treadmill for themselves and hailed it as an economic miracle.

Even so, the growth in the numbers of two-earner families, which now constitute nearly half of all families, has not been enough to sustain living standards and spending in an era in which real wages have fallen. Americans have gone massively into debt, aided and abetted by an increasingly deregulated banking system pumping out credit. By 2000 the stock of household debt had reached an all-time high in relation to household income, driven largely by a growth in mortgage debt. But the greatest increase in debt over the 1990s was incurred by the middle 20 percent of income earners—evidence of how the need to borrow was felt most keenly by those whose living standards were most under pressure. The proportion of income eaten up by debt service has been rising sharply for those on incomes below $50,000—up from 18 percent in 1995 to 22 percent in 1998. For those at the bottom, with incomes of $10,000 or less, debt service is an even heavier burden, taking 32 percent of their income—an extreme pressure reflected in a doubling in the number of pawnshops by some 10,000 between 1986 and 1996. Exposed to extraordinarily high interest rates on small loans, poorer Americans see their chances of being able to enter the housing market diminish as house prices in real terms escalate. These are the dwellers in the mushrooming trailer parks around the country—the flip side of the gated communities. As Barbara Ehrenreich found, rents are so high that sometimes low-paid workers have to sleep in their vans or trucks.

The rate of American employment generation over the last twenty years remains an achievement, but it is wrong to present the American labor market as the philosopher's stone of job creation. This was a particular achievement at a particular moment of time. For example, full-time jobs in the unionized manufacturing sector have held up well over the last twenty years by international standards, a tribute to the strong growth of domestic demand. Again, this has less to do with the structure of the labor market than with the performance of the wider economy. But crucially, the credit that has driven the consumption—and much of the jobs growth—has been taken on by ordinary wage earners even as their wages have been squeezed in real terms; at the time of writing they face highly uncertain economic prospects with enormous cumulative debts. Servicing their current debts will be demanding enough, let alone assuming new debts. The great job-generating machine is coming to the end of its capacity to deliver.

As it does so, the asymmetry of power in the labor market between employers and workers will start to have more malign consequences. Even those who enjoyed the benefits of the talent war of the late 1990s as the labor market tightened, and who declared independence from large companies, making their own careers as consultants, are finding that harsher economic times bring new insecurities. Those working for companies fear another round of downsizing from which nobody at any level is safe. Everybody is under pressure, at risk, and disconnected in an economy where short-term contracts are king. The hours worked continue to climb. The alleged bargain is that this is the price that has to be paid for an efficient, dynamic economy that will deliver opportunity and mobility. But the bargain is a fraud. The conservative proposition is about to come under closer scrutiny than it has faced for twenty-five years.

The Collapse of the Public Realm

Yet the political environment in which any debate takes place has been degraded by the same forces: the United States today, in Michael Sandel's words from chapter 2, is little more than a "procedural republic." The ever onward encroachment of the market and its values has invaded and polluted the heart of the political process. The decline in direct citizen involvement in politics has been associated with and exploited by an enormous extension of corporate and business power as the parties compete for funds. Money, as the billionaire Michael Bloomberg demonstrated by effectively buying the mayoralty of New York in 2001, has become central to political success.

The cost of American elections has grown explosively as politics has grown more centralized and more reliant on the media to extend its message. In House and Senate elections the incumbent, so well placed to raise money, is all but impossible to beat. In 1998, 98 percent of the House and 90 percent of the Senate incumbents were reelected.[38] The community of interest between the Republican party and business described in chapter 3 has given the Republicans a built-in advantage in winning campaign finance. Of those who contributed to parties and candidates in 1997, 81 percent earned more than $100,000 and were over forty-five; half described themselves as conservative while less than a third called themselves liberal.[39] One of the side effects of the enormous and growing inequality of American society is that the Republicans have had an ever richer base from which to raise their finance; if the Democrats try to redress the balance, that serves only to ratchet up Republican spending to stay ahead. Just to enter American politics has become prohibitively expensive.

The American political system has such effective built-in checks and balances that the corporations and rich individuals who furnish the wherewithal cannot buy power in a straightforward cash transaction, however much they would like to. Typically they give "soft" money, according to the stipulation that they can support a cause but not a party or candidate. However, they have an agenda, and they look for paybacks. The influence on Bush's policies, for example, is evident. The shape of tax and regulatory concessions has plainly favored his campaign backers. Ken Lay of Enron personally donated $1 million to the Bush campaign. This is the further pollution of the American political discourse. In order to compete for funds, the Democrats have found themselves being pulled in the same pro–free-market, anti–tax-and-welfare policy directions as the Republicans, so that both parties are huddled around a very particular pro-business centrist political philosophy because that is what makes raising campaign finance easiest. Moreover, the fund-raisers—the individuals who raise money that can be directly spent on the candidates' campaigns, in contrast to soft money—have become the key figures in selecting which politicians will be chosen to represent the party. If they feel they cannot sell a politician to their donors, then effectively they have the right of veto. Thus both the face of the politician and the policies espoused are effectively dictated by money.

The most direct influence of all is that of the lobbyist, directing campaign finance to those members of Congress up for reelection on the quiet understanding that the quid pro quo will be support for a key line change in a bill—or just to lay the groundwork of obligation against a future need to elicit a reply to the telephone call mustering support for an amendment or veto. Jeffrey Birnbaum, Washington bureau chief for *Fortune*, writes in *The Money Men* that President Clinton openly acknowledged at the memorial service for the prominent Democratic fund-raiser and lobbyist Dan Dutko that without Dutko's capacity to raise money he would never have been president. Any number of congressmen and women can say the same. It is this fund-raising power that gives lobbyists and advocacy organizations like the NRA and the AARP (American Association of Retired Persons) their clout. Every presidential nomination for the last twenty years has been won by the candidate who raised the most money. If a democratic political system is meant to offer a means by which a country can engage in public and rational argument in the pursuit of the public interest, and to hold decision makers to account through the ballot box, then the United States is an increasingly dismal failure. It has the form of democracy without its content.

This deformation of the political system has consequences for the rest of the public domain. Expressing public objectives and sustaining the public infrastructure have become increasingly difficult. Federal expenditure on roads, schools, and universities fell as a proportion of GDP throughout the 1990s even under a Democratic president, while few states dared raise their tax base to compensate for the fall-off in federal spending; indeed, many were more hawkish about spending cuts than the federal government. The Bush administration's spending plans are set to accelerate the process still further.

The U.S. transportation infrastructure is increasingly frayed, with endemic traffic gridlock and a decaying public transportation system. The Federal Highways Administration estimates that repairs of 50 percent of major U.S. roads and highways are backlogged, while the Federal Railroad Administration has not inspected more than a third of the United States's highway-rail grade crossings for more than five years. Standards in the public education system are hardly helped by the decline in average starting salaries for public school teachers to 97 percent of college graduates' average starting salary—and an accompanying decline in average SAT scores for new teachers. And the deterioration of the public sector extends well beyond core areas like transportation and education: the Food and Drug Administration, for example, had the resources to inspect only 5,000 food processing plants in 1997, compared to 21,000 in 1981.[40]

The collapse of overt public provision and public investment is only the tip of the iceberg. The quality of public debate and the fabric of American culture have become subordinate to ambitions for individual and corporate profit. Americans thus have ever less protection against the individualization and fragmentation of American life. As work offers less structure and community less meaning to people's lives, companies have used television and the tools of mass advertising to provide alternative sources of meaning with the overt aim of increasing their turnover and profits; branding has emerged as a means to achieve the status and sense of belonging that social and economic structures no longer provide. Starbucks' marketing director, Scott Edby, captures the new intent of the corporations when he says that his company's aim is "to align ourselves with one of the greatest movements towards finding a connection with your soul." For Starbucks read Marlboro, Ford, Nike, the Gap, etc. A disoriented America is seeking comfort in the security of great brands.

Shoppers will have learned about the brands through advertising—most likely through TV commercials. Television is both the ubiquitous form of American communication, and central to its commercial culture. In one respect the ubiquity of television is a pleasure—available alike in the bowling alley and in the waiting rooms of every American airport. But ubiquity has meant increasing trivialization. The average American watches four hours of television a day and the average home receives no fewer than forty-five channels;[41] some 50 percent of Americans watch television during dinner—and a third during breakfast. Only 2.2 percent of viewers watch public television; the rest watch television financed by either sponsorship or advertising. Fifteen hundred commercials are screened daily on U.S. television,[42] and as the rate charged to the advertiser is directly linked to the size and spending power of the audience, there is a relentless battle to ensure high ratings. With attention spans as short as they are and the remote control always at hand, TV schedulers are acutely aware that they must use every contrivance possible across the gamut of programs—from lurid plot lines in soaps and drama to highly emotional talk-show interviews—to sustain their audience's interest.

Hypercompetition in a forty-five-channel marketplace facing increasing diversion of limited viewer time to the Internet is one driver of the character of American television; another is our old friend, shareholder value. GE, the patron saint of the doctrine, took over NBC in 1986; nine years later, Westinghouse's purchase of CBS and Disney's takeover of ABC completed the picture. The American networks' prime obligation is to sustain their owners' share price; with the arrival of cable and satellite channels having shrunk their audience share from 90 percent to 60 percent, the competition has become brutal—as have its consequences. "The product of commercial television is not programs," declared Reuven Frank, the former NBC News president. "If one thinks of making goods to sell, the viewers are not the customers, those who buy the product. Advertisers buy the product, pay money for it. Programs are not what they buy. What they buy, what they pay for, is audience."[43]

In the United States, culture is overwhelmingly popular culture; Americans want to be entertained and diverted, and it is done with élan and professionalism. Some programs are made with spectacular production values. *Seinfeld* and *Ally McBeal* are high-class television by any standards. But the pressing need to capture and hold attention gives rise to a relentless drive to create shows that emphasize human freakery, dramas with plots that border on the surreal. Violence and sex hold the viewer, and there is growing evidence that this skewed emphasis is spilling out into American culture—in particular among American children. By the age of eighteen the average American will have seen 200,000 acts of violence and 40,000 murders on television[44]—and America is tragically familiar with the consequences of "acting out" such violence. The teenage perpetrators of the Columbine High School massacre in April 1999 used the media message—everything from their "cool" hitman black coats to their laughter as they killed—to stylize the atrocity they committed.

In Robert Putnam's view, the length of time Americans spend watching television and the content of much of what they watch are principal causes of the decline in social capital; heavy TV watchers are temperamentally less inclined to be joiners and participants, and the TV they watch leaves them more disconnected from ordinary social realities. Television and its values are a barely accountable instrument in the cannibalization of American culture—and American democracy.

Above all, the intense competition for audience from an ever lower cost base is transforming the way television reports the news and, through discussion and documentary, creates the platform for national public debate. Television is abdicating responsibility. Quality news is expensive, and under GE's ownership the unattractive ratio of expense to audience payback has forced rounds of downsizing on NBC's news operation which have been aped by the other networks. No network has a Supreme Court correspondent any longer, and the foreign correspondent networks have been decimated—but it is not just a question of the *extent* of coverage; the coverage itself has to be either soft or confrontational if it is to hold an audience. Thus policy issues have been supplanted by "human interest" stories: features about oddballs, scandals, and celebrity profiles. The soundbites become ever shorter, news reports more peripatetic, with rapidly changing images. Emotion rules; politics is denuded of nobility, rationality, or any sense that it defines a national conversation—rather, it is reduced to a sport in which every move is about personal advancement and rivalry.

Worse still, independent investigative journalism is in a headlong decline; for it is expensive and risks upsetting important sponsors and advertisers. The numbers of instances where fear of corporate reprisals has checked TV journalism are mounting;[45] for example, during the Gulf War CBS offered to cut its coverage so that every ten-minute segment ended on an upbeat note to benefit the ensuing commercials. During the war against Afghanistan, journalism suspended its critical faculties; the Bush administration was allowed an almost free hand to qualify key American liberties. Its actions might have enjoyed popular support and even have been justifiable; but ordinary American citizens would not have had the chance to reflect on any counterarguments because none was offered. This was a democracy that had simply ceased to operate; for the owners of the channels of communication would brook no debate.

Broadcast journalists themselves, as James Fallows (himself a journalist) argues, have become celebrities, able to command winner-take-all fees on the lucrative conference and punditry circuit; their unwillingness to bite the corporate hand that feeds them is self-evident. Fallows concludes, "The way modern journalists choose to present the news—that the world is out of control, they are governed by crooks and that fellow citizens want to kill them—increases the chances that citizens will feel unhappy, power-less, betrayed by and angry about the political system."[46]

Newspapers and magazines are under similar pressure; institutional share ownership, with its attendant priorities, has come to publishing as well. Fifty-seven percent of the *New York Times* and 52 percent of the *Washington Post* are owned by institutional investors whose priority is share-holder value.[47] The same hollowing-out of newsrooms, accent on the emotional, and growing unwillingness to offend potential advertisers and sponsors are narrowing the scope of written journalism. As a consequence, Americans are becoming less informed and knowledgeable about the world. The great American tradition of serious commentary is under an ever-intensifying siege. Journalism of verification is in retreat before a jour-nalism of assertion, in the opinion of the respected commentators Bill Kovach and Tom Rosenstiel.[48] As one leading journalist commented, "We're not mission driven, peopled by our propensity to inform. We're just here to entertain, to soothe. We're here to sell our wares."[49] Neil Postman summed up the parlous situation in *Amusing Ourselves to Death*: news, as much as politics, has become a branch of the entertainment business.

The United States is, above all, the country of consumption, complete with 28,500 shopping malls. Over half—53 percent—of all purchases are made in these scientifically designed consumption factories,[50] whose loca-tion and internal store layout are calibrated to maximize spending. Financed and in many cases owned by pension funds and insurance com-panies, the shopping mall is the perfect investment proposition—for rising profitability is guaranteed. From the neighborhood mall to the super-regional mall, the principle is the same: the shopper is led through an enclosed and privately policed precinct insulated from anything unpleas-ant—be it the weather or the socially undesirable—and presented with a mix of shops that has been chosen to meet what extensive market research predicts to be the exact profile of the likely shoppers.

The privatization of the spirit and the disintegration of the conception of the civic begin with the retreat of public space. American cities still throb with vitality; at their best they are great tributes to American cosmopolitanism and its democratic spirit and, by British standards, remark-ably well run. Successive waves of immigrants have left their mark, and there is a generosity in the city layout and size of buildings that is awe-inspiring and lifts the spirit. But little by little the downtown areas are becoming sanitized and privatized. Instead of the tumult of the urban city center where public space—for recreation, education, sport, political meetings—interacts with the private, there is a new dominance of the private, symbolized by the corporate skyscraper and the shopping mall. The shopper does not enter a thoroughfare with public rights of way; he or she enters a private space that has been manipulated to make him or her want to spend more. Security is private. The space belongs to the landlord or shop owners, whose objective is the maximization of their rent and sales turnover and who accept no civic claim. As Margaret Crawford writes, "the world of the shopping mall . . . has become the world."[51]

For conservatives, the shopping culture, the weakness of the public discourse, the trivialization of politics and the domination of money all help to entrench their ascendancy and limit the scope of any challenge. The myths about America offering equality of opportunity and high social mobility can be peddled without effective comeback; inequality and the very tough lives of ordinary Americans hardly enter the national public conversation. It is conservatives who protest about the corruption of Washington politics as part of their antigovernment story, even as they exploit the weaknesses in the system to entrench their own position.

Yet the United States is stirring. The first five chapters of this book have rested upon an extensive American literature protesting about what has happened to their economy and society. It is not just foreign critics who believe the United States has not solved the age-old question of how to construct a just economic and social order—or operate an effective democracy. A growing number of Americans share the same view. The argument that Europe should copy the United States is in important respects, as we shall see, the wrong way around. It is European social outcomes and democratic practice from which the United States now needs to borrow; nor is the European economy as sclerotic as U.S. conservatives like to claim. Yet it is the United States—the country that has left so many of its citizens barren and ill at ease with themselves, and which itself is riven by internal concern and criticism—that is held up as a model for the world. How that has happened is where we turn next.

6

The Globalization of Conservatism

This book opened with the concern that the public realm is in eclipse; that there no longer seems to exist a widely shared will or belief that the growth of inequality should be checked; and that our civilization is being consecrated to the interests of a very particular idea of capitalism. We live within the shadow of the conservative conception that capitalism is a sealed, economistic world in which success follows naturally from as little government as possible allowing the maximum freedom to follow the economic imperative of buying cheap and selling dear in the service of making the highest profits. The much-invoked spirit of enterprise is defined entirely in economic terms. It should not and does not rely on any form of social organization or context, whether the internal organization of the company, or the quality and quantity of the intellectual, social, human, and physical capital that surrounds it and in which it is embedded. The watchwords for a successful capitalism are liberty, flexibility, self-interest, and enterprise. Its enemies are the "burdens" of regulation, taxation, welfare, and any form of social obligation. They may be essential to the trust and the social, human, physical, and intellectual infrastructure of a market economy; but in the script of American conservatism they have no part.

This is a hopelessly one-sided account of both what creates a successful market economy and what underpins a just society. The first five chapters of this book have marshaled enough evidence at least to place a question mark over this approach as it has evolved in the United States over the last twenty-five years. America's society has become unfairer; opportunities for all apart from those at the top of the pile are narrowing; its public infrastructure in the widest sense has weakened; and, as the economy comes back to earth, its underlying performance is seen to be much more modest. The American economic achievement over the 1990s rested on the buildup of phenomenal and unsustainable economic imbalances and a stock market boom whose cessation is already having a depressive impact that is likely to restrain the growth of the U.S. economy for some time. Many companies have had their competitive capacities undermined rather than strengthened by the devotion to the pursuit of shareholder value. This is not to deny the record of American job creation, technological innovation, and industrial restructuring, only to place it in a wider and more skeptical context.

Yet this set of—at best contestable, at worst downright wrong—conservative axioms has become the new international common sense. They are marshaled as the intellectual support for the way globalization is advanced and justified, essentially extending the principles by which the United States is run to the world. From the American perspective this has a number of advantages. It validates the American economic and social model. It acts as a crowbar, forcing others to follow the American lead and open up their markets on American principles, thus giving American companies an inherent advantage in the global struggle for market advantage. And it justifies the United States's instinctive unilateralism and reluctance to compromise any economic and political sovereignty in multilateral institutions and processes. The United States can portray itself as an exceptional civilization, with a sacred obligation both to itself and to the world to be the custodian of the only true way. It has successfully fought fascism and more recently communism. Its obligation is to remain an unsullied beacon of what is possible through consecrating an economy and society to the pursuit of liberty.

In both economic and social terms this uncritical and introverted stance leads to a remarkable lack of self-knowledge. This is an environment in which the former chairman of the U.S. Stock Exchange could recently say that "in matters of finance and politics, if not culture, we are becoming the world and much of the world wants to become us"; or a former minister that "Americans should not deny the fact that of all the nations in the history of the world theirs is the most just, the most tolerant . . . and the best model for the future" without any trace of embarrassment or qualification.[1] The national stock-taking after the dreadful acts of September 11, 2001, has been all the more difficult because so much of the American national conversation is wrapped up in this self-congratulatory guff. "We're the brightest beacon for freedom and opportunity in the world," said President Bush, trying to explain the attack to his compatriots.[2]

It is not just that the rhetoric gets in the way of the United States's comprehending how others might see it; fundamentally, it gets in the way of the United States's understanding its own strengths and weaknesses. America, as we have discovered, is *not* the brightest beacon for opportunity in the world. To make this point is not to fall into crude anti-Americanism or to criticize the entire gamut of America's complex relationships with the rest of the globe; for example, there is no doubt that the United States was correct to respond to the terrorist networks in Afghanistan in the way that it did and that the world will be safer rather than riskier as a result. Continuing robustness in confronting terrorism is equally vital. Rather, it is to highlight that the triumph of American conservatism has entrenched an uncritical acclamation of what is by European standards an eccentric and particular view of what makes capitalism work over time—and that a more rounded conception of what delivers a just economic and social order, built around markets and the profit motive, would be not only in the American but the global interest.

Consider the debate in Britain, where the impact of American conservatism is as marked as in the United States. It has taken two landslide general election victories by New Labour finally to convince the political class that it should take seriously the electorate's settled belief that public services need to be improved. For example, at last there is a recognition not only that health expenditure must be lifted toward the European average, but that funding it will necessarily involve an increase in taxation— and that while private capacity, acumen, and expertise may be helpful, even vital, as a change agent in improving public delivery, this does not excuse the state from finding additional resources. Hence the popularity of the proposed tax increases in the April 2002 budget. Better education, health, and transportation needs public initiative and public taxation. Equally, there are limits to how much individuals can provide for their own retirement through individual savings, which is hazardous and insecure. There is a dawning realization that growing inequality has serious social effects—in the housing market, for example, where desirable districts are out of the reach of even moderately well-paid families, or in education, where rich private schools dominate the performance records of academic excellence, making a mockery of equality of opportunity—that in the medium to long term will give rise to intractable social tensions.

Why has it taken the Labour government so long to respond to the voters? Because, for twenty-five years, public policy in Britain has faithfully aped the conservative axioms dominant in the United States, consigning critics to the political margins. UK income tax was last raised in 1977. Labor market regulation in Britain is even lighter than in the United States. Public investment has fallen to new lows. The rail system was privatized, with disastrous results. The litany is familiar. These developments are undoubtedly attributable in part to the British political vulnerability to conservatism and in part to the inability to construct a viable social democratic settlement that culminated in the experience of the 1970s; together, these gave Thatcherism its political opportunity. Laissez-faire nostrums seemed an attractive way out of stagflation and low productivity, and dovetailed neatly with many cultural totems, just as they did in the United States. But they would not have become so entrenched if the American right had not won such complete control of the economic and social agenda, if the propaganda offensive arguing that the U.S. model offers so many apparent advantages had been challenged more strongly, and if globalization had not taken on the character that it has.

The British experience has been echoed in Europe, where, as we shall explore in later chapters, American conservative principles have begun to encroach on liberal social democratic foundations. The European social contract as represented by the welfare state is under fire, blamed for high unemployment by conservative American critics and their converts in Europe; Europeans are being advised to reorganize their financial systems and approach to company law around the American example. The European welfare system has defects, certainly, and there are important shortfalls in European systems of corporate accountability, which often lack transparency. But the attack is one-sided. It takes no account of the benefits the European system produces in productivity, now as high as in the

United States (in some countries, higher), and in social outcomes that are incomparably better, in Rawlsian terms of fairness and equality of opportunity. Europe should not seek to refound itself on American principles; rather, its own principles should be defended while the processes are modernized. In any case, high unemployment in some parts of Europe, the chief excuse for criticism, has much more complex roots than the structure of Europe's social contract.

The international application of the American way, via the integration of financial and trade flows around free-market "Washington consensus" principles, is supposed to be the avenue to global wealth creation. But, in the world as in the United States, to create wealth does not mean that it will be fairly distributed. Just as inequality within the United States and Britain, and in the majority of OECD states, has risen over the last twenty years, so it has grown internationally on seven out of eight possible measures. As the international economist Professor Robert Wade argues, the distribution of international income now represents a champagne glass, with a wide shallow bowl at the top, representing the richest 20 percent, who have 82.7 percent of the world's income, and a long stem at the bottom. Astonishingly, 60 percent of the world's population enjoy a mere 5.6 percent of its income.[3] The same low commodity prices that helped the United States to experience its ten-year boom by permitting low inflation and cheap money have entrenched much of the rest of the world in grinding poverty, and borrowing on the private capital markets to lever themselves out of their situation incurs the risk of financial crisis and massive capital flight. Winner-take-all effects make matters worse; technological innovation and investment flow to—and are created by—richer markets. Without intervention, debt relief, and aid transfers it is difficult to see how the condition of the less developed world is likely to improve relative to that of the first world; and while there is not a simple relationship between this prospect and the creation of Third World terrorist networks, plainly it not unreasonably provokes an immense feeling of injustice, which the West needs to address. Yet American conservatism rules otherwise, for to do so would offend its canons. The same indifference pervades global attitudes to inequality.

It is easy to interpret this new world order as a form of American empire; after all, the United States has been indisputably the world's leading capitalist power ever since 1945 and the world's only superpower ever since the collapse of the Soviet Union in 1991. It is palpably self-evident that, if it had wanted different outcomes, it had the power to will them. Yet such an analysis fails to capture the complexity of what has happened, the compliance of other countries in the creation of the world system, and the real benefits that some—notably Japan and the Asian tiger economies—have experienced as the result of how it works. Nor is Washington politically structured to deliver the sustained and coherent policies that can create and manage an empire; it is cross-cut by different conceptions of the national interest held by the various departments of state and political parties, and above all by the Senate, House, and president, which in turn superintend a continental economy with a vast array of different and competing interests. American manufacturing and its workforce, for example, actively oppose the Wall Street view of what constitutes an appropriate U.S. economic and foreign policy.

While it is wrong to characterize the United States as monolithically and single-mindedly building a world order around a coherent strategic plan, it is equally wrong to characterize globalization as some politically neutral force springing from ICT and the anonymous forces of trade and financial liberalization—as, for example, the leading globalization theorist Professor Tony Giddens of the London School of Economics tends to do.[4] Globalization has been politically shaped by the United States's deploying three simple guiding principles in an ad hoc but increasingly determined fashion. First, the United States looks to exercise its power unilaterally rather than have its autonomy constrained by international alliances and treaty obligations. Second, it focuses aggressively and unilaterally on promoting the interests of those sectors and companies that plainly benefit, because of their ascendant market position or technological lead, from globalization—notably financial services, ICT, and, latterly, those with leadership in intellectual property. Third, it instinctively looks to market solutions and remedies, both as a matter of intellectual and ideological conviction, and because over a period these render it more likely that American interests will prevail. The bigger and more powerful tend to succeed in "free," unregulated markets.

These three predispositions have always been present in the United States as an autonomous continental great power, supported by its own conviction of its special destiny as an exceptional civilization. But as conservatism has grown in influence and the various countervailing, international checks to the deployment of American power have fallen away, so each has become more marked. The world could certainly have a more threatening and malevolent power at its center, and if this power is to have an overweening ideology, better the advocacy of liberty than the fascist and communist ideologies that disfigured Europe in the first half of the twentieth century. That does not mean, however, that the particular economy and society that the United States has become represents the acme of a just economy and society. If we care about the public realm, equality, and the importance of the social contract; if we wish to promote fairness and equality of opportunity; if we believe that these values should underpin the global order, then U.S. conservatism needs to be challenged and the country needs to be repersuaded that even America depends on others for some things and that forms of multilateral cooperation are in its interests. Even the United States is interdependent. There is only one source of countervailing power and values: Europe. This is where the argument next leads; but first we need to understand how the modern world has been shaped by those three American predispositions—and how the rise of conservatism has made them more acute.

Unilateralism, Power, and Free Markets

Power politics is always rough and tough, and there has never been a period—nor should one be expected—when the United States has somehow subordinated its perceptions of its own interests to some idea of the global public good. All states at all times prosecute their interests. What is true, however, is that for twenty-five years after World War II the United States chose to prosecute its interests through a web of multilateral treaties and alliances—albeit always as first among equals—through which it believed its interests could best be served. In the great war against communism there was a common Western interest, and the United States knew that if it was to lead the West there needed to be common rules of the game that were accepted by itself as much as by lesser powers, although it was careful to entrench its own leadership position. What has changed since the collapse of communism and the triumph of conservatism is that the United States increasingly believes that there is one set of rules for it and its nationals, and another for the rest of the world. September 11 has reinforced this proclivity. Thus every country can extradite and sue the perpetrators of terrorist acts as long as they abide by international law in their courts—except the United States, which reserves the right to try by American military law. Thus the extraordinary period in the aftermath of the Afghan war during which the Bush administration unilaterally decided to suspend the rules of the Geneva Convention for captured Al Quaeda and Taliban fighters. This was only partially reversed under intense international pressure so that Taliban detainees enjoyed the conventions—but neither group prisoner-of-war status.[5] This is an assertion of exceptionalism that stretches across the board, from financial regulation to how the United States should organize its security.

In the years after World War II the story was different. As the war came to an end urgent negotiations took place between the Americans and British about how to prohibit the neighbor-be-damned trade and competitive devaluations of the interwar period when countries had tried to export their economic problems, provoking the implosion of trade and credit that turned recession into the 1930s depression, and which became the seedbed of fascism. Instead, world trade and finance were henceforth to be conducted within a framework of universal rules that favored economic openness and internationally agreed responses to individual economies' difficulties. Under the system agreed to at Bretton Woods in New Hampshire in 1944, every member currency was pegged to the dollar, whose value in turn was pegged to the price of gold and freely convertible into it. To join the system, states undertook to adjust their domestic economic policies to sustain their exchange rate, and to devalue or revalue only after consultation and agreement with the International Monetary Fund (IMF)—which would in turn advance them transitional loans in vital hard currency, dollars, in exchange for their implementing austerity programs while they traded their way out of unfinanceable trade deficits. The World Bank, established at the same time, functioned as a multilateral institution to channel aid and loans to support third-world development. Three years later the General Agreement on Tariffs and Trade (GATT) was signed, pledging to work for progressive reductions in the postwar legacy of protectionist tariffs.

The system worked, underwriting the postwar economic boom. The Europeans became steadily more confident about lowering tariffs and opening up their borders as they began to earn trade surpluses convertible into dollars backed by gold—and there was always the reserve option of an organized devaluation to adjust their international balance sheet if they hit the economic rocks. Trade grew explosively as tariffs fell by 73 percent between 1947 and 1961. The counterpart of the surpluses established by Japan and Europe—with the painful exception of Britain, which still ran deficits—was a burgeoning American trade deficit. The prosperity the United States had wanted to foster was coming into being—and in a multilateral context.

At the negotiations in 1943 and 1944 the United States had insisted, in an exercise of raw power, that the dollar (backed by gold), rather than a new international currency, bancor (again backed by gold), should be the international unit of account, for which Keynes had pressed. Moreover, the United States gained decisive voting rights in both the IMF and the World Bank. But this was a power play within a multilateral framework. In philosophical terms America's New Dealers accepted that the new system should operate along liberal, Keynesian lines. "Strong," creditor countries should be under just as much obligation to adjust their economic policies as "weak," debtor countries; and government management and regulation of national economies was accepted as inherently vital to achieve more income equality, employment, and economic stability. Harry Dexter White, the chief U.S. negotiator and special assistant to the secretary of the Treasury, fought off Wall Street pressure for the system to be run with no capital controls, agreeing with Keynes that controls were imperative if national governments were to control domestic interest rates to achieve full employment—even if they might inhibit the growth of Wall Street internationally. Thirty years later, no such inhibition on U.S. financial interests and autonomy of U.S. action would be acceptable. But the 1940s was the time not only of the IMF, World Bank, and GATT, but of full-hearted American support for NATO and the UN.

From the American point of view, the Bretton Woods system had one chronic defect. It might make the dollar the effective world monetary standard, so permitting the United States to pay for whatever it wanted worldwide with its own currency; but the quid pro quo was that the dollar should hold its value against gold. The United States could never devalue, and that set a constraint on American economic policy. Eventually the dam would break. Not even the giant American economy with its legendary productivity could permanently underwrite the value of the dollar in terms of gold—and from the late 1950s and over the 1960s American gold reserves steadily fell.

No great power can sustain its position for long unless it can pay its way, and the first great assertion of conservative U.S. interests and harbinger of the consequent recasting of the world economic order was the American refusal between 1971 and 1973 to continue its role as banker of last resort to the world financial system. This ranks with the collapse of the Soviet Union in 1991 as a pivotal event in postwar history.

There were two potential solutions to the problem of America's hemorrhaging gold reserves. The first was to reform the system multilaterally with international agreement and even go so far as creating a new world paper reserve currency, which would relieve the pressure on the dollar and would be managed by a strengthened IMF as a kind of world central bank. Or the Americans could throw down the gauntlet, insist the rest of the world revalue their currencies so that the dollar could have the same relationship with gold—and if it refused, simply scrap the system and create a de facto world dollar standard. Throughout the 1960s the Kennedy and Johnson administrations tried successive administrative and regulative schemes to support the dollar—notably imposing restrictions on American companies' investment overseas through capital controls, together with voluntary restrictions on U.S. bank lending to foreigners—and so keep the international bargain America had struck. But so large were U.S. demands for foreign capital that they could only delay the ultimate reckoning.

As banks fled the United States to escape the controls, and the financial pressure mounted, criticism from Wall Street was reinforced by a vocal group of articulate conservative economists, famously including Milton Friedman and Alan Greenspan. Together with economists from Chase Manhattan, Morgan Guaranty, and First National City Bank of New York (all chafing against capital controls) they unashamedly advocated the unilateral option as, in 1969, the U.S. Treasury canvassed opinions on how to react. The world's currencies should float against the dollar, they argued, which had no serious rival, and the United States should stop guaranteeing that the dollar was worth a fixed amount of gold. Such a system of market-based floating exchange rates would work better than the government-managed system of Bretton Woods. Exchange rates would quickly find the correct natural market rate; the system would be stable, and the outflow of American gold would stop immediately. Moreover, America could scrap all its controls on movements of capital so that the U.S. government, financial institutions, and corporations could spend as freely as they liked. Instead of the United States's having to make any kind of economic adjustment, the rest of the world could adjust to America's ambitions. As it was shouldering the burden of defending "freedom" worldwide against the ambitions of communism, it was a fair deal. The world, after all, was lucky to have the United States.

And that was what happened. In the eighteen months up to August 1971 the strain of financing both the Vietnam War and the U.S. trade deficit obliged the U.S. government to insist that foreign central banks buy over $40 billion (over $100 billion in 2000 prices) to balance America's international books—a potential catastrophic liability if they insisted simultaneously on converting their dollars into gold. In May 1971 a European bloc, led by the Germans and including the Netherlands, Austria, and Switzerland, decided to let their exchange rates float upward—detaching the fixed link with the dollar—rather than be forced to reflate their economies to relieve pressure on the dollar, which they considered inflationary. This was the end of a grim two-year battle to hold European exchange rates in a pattern consistent with plans for European integration and even monetary union. The Europeans saw themselves as bearing the brunt of America's fiscal and monetary indiscipline, their nascent exchange rate system attacked by floods of dollars; the Americans saw the Europeans as ungratefully pursuing their own advantage.

In an atmosphere of gathering crisis President Nixon struck back. He simply suspended the convertibility of the dollar into gold and slapped a 10 percent surcharge on all imports into America. Over the next two years the United States, resisting any attempt by the rest of the world to persuade it to accept any economic constraints in the reconstruction and potential reform of the system, arm-twisted and bullied its way to the establishment of a world financial system in which the dollar would necessarily be the number one currency against which other currencies would float. When the last attempts to gain agreement on a multilateral system were shattered by the quadrupling of oil prices in the autumn of 1973, the world moved from a gold exchange standard managed by international agreement to a dollar standard in which the United States accepted no obligations whatsoever in the management of its own currency. Treasury Secretary John Connally, coauthor with Nixon of the policy, captured American indifference to others' views: "We had a problem and we are sharing it with the rest of the world—just like we shared our prosperity. That's what friends are for."[6]

Connally's hard-headed assessment that, whatever complaints America's "friends"—Europe and Japan—might make, the United States could and should do just what it liked, laid down the essential parameters of American foreign economic policy for the next thirty years. The United States needed to appropriate 80 percent of the industrialized West's current surplus for its own strategic and military purposes, as Nixon told Germany's central bank, the Bundesbank, two days after he had suspended dollar convertibility into gold.[7] If its allies would not agree to this voluntarily, the United States would find another way to deliver the same result.

On New Year's Day 1974 the United States lifted all its capital controls. The dollar fell sharply, but that was of little consequence; it had no rival. American free-market conservatives, the Wall Street financiers and their allies in government, schooled in realpolitik, had claimed their first major scalp: the international economic order was to be built unilaterally around American interests. And it was the conservative ultras who had provided the intellectual underpinning for this démarche—even if they had no clear idea of where it might lead.

The first immediate impact was evident in how the United States approached the buildup of dollar surpluses in the Arab oil-producing countries as the oil price quadrupled, and was kept high by the Organization of the Petroleum Exporting Countries (OPEC) making production cutbacks. The multilateral approach of the postwar period would have been to organize the deposit of the OPEC dollars with the IMF and World Bank so that they could be recycled into the Western industrialized countries and Third World alike in an orderly and predictable way, financing the trade deficits that emerged everywhere as a result of the oil shock and so averting a synchronized recession as demand fell everywhere simultaneously. With capital controls lifted on the dollar alone, another option was created. The petrodollars could be deposited with U.S. banks and recycled as loans to national governments and corporations wholly through the private American financial sector; as the United States no longer had any capital controls, dollars held anywhere were part of the same vast pool of dollar liquidity. Between 1976 and 1981 U.S. banks increased their overseas assets from $80 billion to $300 billion, lending largely out of London, where the remaining American rules on interest rate ceilings on deposits did not apply. Bank lending to national governments, especially in the less developed world, exploded, rising sixfold over the decade.[8] National governments do not go bankrupt, wisecracked Walter Wriston, the buccaneering chairman of Citicorp, as the proportion of his bank's profits made from overseas transactions soared to 80 percent.[9]

As Leonard Seabrooke describes in *US Power in International Finance*, increasingly the New Deal apparatus of financial regulation began to creak at the seams. In 1980, to keep the petrodollars flowing into New York after the second oil shock, the Americans decided to allow banks to create "international banking facilities" in the United States without any interest rate ceilings nor any requirement to lodge a proportion of the cash with the U.S. Federal Reserve as a so-called reserve requirement. Now, not only was there an indivisible dollar market at home and abroad, but dollars everywhere carried the same interest rate free from any regulatory inhibition. Going it alone around market-based solutions was proving the biggest shot in the arm the U.S. financial system had had for fifty years; its deposit base and lending ambitions were moving beyond the United States to become global.

Nor was this the only advantage. Since the early 1970s the United States has run a large and growing trade deficit while simultaneously financing a steady buildup of overseas direct investment, cumulatively worth at the end of 1999 some $1.1 trillion, and sustaining its vast military operations overseas. Nixon's target of winning 80 percent of the industrialized world's current account surplus has been achieved comfortably. When there have been strains, the United States has responded with further acts of market-based "liberalization" to step up the vital inflow of dollars. In 1984, for example, Ronald Reagan abandoned the tax deducted at source on interest and dividends paid to foreign holders of American financial assets—withholding tax—making it more attractive for foreigners to finance America's burgeoning deficits. The United States then complemented that action by twisting its partners' arms to relax and indeed abandon their capital controls, making it easier for other countries to export capital to the United States. In 1988 the Basle Accord was signed, under which banks had to raise the levels of core capital in their balance sheets to underwrite their lending; it was deliberately aimed at raising the demand for U.S. government securities, which counted as part of banks' core capital. Japanese banks alone, reports Seabrooke, as a result had to buy over $20 billion of U.S. treasury notes and bonds after Basle.

By 1989 every major European economy had been forced to drop capital controls, as powerful offshore markets in marks, francs, pounds, lire, guilder, and kroner developed—all created by the United States's decision to have no capital controls so that there was an offshore foreign exchange market in each currency; and the boundaries between the domestic and offshore market were impossible to police. So it has continued. As the pool of dollar liquidity has increased yearly with the size of the U.S. trade deficit, U.S. banks have wanted to exploit the pool to lend more, both at home and abroad, and break down regulatory barriers to the growth of their business. Thus in 1991 the Fed allowed J. P. Morgan to become the first bank to underwrite issues of public stock since 1933—the forerunner of the bonfire of financial controls over the 1990s described in chapter 4.

Liberalization, by integrating the world's principal capital markets but around a dollar standard, has thus served U.S. interests twice over: it has enlarged the dominance of U.S. financial institutions and made financing the U.S. trade deficit much easier. In one year alone, 1995, foreign central banks bought $70 billion of new U.S. treasury securities—half the total issued.[10] Foreign exchange turnover has grown exponentially, as have flows of capital and bank lending. Investment in finance and insurance now constitutes a third of all American investment overseas, with Citicorp, Prudential of

America, and State Farm Insurance leading the charge. American banks'
share of the world financial services market has doubled in the last twenty
years.[11] Goldman Sachs, Morgan Guaranty, and Merrill Lynch now dominate
investment banking in London, an American takeover that is a by-product of
the developing monetary system.

At times it has been the Europeans (as in the late 1990s) and at other
times the Japanese (as in the late 1980s) who have shouldered the burden
of providing the United States with its necessary dollar inflows, through a
mixture of direct and indirect investment. From the American perspective,
the identity of the source of the investment has not mattered, any more
than the roller-coaster ride of the dollar has mattered. What *has* mattered
is that the system is constructed to maximize U.S. economic and financial
autonomy. The dollar's value has alternated from periods of extreme
weakness, as in the mid-1980s, to extreme strength, as in the late
1990s—but with little impact on U.S. economic policy, which has been set
wholly around domestic priorities. When George Bush senior was asked
about the dollar, at that moment declining, he signaled the insouciance of
every U.S. president since the breakup of Bretton Woods in his reply:
"Once in a while I think about these things, but not much."[12]

Thus the capacity to finance the enormous trade deficits of the 1990s
without any constraint on the evolution or growth of the U.S. economy
has not been a happy by-product of something technical and anonymous
called "financial deregulation." The stock market boom and the role of the
financial system in attracting inward flows of capital on a vast scale have
been the results of a series of consistent policy choices over thirty years
reflecting those essential U.S. reflex predispositions toward unilateralism
and markets. Nobody in the 1970s could accurately foresee what might
happen; but by pushing the scope of U.S. financial autonomy outward,
enlarging the role of the New York markets as financial intermediaries and
insisting on the pivotal role of the dollar, the United States has created an
environment in which essentially the rest of the world adjusts to U.S. economic choices—and becomes enslaved to the prevalent U.S. financial and
economic ideology. And that is not liberalism.

Handmaidens of the New Conservatism

The transmutation from a liberal to a conservative world order is most obvious in the transformation of the two great Bretton Woods institutions—the IMF and the World Bank. Originally cast as liberal custodians of a global public interest, they have become de facto agents of the U.S. Treasury in its quest to sustain American financial hegemony and policy prescriptions irrespective of the consequent contradictions and strains.

The collapse of Bretton Woods in the early 1970s removed the liberal rationale for both institutions. There was no longer a system of exchange rates to be policed and managed by the IMF; if countries wanted short-term credit, they could negotiate terms with American banks now freed from the controls that had inhibited their lending—a trend that undermined the importance of the World Bank just as dramatically. Countries at any stage of economic development could borrow directly from Wall Street, or from international banks operating in the eurodollar market in London. This market in vast sums of expatriate dollars had sprung up during the 1960s as governments, central banks, and multinationals borrowed and lent the dollars they had acquired from the United States offshore in London, free from American controls. As mentioned earlier, once capital controls were lifted, American banks rushed to capture the markets they had lost to London, and pushed their lending aggressively.[13] But the loans, denominated in dollars, carried American interest rates, which went up and down as the U.S. Federal Reserve changed American monetary policy to suit the needs of the U.S. economy. A disaster was waiting to happen.

It duly occurred in 1981. Paul Volcker, the incoming chairman of the Fed, following the prescriptions of the Chicago school, doubled U.S. interest rates to check the growth of American money supply. Less developed countries suddenly found that their debt service requirements doubled too, and in August 1982 Jesús Silva-Herzog, Mexico's finance minister, announced what Walter Wriston had said was impossible. Mexico simply did not have the financial wherewithal to service its $94 billion of debt; it was technically bankrupt. Worse still, the American and European banks that had been so ready to lend in 1981 and the first half of 1982 simply turned off the tap. The privatization of the world financial system was exemplifying the volatility against which Keynes and the New Dealers had wanted to guard when they founded the Bretton Woods system in 1944.

The situation could not be left unaddressed. If Mexico was not bailed out, then the loans made largely by American banks would be worthless; they would have to be written off, imperiling the banks' own creditworthiness and their capacity to support the U.S. economy. Loans to Mexico and Brazil alone equaled 90 percent of the total capital of America's top nine banks.[14] There had to be a rescue package. But Mexico in 1981 was not confronting the United States of Harry Dexter White, Roosevelt, and Truman. The conservative revolution described in chapter 2 had now embedded itself in Washington under Reagan's presidency, and it intended to extend the gains it had made abroad as much as at home. If Mexico, or any other indebted borrower, thought it could change the terms of the international system so that it could protect employment and growth at home—the essential underpinning, after all, of Bretton Woods—then it had better think again. Nor should there be any symmetry of adjustment, with the United States accepting some responsibility for the situation—it was the U.S. banks, after all, that had pushed their lending so aggressively. In the moral universe of the U.S. conservative, it was the borrower, not the American lender, who had displayed moral turpitude, and there would be no indirect support for Mexico by helping American banks. Mexico had to accept that the rules of the international game would remain exactly the same, and that if it wanted to borrow from private banks in the future it would have to earn that privilege by imposing an extraordinarily tough austerity package right now. Only then would the United States support any international bailout; and, given the U.S. veto in the IMF, this was the precondition for any negotiations.

Imprisoned by the new U.S. intransigence, the IMF began to jettison the notions of balanced adjustment and noninterference with the political philosophy behind national economic policies. Instead, it required not just austerity but detailed changes in Mexico's policy, changes that were to foreshadow the "structural adjustment" demanded of applicants for loans and aid in the late 1980s and throughout the 1990s. This was a pseudonym for a raft of hard, free-market fundamentalist policies that went well beyond the legitimate requirement to tighten monetary and fiscal policy in order to free resources for export while cutting imports—the only path any capitalist economy can take to restore financial probity, whether it is run on conservative or liberal principles.

Mexico, along with the rest of Latin America, had to accept the medicine; for there was no alternative. In exchange for an IMF support package, Mexico, and latterly Brazil and the rest of indebted Latin America with similar arrangements, had to accept whopping cuts in public expenditure and structural adjustment programs imposed with increasingly ideological fervor: basic programs of health, education, and poverty relief were regarded as wasteful and extravagant—and thus were savaged. And because most of Latin America was retrenching simultaneously under IMF guidance, the consequences were multiplied; recession spread across the continent. In Mexico, where half the population had no running water, per capita incomes were to fall 40 percent between 1983 and 1988. For Latin America as a whole it was a lost decade, precisely the kind of economic and social disaster that the liberal designers of Bretton Woods had tried to avert—but a disaster that American conservatives, now in control of the system, were prepared to countenance as the price of U.S. dominance.

Calls for reform of the system, for an orderly approach to debt relief, and for a return to a more managed system of exchange rates were brushed to one side. It was not just that they demanded a willingness to exert some control over the now gigantic financial markets, with an explicit loss of autonomy for the United States; any such control went against the mantra that free markets worked perfectly—certainly better than any comparable system managed by government. But as the 1980s wore on, it became clear that the predictions of conservative ideologues like Milton Friedman, that floating exchange rates would tend to produce stable currency values, were wildly wrong. The foreign-exchange markets became a byword for market irrationality, with exchange rates experiencing prolonged periods above or below any reasonable judgment of their sustainable level—pitched to excessive heights and depths by a succession of speculative short-term bets that once a trend had been established it was more likely to continue than to break. Speculation on the basis that "the trend is my friend" reinforced the misalignments, wholly against the predictions of market theorists that it would be against such absurd valuations. But while the overvaluation of the yen, for example, in the late 1980s and early 1990s would be an important cause of the long recession of the

Japanese economy, periods of dollar overvaluation had no parallel impact on the U.S. economy. The United States was a continent in which exposure to international competition was less significant, and in any case the system was constructed to permit it to run large trade deficits with no consequences for its domestic economic policy

Over the 1990s the characteristics of the system became yet more exaggerated. Foreign-exchange turnover continued to grow exponentially as new and more innovative techniques were developed to hedge against individual risk—although the system could not insure itself against the risk that the system was at fault. Distressed borrowers or those who wanted U.S. trade and assistance had to submit to the new canons of the U.S. right, embodied in the now toughened and honed version of structural adjustment: they should lift controls on their financial system; they should lower taxes generally, but especially on corporations and the rich; they should privatize; they should open up to foreign investment; they should deregulate; they should reassert private property rights; they should cut back spending on welfare, health, and education; and they should place price stability as the top economic priority. In short, they should adopt the same economic program that the American Business Roundtable and the Chicago school had recommended for the United States. Equality of opportunity, the sharing of risk in a social contract, the redistribution of income, investment in social, physical, and human capital, and any attempt to manage capitalism or develop public enterprise should be forsworn.

Pressure on all countries to pursue this Washington consensus mounted—in particular, pressure to open their financial systems to American participation under the rubric of liberalization. Thus, for example, between 1990 and 1993 over $90 billion—a fifth of net capital flows to developed countries—migrated to Mexico in search of the high interest rates to be found by investing in Mexican securities denominated in dollars.[15] In December 1994 the dollars threatened to leave the country in days as U.S. investors and mutual funds worried about Mexico's capacity to service its debts. The "Tequila crisis" prompted a second joint U.S. Treasury–IMF bailout, demanding in return for $40 billion an aggressive structural adjustment program. The IMF's dependence on, and synchronization of its actions with, the U.S. Treasury was now open. But this was not a bailout of U.S. and Western banks, as it had been in 1982; it was a bailout of U.S. investors who had wanted the 14 percent interest rates available on Mexico's dollar assets rather than the 5 percent on U.S. Treasury bills, but were unprepared to accept the consequential risk. Again Mexico had to swallow its reluctance; it floated the peso, which halved in a matter of weeks, while interest rates doubled in two months. But U.S. investors got their money back in full, in part from the U.S. Treasury and in part from the IMF.

As the 1990s wore on the IMF became yet more subsumed under the U.S. Treasury, with more damaging effects. Their joint response to the financial crisis in east Asia between 1997 and 1998 was another calamity, echoing the experience of Latin America in the early 1980s but involving much greater volumes of debt. The financial deregulation in east Asia pressed for by the U.S. in the early 1990s had sparked credit booms and escalating trade deficits across the region; but these interacted with the pegging of Asian exchange rates to the dollar both to ensure price stability and to minimize the risk of exchange rate losses to American investors. The fixed exchange rates were impossible to hold and became irresistible targets for foreign-exchange speculation. One by one the so-called Asian tigers found their exchange rates devastated by speculative attacks, and looked to the IMF for assistance.

But the IMF was now totally in hock to the U.S. Treasury. Compared to the size of the speculative flows, the sums it could raise from its own resources were trivial; so it needed the firepower of the United States to support its lending programs. This was a position of weakness that the United States happily exploited. Korea, Indonesia, and Thailand had not only to undertake the austerity program demanded of Latin America in the early 1980s, but also to restructure their economies around American conservative principles. For example, the journalist Paul Blustein describes in *The Chastening* how in Korea, the U.S. and IMF teams checked into the same hotel, the U.S. Treaury team insisting that the IMF extract further drastic reforms from the Koreans even as it negotiated in tandem with the Korean ministry of finance.[16] In the fire sale of assets to pay off debts, American multinationals picked up a whole range of companies at reduced prices: U.S. firms spent $8 billion on Asian businesses in the first half of 1998 alone. Asia pledged to accelerate its Americanization. The result of the austerity programs imposed simultaneously across east Asia was a regional depression, making the recovery plans of individual countries harder rather than easier to achieve—precisely in accordance with Keynes's dictum that recession in one country reinforces recession in another.

Yet apart from criticism in Japan and by some American economics professors like Harvard's Jeffrey Sachs and Princeton's Paul Krugman,[17] the IMF got off largely scot-free for what was by any criteria a massive policy mistake. The American financial establishment had been bailed out—again—from the results of its imprudent lending. Abroad, the adjustment was borne by the peoples of the countries to whom it had lent, and on terms that would lead to a greater opening to American capital in future. The system could continue. It had the protection of the U.S. Treasury. Those who argued that it was flawed because smaller countries simply could not cope with the consequences of violent inward and outward flows of freely flowing capital got short shrift; all that was required was more transparency and information for the market to make its judgments, and all would be well. After all, markets worked perfectly if allowed. Yet in 2001 greater transparency did not prevent Turkey and Argentina from suffering sudden capital flight on just the same scale, and with the same consequences.

It is not that there is no viable alternative to the current system; it is that any alternative would qualify American hegemony and reduce the benefits the United States enjoys from the current structure. And anyway, the new conservative orthodoxy insists that the IMF and U.S. Treasury have been right to focus on austerity and structural adjustment, and not to be concerned with the wider economic, financial, and social consequences of what they do—even on the occasions when these consequences impinge on the New York banking system. The bailout of the hedge fund Long Term Capital Management, led by the New York Federal Reserve in September 1998, with some $200 billion of off-balance-sheet liabilities and a chief executive, John Meriwether, as gung-ho about free markets as Enron's Ken Lay, might have prompted some reappraisal about the risks of running the international financial system as it was. Nothing of the kind. The bigger game was and is to attack statism and governmental influence wherever it is found.

The transformation of the IMF's role was mirrored over at the World Bank, which over the 1980s was progressively invaded and influenced by the new right. Its annual *World Development Reports* became more conservative as the right's grip on Washington tightened; in 1987 the Bank argued that the very interventionist principles upon which it had been founded were now disruptive for private-sector growth.[18] Its "structural adjustment loans" matched the thinking of the IMF as reflected in its structural adjustment programs, and indeed the Bank became as fervent an advocate of the conservative cause as the Fund.

Then in 1995, under its new president, James Wolfensohn, the World Bank began to strike out in a different direction—arguing for debt relief, and insisting that good government, education, and health were as important as adhesion to the Washington consensus in promoting economic development. But it was bucking the tide. In November 1999 Wolfensohn's chief economist, Joseph Stiglitz, resigned—evidence that in any attempt the World Bank might make to return to its liberal roots, its scope for maneuver was very limited. Stiglitz had been restless about the Washington consensus throughout his tenure of office, arguing in a 1998 lecture that the obsession with price stability is counterproductive and that economies can tolerate a low level of inflation without it accelerating, as the consensus argued.[19] Recessions, he argued, need to be countered by allowing automatic stabilizers to work; and the financial system, far from being accurately characterized as a market, is an economy's "brain," and is impaired rather than improved by deregulation. Stiglitz further insisted that privatization would fail in the absence of investment in the institutional framework of an economy—its legal system, for example. He later explained that he fought against the IMF austerity programs in Asia, on the grounds that they would lead to a synchronized Asian recession, but to no avail.[20] If anything, the IMF wanted to be more severe.

Stiglitz's criticisms are right, and come from inside the belly of the beast. But the system has built up too much momentum to give way to such rationality, which in any case for the conservatives is beside the point. The point is to entrench the dominance of the dollar, now accounting for 77 percent of all international loans and 83 percent of all foreign exchange transactions[21]—proportions as large as in 1945, even though the relative weight of the U.S. economy in world GDP has shrunk since then. Stiglitz might complain that "all too often the dogma of liberalization became an end in itself, not a means to achieving a better financial system,"[22] but this was no irrational economic dogma. It was the dogma of the expanding superstate. The international financial system has been shaped to extend U.S. financial and political power, not to promote the world public good. And that is what it has done. In the process it has opened up a bridgehead that has created opportunities for many more U.S. corporate interests besides those of finance.

Globalization as Americanization

As early as 1974 it was becoming clear that the character and structure of American capitalism were changing. For twenty years American prosperity had been consistent with a growing trade deficit; as long as the rest of the world accepted dollars and workers in the displaced industries in the United States moved on to find work elsewhere, the deficit seemed of little lasting consequence. Trade unions and the industries affected protested loudly, but the overall balance sheet was plainly good for most American consumers and the Fortune 500. Indeed, as half of all U.S. imports were from the affiliates of U.S. companies abroad that had sourced production overseas to boost profits, the deficit was the inevitable concomitant of profit-maximizing U.S. multinationals tending to manufacture in low-cost countries—and as such, a positive benefit to corporate America. What was beginning to matter was less the location of factories and nationality of workers than the intellectual capital embodied in whatever was being produced and the necessary access to overseas markets that delivered the extra sales and profits growth that were crucial given the saturation of the U.S. market. In 1970 IBM had emerged as the world's largest computer company with its 360 series; Texas Instruments was the world's leading manufacturer of integrated silicon chips; AT&T was the largest corporation in the world in sales. Over the 1970s U.S. leadership in the new information industries strengthened, so that by the early 1980s Microsoft, Apple, and Intel were already well established. In January 1983 *Time* magazine gave the personal computer its "man of the year" accolade; the ICT revolution had begun in earnest, and what the United States wanted was to open the world to its lusty high-tech champions.

For if intellectual property and control of information flows were beginning to matter more, that in turn meant that market access to service industries like finance and telecommunications began to rank alongside market openness in conventional manufactures as a prime policy concern. A new hierarchy of priorities was emerging in which sustaining leadership in the information economy and opening up the service sectors—notably finance and telecommunications—of the world's principal economies became at least as important as ensuring free trade in commodity manufactures, where in any case the United States hardly had a comparative advantage.

Again, it is hard to argue that there was any blueprint. The United States simply threw its weight behind those companies and sectors that it felt could exploit trade openings, and used free-market, free-trade theory as the intellectual lever to achieve its strategic ends. It could allow its transnational corporations to locate production according to their best judgment on profitability, and as long as the dollar was the world currency it was of no concern if the resulting pattern of production meant U.S. trade deficits. In any case, if the United States could dominate services, ICT, the flow of information, telecoms, and intellectual property rights, then it controlled the framework in which all trade flows took place.

From the launch of the first American satellite in 1962 the United States had been alert to how this new technology would equip its companies to take the lead in controlling and disseminating information; the 1962 Communications Satellite Act allowed private companies to take stakes in NASA's direct broadcasting satellites for commercial usage, and provided for AT&T to extend its monopoly on long-distance communications into space. The company's Telstar made the first transatlantic satellite transmission of television later that year. The United States shrugged off attempts by the French in 1970 and the Russians in 1972 to establish a multilateral framework for the use of satellite broadcasting and telecommunications within which the prior consent would be required of nations that would be impacted from space; the United States refused to accept any infringement on its sovereignty. Rather, it became more interested in how its nascent and unchallenged grip on the new communications technologies could be exploited to support the growth of its overseas economic interests. The Hollywood studios had built up an unrivaled distribution network in the first half of the century that had entrenched their global leadership of the film industry; now the same possibilities were opening up for American television, ICT, and telephone companies. If government control of television and telephone services in Europe and Japan could be broken down, the United States would dominate the new information age as it had the twentieth-century industrial age. The pivotal year was 1974, when the Trade Act empowered the U.S. government for the first time to include services in the industries over which it was mandated to negotiate tariffs and access, and also empowered the United States to act unilaterally—the infamous 301 clause—in defense of particular trade interests. When the United States had to choose between loyalties to multilateral arrangements such as GATT and equipping itself to act unilaterally, already the United States was unhesitatingly coming down in favor of the latter.

Over the next three decades the same predispositions that had been deployed to recast the world financial system would be used to recast the world telecommunications and information system—and used ever more aggressively as U.S. power and the conservative ascendancy grew. This was globalization led by the U.S. pursuit of its interests. Financial liberalization and telecom deregulation went hand in hand. American financial expansion abroad relied on the new ICT and telecom technologies; if U.S. banks were forbidden to use them they could not create their twenty-four-hour global financial networks. By 1985 Citicorp had linked its offices in ninety-four countries, and was trading $200 billion daily in the foreign-exchange markets; without satellites, PCs, and a dedicated global telecommunications network such turnover would have been impossible. It needed telecom deregulation as much as capital market deregulation to pull off the coup. Between 1972 and 1985 the 1,000 largest U.S. banks increased their dedicated spending on telecommunications from 5 to 13 percent of their total operating expenses.[23] Over the 1980s and 1990s a parallel axis to that between the U.S. Treasury and the IMF and World Bank grew up between the U.S. Department of Commerce and first GATT and later the World Trade Organization—and for similar reasons. The multilateral institutions' choice was stark—if they did not accommodate the United States's unilateral ambitions then the United States would achieve its ends without them. So, better to keep some multilateralism than have none at all. The GATT could no more launch a round of tariff reduction negotiations without U.S.

support than the IMF a bailout, and when the so-called Uruguay round of tariff reductions and market opening began in 1985 the United States insisted that intellectual property rights, service sector trade, and in particular telecommunications were on the agenda—thus bypassing what the Reaganites saw as the statist International Telecommunications Union (ITU), the intergovernmental agency that regulated international telecom business. Four years later the ITU agreed to take part in the GATT talks, recognizing the reality that the United States was going to drive through telecom liberalization and that its only chance of saving even minimal public interest obligations was to work through GATT. In 1990 GATT ruled that American multinationals should have access to all the service markets of GATT's signatory states. Four years later the United States used GATT to compel the European Union to agree to open all its voice communications (post, telephone, and telegraphs) to competition. In 1995 the United States forced through GATT a framework agreement on trade-related intellectual property, or TRIPs, protecting the enforcement of intellectual property rights, with the result that the U.S. Patent Office—as the gatekeeper controlling the exercise of patents in the world's largest market—would become the de facto upholder of all advances in the information age. In April 1996, by which time GATT had been succeeded by the World Trade Organization (WTO) the U.S. delegation walked out of the WTO talks, declining to take further part unless telecom liberalization was made global; a year later the WTO gave in and opened up seventy countries to U.S. telecom companies on American terms. With the World Bank and IMF insisting on telecom deregulation as the price of every structural adjustment program, the United States was succeeding in deregulating global telecoms in the 1990s as it had finance over the 1970s and 1980s. By the early 1990s the U.S. trade surplus in services had quadrupled to $60 billion a year.

To capitalize further on these hard-won openings the U.S. telecom industry needed to reorganize and consolidate at home. It pressed hard for deregulation that would allow it to form new domestic groupings and alliances as a platform for expansion overseas—and it wanted to move fast. New Deal and liberal notions that access to telecommunications should be universal and that there were public service obligations associated with information dissemination in general and broadcasting in particular had been undermined throughout the 1980s as part of the conservative grip on U.S. thinking. Conservative appointees to the key Federal Communications Commission (FCC) repudiated notions of the public interest and social equity in determining communications policy, insisting instead that information should be structured as a marketplace.[24] The Democrats, swept up in enthusiasm for the New Economy, became apostles of liberalization—hoping vainly that they could create a genuinely competitive marketplace that would deliver an information-based economy free from overwhelming corporate power with only light or minimal regulation. They should have thought again. In any case, the now vastly expanded role of money in American politics meant that if they wanted to receive the largesse of the PACs or political action committees (see chapter 3), they would have to talk the language of deregulation and liberalization. By 1995 AT&T was the largest single PAC donor, and the lobbyists for deregulation were the cream of former White House staff from both main parties.[25]

Before the onslaught of lobbying and assertive private interests there was no defense, and the 1996 Telecommunications Act was the inevitable result. Democrat Congresswoman Marcy Kaptur called the process leading up to the act "living proof of what unlimited money can do to buy influence and the Congress of the United States." That did not trouble Citicorp any more than AT&T. The telecom companies wanted less regulation, they wanted the right to build their own freestanding networks and they wanted to use their allocations on the terrestrial spectrum as free as possible from public service obligations; long-distance carriers wanted to enter local markets; all wanted cross-ownership rules relaxed. All that they wanted, they got. In contemporary Washington, dollars, informed by the self-righteousness of the new conservatism and aided and abetted by lobbying, buy anything.

The Telecommunications Act was the trigger for the most infamous financial bubble in world financial history, which would ultimately waste, according to the *Financial Times*, $1,000 billion of real cash around the world in write-offs and losses from absurd investment—and yet more trillions of dollars in falling telecom share prices.[26] The deregulation of the financial system in the 1980s followed by the forced opening up of the world telecom market in the 1990s were the preconditions of the madness; every semiprivatized or wholly privatized telecom company in the world could become a player, borrowing money on global financial markets to finance its global ambitions to be the owner of as many complementary networks as possible. All bubbles are animated by a big idea, and the telecom bubble's big idea was that in the new knowledge economy waves of digitized information would be pumped through a multiplicity of broadband cable networks; the notion that each country needed only one network, giving universal access, was old-fashioned socialism. There would be enough information for many networks, and private enterprise would show that competition would deliver what old state-owned telecom companies could not. This was American conservatism's gift to the globe. It was to prove a total disaster.

The first-round effect of the Telecommunications Act was an orgy of takeovers in the United States; in the first half of 1998 136 merger deals worth $120 billion were announced between U.S. telecom companies. Long-distance carriers merged, and paid extraordinary prices to buy local networks; for example, WorldCom paid between six and nine times the value of the telecom infrastructure of two local carriers (MFS and Brooks Fiber) in order to construct a national network. Then they paid $30 billion for MCI, trumping the bid from British Telecom by $12 billion. It now faces dismemberment as its debts overwhelm it. Cable companies merged with telephone companies; AT&T paid $44 billion for the cable giant TCI. Simultaneously a wave of mergers and conglomeration hit the providers of all the digitized software that would allegedly be pumped through the new networks. Time Warner, already a presence in terrestrial, cable, digital and satellite TV, film, music, books, newspapers, and online publishing, merged with the Internet portal and search engine AOL to gain dominance over every possible piece of the converging markets in digital information. Disney bought ABC for the same reason. And once they had captured market share in the United States, all had eyes for the new opportunities opening up in Europe and Japan—whose companies themselves began to consolidate in anticipation of the American advance. A fifth of all mergers worldwide in 1999 were initiated by global telecom companies. Most have proved disastrous.

The consequences for American consumers have been baleful. Although long-distance rates have fallen, local telephone and cable rates have soared. Absurdly, some sixty companies emerged as aspirant network builders and carriers in an industry which, even in a continental economy like the United States, is a natural monopoly: there is no more reason for rival cable networks than competing road networks. Telephone companies have been "slamming" (signing up customers without permission) and "cramming" (billing customers for services not provided) with impunity; a million people a year have been signed up without their agreement, and millions more are charged for services they have not used. Only 2 percent of U.S. telephone lines are served by new competitors. A mere 6 percent of American consumers are connected to the Internet through broadband networks. Educational programs for children have virtually disappeared; low-power television stations to serve ethnic minorities have been neglected and their program standards have fallen; community-based broadcasting is disappearing.

The catastrophic effects did not stop there. There was a global frenzy as telecom companies all tried to ape the American lead, combining the ownership of cable networks, mobile phone networks, communication satellites, and sometimes even the manufacture of equipment: the assumption was there would be enough traffic to support many competing networks outside the United States as well. All paid absurd prices to realize their ambitions, offering ridiculous sums in Britain's auction of the radio spectrum for third-generation mobile phones, for example, or making acquisitions at ludicrously inflated prices. Global stock markets chased up their share prices, encouraging everyone to join in the game. But there never was the avalanche of digitized information, and when the dot-com bubble burst it was followed inevitably by the end of the telecom boom—in which trillions of dollars were at stake. We are left with vast overcapacity, threatened bankruptcies, and a massive debt overhang in which only a fraction of the capital invested is remotely recoverable. British Telecom, Deutsche Telekom and France Telecom were by the autumn of 2001 saddled with $160 billion of debt compared to combined earnings of $40 billion. Share prices have been decimated. In Britain, new cable operators like NTL and Energis are engulfed by debt and struggling for survival: again, the notion that there would be sufficient traffic to justify the business model of companies competing in an industry which is a natural monopoly was ridiculous. Equipment manufacturers like Marconi, as described in the following chapter, have been sucked into the disaster—all chasing that other icon of the U.S. conservative revolution, shareholder value. The U.S. Securities and Exchange Commission is even investigating sham transactions between rival telecommunications carriers, including British companies, set up to inflate revenues. And despite it all, no country can boast a complete broadband cable network. If the public sector in the leading industrialized countries had spent a fraction of the lost cash in each building one public network, the spread of the information economy would have been faster by years. That was forbidden by the conservative orthodoxy.

The act and its consequences have been a global fiasco, just as IMF structural adjustment and austerity programs have been. But to conservative America that does not matter. The greater game lies elsewhere. The global system has been constructed to disallow government autonomy and give the maximum freedom to business, whatever the irrationalities and extravagant waste. The object is not to promote notions of equity, the social contract, equality of opportunity, or the public realm. The object is to promote the autonomy of action of American transnationals in general, and American control of the global financial and information technology systems in particular. Others can join in the system the United States has done most to create, and benefit if they can. But with 62 percent of global information technology business originating in the United States and American companies owning 75 percent of the global software market, there should be no illusions about who the winners are. One hundred and eighty commercial satellites orbit in space; all but half a dozen are American-owned. The United States controls the information age as it does the world financial system. American conservative ideology has served its purpose, although many ordinary Americans might wonder if it has done them any good. The question is whether it serves anybody else's purpose—and how the world might be different.

7
Britain in the American Bear Hug

American conservatism is a phenomenon whose reach goes far beyond the shores of the United States. Britain's intellectual and political history over the last twenty-five years has mirrored America's remorseless drive to the right. Because Margaret Thatcher was such a formidable conservative force, it is easy to characterize the rise of British conservatism as a purely British affair, drawing on Britain's conservative traditions to contest the products of British socialism and the labor movement. But hers was a conservatism that always had one eye on the other side of the Atlantic—inspired by it and looking for ideas from it. "The fundamental strength of the American economy is the underlying enterprise culture of the American people," she said in a speech in the mid-1980s. "It is, therefore, vital to secure in this country that same enterprise culture." It was an oft-repeated mantra.

The same sentiment has been expressed in almost the same tones by both Tony Blair and Chancellor of the Exchequer Gordon Brown, who, no less enthusiastic about U.S. economic dynamism, equally uncritically accept the American explanation of how its "success" has been achieved. "In the 1980s Margaret Thatcher rightly emphasized the importance of the enterprise culture," wrote Gordon Brown in the *Wall Street Journal* in June 2001, "but this did not go far enough."[1] Brown wants to extend this culture to ordinary people as an instrument of individual advancement.

The British political class accepts the American success story, as much as its account of high social mobility, on its own terms, with little challenge; there is little investigation into whether these claims are true and even less into the associated costs and deficiencies.

Yet the "success" and ideas so many British leaders want to copy are, as previous chapters have made clear, not only very contentious but—and increasingly—no less than the successes and ideas of American conservatism. This very particular doctrine has had a huge influence in Britain over the past quarter-century, challenging "one nation" Conservatism and Labour's social democratic tradition alike. The depiction of taxation as an unparalleled economic burden and moral offense could never have happened, for example, without the ammunition supplied from the United States, just as the "flexible" labor market could never have reached its iconic status. The lazy way in which American conservatives identify any activity of the state with socialism has been imported wholesale, so that British conservative writers can pitch the British Post Office on a continuum of statism/socialism that culminates in the Soviet gulag.[2] As the entire American political discourse has moved to the right, Britain's has faithfully followed.

Britain is peculiarly vulnerable to trends in American politics. The British relationship with the United States is necessarily more complex and unique than that of any other country. The original thirteen colonies were, after all, British; the War of Independence was fought against Britain; the two countries not only speak English, but share the same philosophical roots. Neither country's economic development was state-led; Britain's industrial revolution happened as spontaneously as the United States's industrialization. In both countries, the state's contribution was primarily to provide the overarching framework within which private property–based capitalism could flourish, whether by setting tariff walls (which both countries paradoxically did aggressively until they became the dominant economic power) or by defining a powerful legal framework in which contracts could be enforced. Neither country deliberately set about building a financial, educational, and scientific infrastructure—as did France, Germany, and Japan—in order to industrialize. Development and its institutions were market-led.

Nor is that all. If over the nineteenth century both Britain and the

United States grew similar models of capitalism justified by the same essential philosophy, over the twentieth century both shared the same enemies—fascism and communism. As its economic power waned in the first half of the twentieth century, Britain increasingly took the view, dramatized as the U.S. Army proved the decisive influence in settling the World War I, that its international interests were best served by defining itself as a partner, if increasingly a very junior partner, in a relationship whose aims were shared. Britain has actively sought to enmesh its military, financial, and economic decision making with that of the United States, accepting that while this brought important losses in sovereignty, they were more than offset by the gains.

This "special" relationship, affirmed once more during the war in Afghanistan in 2001–2, allows Britain to define itself as the representative in Europe of the English-speaking Anglo-Saxon model—a stock market–based capitalism, complete with a minimal welfare system and flexible labor markets, which has both global ambitions and thus necessarily global defense and security concerns. Britain may have some of the features of the European model, but the more it can behave like the United States the more efficient it will be. Euroskepticism is presented as a noble assertion of the country's real roots and values.

Think back to chapter 2. Of the four clusters of values that define Europe's distinction from the United States, Britain is unambiguously European in its attitude toward the social contract, equality, and the public realm. The British are firmly in the European camp in their attitudes toward the reasonableness of the state acting to provide a basic income to the disadvantaged and maintaining the social contract. Just a casual glance at the World Value Survey (a detailed survey of values in forty-three countries) identifies Britain as a member of the European camp over attitudes toward areas as disparate as religion and work. For example, 36 percent of Britons, 30 percent of West Germans, 29 percent of French and 37 percent of Spanish say that "life is meaningful only because God exists"; in the United States, the proportion is 61 percent.[3] Equally, the British would no more abandon universal health provision or their welfare state than any European.

It is on attitudes toward property, the financial system, and the market economy that British values and institutions are closer to the American—John Locke, the apostle of private property, and Adam Smith, the apostle of free markets, have left their indelible mark on both countries—but even here the proximity is overstated. The British do not believe in the absolutism of proprietorial rights as strongly as the Americans. Processes that qualify property rights—taxation or planning laws—are fundamentally more legitimate in Britain, and there is much less tolerance of inequality. In the latest *British Social Attitudes* survey, 81 percent of respondents thought the gap between rich and poor too wide, with 73 percent arguing that the government had a responsibility to narrow the gap.[4]

Yet while the patrician Tory one-nation tradition has been happy to accept Britain's essential Europeanness and take what in Europe would be characterized as a liberal, Christian democrat position toward the social contract and regulation of capitalism, another strain in British conservatism has wanted to identify more completely with the United States. As American conservatism launched its ideological counteroffensive against American liberalism, this brand of British conservatism rose in tandem—importing the whole paraphernalia of antistate ideas that have been outlined in the last half-dozen chapters. But if these concepts have had a malevolent impact on the United States, they have had a doubly malevolent impact in Britain, distorting the national conversation and preventing the British from understanding who they are and how they work. In the process the Tory party has been wrecked, British social democracy compromised, and an endemic Euroskepticism allowed to flourish. Nor has underlying British economic performance notably improved with productivity lagging, or our Rawlsian infrastructure of justice been protected. It is not a happy story.

The Story Begins

It is no accident that the British free-market think tank the Institute of Economic Affairs was set up in the same year, 1955, as the American Enterprise Institute. From its foundation the IEA, which drew upon the increasingly frenzied output from the University of Chicago, the public-choice school at the University of Virginia (which argues that all public agency is self-defeating because it is captured by vested interests), and the great U.S. right-wing think tanks, was one of the principal conduits by which American conservative ideas were introduced into British conservatism and the right-wing press. During the 1960s and 1970s the IEA was to parrot the great U.S. conservative causes, from the rise of monetarism to the application of free markets as a universal economic panacea. At the high-water mark of British social democracy it advocated private rather than state pensions, education vouchers, and the privatization of state utilities. In 1974 the dedicated Conservative party in-house think tank, the Centre for Policy Studies (CPS), was established; and in 1977 the Adam Smith Institute followed, completing a fateful trio of free-market propagandists, all looking to the United States for ideas and inspiration.

The decisive moment came with Mrs. Thatcher's general election victory in 1979. Thatcher was at heart a simple, right-wing Tory with a gut hatred of trade unions and nationalized industries together with a powerful belief in the virtues of the English middle class, whose privileges she set out to defend and enlarge. What the new think tanks gave her, relayed straight from their American conservative mentors, was an intellectual rationale to justify her instincts. Her grip on the high theory of monetarism and free markets was never very solid, so that the inconsistencies, say, in wanting to roll back subsidies to nationalized industries in the name of markets while retaining them for farmers and home buyers never troubled her. What she wanted was a justification for attacking traditional Tory enemies and helping traditional allies, both of which she did with gusto. Moreover, she was at home in the United States; she liked its lack of unions and nationalized industries, and its welfare state, and bought the proposition of American conservatism that liberty meant enterprise.

Much of the Thatcherite program should be seen as a twofold mission: to pull down the social democratic settlement and to construct in its place a simulacrum of the United States. Thus the nine employment acts that made the UK the least regulated labor market in the OECD. Thus the accent on tax cuts for the rich and incentives for enterprise. Thus, as her government grew more confident, the constant insistence on "market" and "private sector" solutions. Thus the great drive toward financial and telecom deregulation. Thus the creation of planning-free zones as a tool of urban regeneration. Thus the tougher and tougher approach to the welfare state—a case study worth exploring in a little more detail.

The great social achievement of the Labour government elected in 1945 had been finally to lay to rest the distinction between the deserving and undeserving poor that had disfigured a hundred and fifty years of British social life from the industrial revolution. The nineteenth-century workhouse and the twentieth-century means test had rested alike on the pitiless view that the poor were poor because of their moral deficiencies, and did not deserve to be treated as potential fellow citizens. In establishing a strong welfare state in which welfare benefits were available as a matter of right, Labour broke with this entire tradition.

This departure was never likely to appeal to Margaret Thatcher. In 1987 a London conference of American dependency theorists—the avant-garde of the American right—was held at the instigation of the CPS to put the argument that welfare caused poverty by undermining the moral character of those who depended on it and thus made them unable to escape welfare—one of the key tenets of American conservatism, whose lineage, as we have seen, can be traced back to Leo Strauss. This is part of a wider argument in which to be poor and accept welfare is characterized as a personal choice arising from moral weakness—marking out the undeserving poor. One of the contributors, Charles Murray, had gone further, claiming to demonstrate that welfare directly created a dependent and self-generating underclass—and his theories were uncritically celebrated in the (London) *Sunday Times*. America's underclass is largely black, and its plight is impossible to understand outside the particular history of American slavery and racism; equally, the idea that the poor choose to be poor flies in the face of reason. This was the theory of the workhouse in modern guise. But none of that mattered to the British conservative propagandists. They wanted to undo Labour's settlement, and were happy to make use of any ammunition.

The policy conclusion was that welfare should be made contingent on a willingness to work, the underlying assumption being explicitly that the poor are feckless and do not deserve to be treated as equal citizens. By 1987 Department of Employment ministers had made six official visits to the United States to examine welfare-to-work programs,[5] and the conference was but another step on the journey. Over their eighteen years in office the

Conservatives were to make welfare benefits increasingly contingent on the willingness of the unemployed to look for work—an approach directly modeled on the U.S. 1988 Family Support Act (FSA) and various state welfare-to-work initiatives—and progressively to reduce unemployment insurance as a citizen's right. But while the FSA did not compel workers to come off welfare if they could show they would be worse off as a result, and required states to increase their training investment, Thatcher's initiatives made no such concession; they were more punitive even than the new American system.[6] By the end of the Tory period in office, unemployment insurance for twelve months had become the job seeker's allowance, available as a non–means-tested citizen's right for only six months—under tight scrutiny—and its value in real terms fell as increases in the rate were linked to inflation rather than the growth of average earnings, which rises faster than inflation. As a result, those living on welfare became progressively poorer in relation to those with average earnings.

The notion that the proper objectives of an active labor market policy, including helping the disadvantaged to find and hold work, were perfectly consistent with the maintenance of social insurance as an entitlement and reasonable levels of welfare benefits that did not pauperize the recipients, together with even greater investment in education and training, passed the conservatives by in both Britain and America. It was not until New Labour's New Deal that a more enlightened conception was launched with a guaranteed commitment to training. The introduction of the minimum wage meant that all those who came off welfare were better off. But enlightenment was limited. While insisting that recipients of unemployment benefits and income support be aggressively tested for their willingness to look for and find work—a fair enough quid pro quo for receiving benefits—actual benefit levels remained niggardly. There was no substantive improvement in their level or structure, which remained means-tested and indexed to the lower growth in retail prices rather than the growth in average earnings. The revival of social democracy did not dare challenge the heartland of conservatism; the poor had better stay poor.

The American imports did not stop there. In health, an eccentric paper by the conservative Alain Enthoven of Stanford University in 1985, suggesting that "there seems to be no substitute for competition and consumer choice" to improve the dismal performance of the NHS, which was deemed to be "frozen by an excess of egalitarianism," was adopted wholesale in the NHS reforms of 1990, with disastrous results. Ignoring the fact that health outcomes had improved remarkably over the 1980s while costs had remained stable—between 1980 and 1988 NHS hospitals increased inpatient treatment by 16 percent, emergency treatment by 19 percent and day surgery by 73 percent, without a significant real increase in costs—Enthoven argued for an internal market to improve responsiveness, punish the weak performers, and reward the effective. He suggested that health authorities should essentially contract with each other and with GPs for business.[7]

Enthoven's ideas were not even given a trial run; they conformed to the conservatives' prejudices, and thus were legislated for on the basis of only a computerized simulation of what the impact might be. The breakup of the NHS into elements that contracted with one another in a quasi-market, as Enthoven recommended, immediately lifted costs by creating an expensive bureaucracy through which the contracts were audited. More seriously, access to treatment became dependent upon the bargaining skills of doctors and hospitals, with no parallel system for allowing successful units to invest and expand or unsuccessful units to turn themselves around. A two-tier system was created, entrenching health inequalities and jeopardizing the core principle—universality of access—upon which the NHS was founded. New Labour was to abolish the internal market; but again the reform was incomplete. The NHS remains structured around a balkanized network of trusts and primary care groups that have to contract with each other to produce health care. The notion that the NHS must be respected as a social organization with a unique culture is in danger of being lost.

The greatest bequest of American conservatism was its assault on taxation and the ludicrous advocacy of the Laffer curve (described in chapter 3), purporting to show that the incentive effects of low tax rates were so great that they produced a greater overall tax take than higher rates. British Conservatives took up the battle cry of Reagan's Republicans with even greater enthusiasm. It became part of the accepted wisdom that high taxation is a massive economic disincentive and the source of wider economic underperformance (which at absurdly high marginal rates it is; but beyond that there is no economic proof of any disincentive—indeed, there is some evidence that the higher the overall tax burden the better the economic performance as a result of a stronger public infrastructure),[8] that it is no solution to "throw money" at severely underfunded public services and that public spending is definitionally inefficient and wasteful. The only direction for income tax rates is downwards; as more taxation has been raised from indirect taxes that impact more heavily on the poor, so the system has become less progressive. To tax and to spend became the greatest sins in the lexicon, even though British public services and the quality of the British public infrastructure were to become among the worst in Europe.

So it was that Thatcherism owed its intellectual inspiration to the conservative movement in the United States. Even the apparently home-grown initiative of privatization would have been less intellectually defensible had it not been launched at a time when the U.S. economic, business, financial, and political establishments had become converted to a purist conception of the efficiency and creativity of the market. Privatization merely took the logic of deregulation, already well established in the United States, to its logical conclusion.

The passionate belief in the efficacy of markets had its most complete expression in the recasting of the British financial system, which has become almost an exact replica of New York, but within the European time zone. Its financial assets are as freely tradable; there are no controls on the international convertibility of sterling any more than there are on the dollar; regulation is minimal. In the stock market, individuals own only 20 per cent of the shares; the rest are held by institutional shareholders—just over half by British pension funds and insurance companies, and some 30 percent by foreign, mainly American, institutions.[9] The value of shares held by institutional investors represented 197 percent of British GDP in 1998—176 percent in the United States.[10] The same investment and business philosophy, the maximization of shareholder value, prevails; the same investment banks and management consultancies who promote the doctrine in the United States operate in almost exactly the same way in London. Takeover and the deal are king, facilitated by the same domination of share ownership by financial institutions.

This is no accident. London's role as an international financial center, waning as the sterling area and empire became progressively irrelevant, was reinvented during the 1960s as the intermediary where offshore dollars could be deposited, re-lent, and invested in the new eurodollar and eurobond markets—driven by the process outlined in chapter 5. When in 1980 capital and exchange controls were lifted, following Nixon's example, and then in 1986 membership of the stock exchange was opened in the so-called Big Bang to international banks and investment banks that could buy the existing stockbrokers, the process was complete. London was wide open to any bank or financial intermediary that could pass the Bank of England's undemanding creditworthiness tests; shares and bonds could be traded between banks in an electronic, screen-based market—with foreign banks and bankers enjoying a light tax and regulatory regime designed to attract Americans.

Against this background New Labour has struggled to establish even a moderate strain of social democracy. It has not dared to challenge the doctrine of shareholder value or the system of corporate governance, as the economic historians Richard Roberts and David Kynaston outline in their honest assessment of the entrenched dominance of the City of London and its values, *City State*. Its attempts to improve the quality of working life through regulation have been modest and voluntaristic; it has proudly defended the least regulated labor market in the OECD. It spent four years resisting the introduction of the EU directive requiring British companies to inform and consult their workforces over key decisions, and accepted the directive only grudgingly in the immediate aftermath of a second landslide electoral victory. It has promised not to raise income tax rates for a second successive parliament. It has been carefully selective in raising welfare benefits only to the "deserving" poor—lifting income support for children and devising a tax credit for working families. It has presided over the fall of public investment to its lowest proportion of GDP since 1945, and permitted gross underspending of even modest plans. It has carried on the means-testing of the welfare system, extending it to disability benefits. Its loss of confidence in public enterprise and need to justify public spending by demonstrable efficiency gains is evident in its rigid commitment to public/private partnerships and the financing of public investment through the private finance initiative—even in contexts where the gains are dubious, like the London Underground and hospital building in the National Health Service (NHS). Under the

London Underground Public Private Partnership, it will, astonishingly, be 2008 before the first new trains—twelve in total—will be introduced, an abrogation of the public interest that tests new limits.

New Labour has made gains, but famously they have been either by stealth or very cautious. A large increase in public spending that began in 1999 is beginning to turn around two decades of public neglect. Further spending increases, announced in summer 2002, will take Britain's health expenditure as a percentage of GDP to the EU average by 2006. Education spending is not far behind. The government has dared to open a debate about how an improved NHS is to be paid for. In the criminal justice system it is committed to the rehabilitation and education of prisoners and has relaxed British drug laws. There are signs of significant improvement in educational performance. Britain's aid budget is to be increased.

These are all important signs of movement; but in its essentials, Britain's economic and social model remains profoundly shaped by conservatism. The great themes of our age—the rise of inequality, the overriding priority of business and the decline of the public realm—have not yet been intellectually and politically challenged, nor has any popular narrative been developed that might do the job. Conservatism's grip may be weakening, but it remains ascendant.

The World Gone Mad

Yet the benefits of this marriage to the precepts of American conservatism have been at best qualified, at worst illusory. Britain's inflation and employment performance has certainly improved, both absolutely and relatively, and this is trumpeted as proof that Britain is making better progress toward emulating American "success" than other European countries;[11] but the gains are only modest. Historical data from 1999 and projections up to 2003 assembled by the OECD (the Paris-based club of government economic analysts and forecasters) suggest that Britain's growth in GDP and employment will be lower than France's and only fractionally higher than Germany's; even Italian employment growth will be higher. It is true that Britain's unemployment rate will have been markedly lower than all three over the period, but the economic slowdown in 2002 and 2003 will see a similar proportional rise.[12] After decades in which Britain was unambiguously the worst-performing economy in Europe its recent improvement is cause for relief, but hardly so stellar as to support the argument that its progress towards Americanization should be followed by the others—or that pursuit of the U.S. model has brought unadulterated rewards.

Indeed, drill a little deeper and the results are profoundly disappointing. After more than twenty years of importing the nostrums of American conservatism Britain is no nearer to developing an "enterprise culture"—if that is to be measured by the growth and level of productivity, new patents, and presence in new technologies—than it ever was. The British government's own survey of business investment shows that the top 500 British companies invested only 7.9 percent of their revenue, while the top 500 international companies invested 9.6 percent of their revenue. Only 44 British companies ranked in the top 500 international companies; if they are excluded, the other 456 British companies invested a paltry 5.8 percent of sales.[13] Moreover, while the top 500 international firms raised their investment by 12 percent per year, the British 500 managed only 10 percent. So it is that while France, Germany, and Italy have dramatically closed the productivity gap with the United States, Britain's relative improvement has been slight; the gap, although narrower than it was, is still yawning. Output per hour worked is 32 percent higher in France, 29 percent higher in the former West Germany, and 21 percent higher in the United States,[14] and with current investment behavior it will widen.

Britain has an American-style deregulated labor market, weak trade unions, indifferent social protection, and a fierce market for corporate control to keep the management of quoted companies, as the conservatives would argue, on their toes. It has, as a survey in *Management Today* reported in July 2001, rewarded its chief executives more handsomely than other European countries, so that in 1999 and 2000 executive pay rose by 29 percent to an average annual salary of $760,000 compared to $573,000 in France and $447,000 in Germany. Meanwhile, ordinary workers' pay was the lowest of the same countries. With these advantages, if the conservatives are right the British economy should be clipping along. Instead, its performance is only modest.

For the zealots—rather like ancient Druids or the cargo cult islanders—

this is proof only that something is wrong with their rituals and they must redouble their efforts, not that their whole belief system may be awry. Others do not acknowledge the reality at all. The *Sunday Times* Business Section's economic columnist and conservative zealot Irwin Stelzer is a classic of the breed, who rehearses his prejudices as the truth, selectively choosing his facts while omitting others, week after week—a tendency, as we have seen, that extends to conservative academics like Alain Enthoven. In Stelzerland a "sclerotic" Europe has lagging productivity generated by a "eurocracy" that delights in setting burdensome regulations that "drive entrepreneurs mad." His view is that European governments set tax, cost, and regulatory burdens that are the sole cause of uncompetitiveness; his hero is the individualistic entrepreneur chasing the next idea, rightfully worth billions, and that America's pro-enterprise approach can be relied upon to beat all other economies over time. He has no interest in any social capabilities that might create organizational creativity or support high-performance companies; that is "corporatism."[15] The notion that output per man-hour might be higher in the former West Germany and France than the United States is plainly preposterous, as is the idea that, apart from one or two exceptions, the European corporate sector is anything but deadbeat. Yet Stelzer's partisan effusions go unchallenged in a way impossible for anybody who takes the alternative view. Offered a platform in an American-owned newspaper (in addition he writes for the *Sun*) to propagandize the Washington consensus and the new conservatism with no health warning, he is part of the internationally accepted common sense. Typically, he was a member of an advisory council for the now-bankrupt Enron, where his constant advocacy of minimal regulation in exchange for more than useful remuneration helpfully contributed to an intellectual climate supporting Enron's fraudulent operations. He is an adviser to the Smith Institute, a think tank close to Gordon Brown, where he rehearses the familiar free-market litanies. He also advises Rupert Murdoch, acting as a key intermediary with the British government: during the negotiations over the relaxation of Britain's media ownership laws in 2001 and early 2002, for example, the ministers concerned were obliged to offer him any access he wanted where he pressed his antiregulation case. At the heart of the economic, government, media, and business establishment he can get away with consistent presentation of unsubstantiated ideology as the truth—and does so regularly.

It is an analysis that infects the entire economic and consultancy establishment. The McKinsey report into productivity, commissioned by Chancellor of the Exchequer Gordon Brown soon after the 1997 election, reveals just how deep the prejudices go, and how perverse the recommendations are that flow from such flawed and ideologically informed "analysis." McKinsey starts its report with the unashamed and explicit view that the benchmark economy is the United States, and that the puzzle for Britain is how to import more American best practice. It adopts the unconventional view that the core of the British problem, far from lack of investment, is land use planning: "regulations governing land use determine corporate behavior, investment and pricing." These, it concludes, are the "pervasive explanation" for lower British productivity. A shake-up in overly restrictive British planning rules to allow firms more freedom to expand and enter new industries along American lines is the single most important contribution the British government could make to lifting productivity.

At first sight this seems like an innovative idea—until the evidence is examined closely, when it plainly becomes batty. McKinsey's "insights" were foreshadowed in the early 1980s by the Adam Smith Institute, which inveighed against the "planning class" and cited Houston as an example of the benefits of a laissez-faire approach to planning: the only American city then without politically authorized zoning, it was growing rapidly.[16] However, it is now clear that Houston's growth in these years was part of a much wider renaissance of the southern and specifically Texan economy—which proved limited when pollution and toxic waste grew over the decade, choking its growth; a trend accompanied by the quiet relegation in order of priorities, even by American conservatives, of the notion that planning laws inhibited growth. McKinsey had not read the literature. Nor had the authors of the report broken down the sources of productivity growth to identify correctly the importance of the emergence of new firms in contributing to productivity. If they had done so they would have realized that the ideological assumption upon which they based their analysis had wildly overestimated the role of firm entry. The OECD has demonstrated that firm entry and exit is relatively trivial as a cause of productivity growth, and that notwithstanding British planning laws, firm entry is considerably easier in Britain than in the United States, where in any case it makes a negative contribution to productivity growth.[17]

In fact, most productivity growth in both countries is achieved within the firm—as it is in every country the OECD surveyed. McKinsey might make grandiloquent boasts about how its judgments are informed by global experience, but in truth it—like Irwin Stelzer and Alain Enthoven—is a simple propagandist of the conservative Washington consensus, right or wrong. There is even an argument that planning laws, by generating higher-density urban areas, help to increase productivity by clustering skills in close physical proximity so that there is a much greater chance of interfirm and interemployee learning. But this is not what McKinsey's brand of economics teaches, and so the point is not even considered.

Indeed, in assessing the causes of productivity growth, conservative economics looks in entirely the wrong direction. Conservatives want to prove that markets are economically and morally superior to all other forms of organization. Economic efficiency, for them, is about the permanent freedom to complete the most cost-effective contract and to move on to another if there is a better opportunity; in this world, the aim is to allocate resources effectively through buying cheap and selling dear. The assumption is that productivity is delivered by firms being able to exit from costly contracts, whether with their workforce or their subcontractors, and enter into new ones quickly and flexibly; that production is simply a matter of combining workers, machines, and technology in the best technical configuration through top-down managerial direction; and that the optimal production configuration is self-evidently obvious once costs and prices are known. The organization in which these choices take place is beside the point. Its history, the quality of its leadership and internal organization, and the uncertainty in which it makes strategic choices about what to do and how its market might evolve are abstracted out of the account. These "soft" issues are not allowed to muddy the "hard" message: productivity is about entrepreneurial freedom to cut deals independent of any consideration other than cost minimization and profit maximization.

Yet, as the OECD has established, the heart of productivity growth is what happens inside the firm, and firms are human organizations. Mary O'Sullivan, assistant professor at INSEAD, Europe's leading business school, argues persuasively that innovation cannot be conceptualized within the market contracting framework, for it is an organizational quality that flourishes better in some environments than others. In the first place, organizations cannot be scrapped and rebuilt at will; they develop cumulatively over time and what they have been determines in part what they can become. A major steel or chemicals company cannot easily transmute into a bank or insurance company if it believes that might maximize its profits; it has sets of skills and competences that are unique to a particular industry, even to that firm. Its directors, managers, and workers know what to do to make that particular firm function in that particular industry, and they will necessarily be at a disadvantage if they try to migrate wholesale to a different industry or economic function. Their success depends on their ability to innovate within their organizational capacity, and that in turn depends on their learning capacity—on their ability, at every level, to move on. Even if managers choose to command and control in a top-down way—as on occasion they must—they have to act on information that is passed up to them, and that in turn demands that the organization operate as a successful social process. Information is collectively gathered and synthesized by the organization as a whole, and necessarily account has to be taken of competitors' strategies. Put bluntly, this is a social and leadership process that too much reliance on individualistic market contracting obstructs. The more conservative economics rules, the less innovative the organization.

The evidence marshaled by O'Sullivan shows that across countries, industries, and firms there are certain golden rules conducive to innovation. The directors who make decisions over investment need to be closely aligned with and understand those who are at the competitive front line; they need to be close to their key managers and operators, who need to be constantly feeding back to them information about market conditions and new technologies. Equally, there needs to be a shared loyalty to the organization's goals; and this is easier the fewer individual members break away to sell their own skills on the open market. And finally, there needs to be a consistent commitment to continue to make investment—in skills, knowledge, and physical assets—over time, so that obsolescence is counterbalanced by new resources. Planning restrictions, regulatory burdens, and high taxation are seen for what they are: at most, second-order problems; at worst, intellectual red herrings because they obscure the real drivers of innovation. Just to enter this universe is to realize how feeble the

McKinsey/Stelzer/conservative approach to understanding enterprise and innovation is. They are not even at first base.

For what becomes immediately apparent is that conservative economics, with its emphasis on maximizing shareholder value and market flexibilities, is actively inimical to innovation and productivity growth. External shareholders impose their views on what constitutes appropriate investment, setting criteria and goals that are inevitably removed from the organization's competitive day-to-day exigencies. Moreover, the company with a quotation on the London or New York Stock Exchange faces a shifting and volatile base of owners, always ready to sell the company to a predator if its performance falls below their expectations—sometimes a judgment that is made after just two or three quarters' poor results. Moreover, if directors, star managers, and key income earners are always ready to put themselves on the labor market to maximize their incomes, then their loyalty to the organization over time is necessarily weakened. Individual wealth generation comes before that of the organization. In the world created by conservative economists, innovation becomes more difficult.

McKinsey, for example, uncritically accepts that Britain's capital markets are good for productivity because they are market based and flexible. Wrong. The increasing emphasis in Britain's capital markets, like those in the United States, is not on increasing investment and innovation; rather, it is on trading financial assets for immediate financial gain, so that the focus continually transmitted by the markets to the corporate sector is on the need to increase profits—by whatever means. If the result of some historic innovation has been to deliver the desired financial return, then the markets readily welcome it—but no more than they would welcome increased profits achieved by any other means: layoffs, asset-stripping, a clever deal, tax avoidance, or even smart manipulation of the corporate balance sheet—although, as the markets have discovered with Enron, sham traffic between telecom companies and hideous fraud in the financial sector, when the process of manufacturing profit by any means goes too far, it is self-defeating. Indeed, as I argued in *The State We're In*, the perennial problem in capital markets structured as they are in Britain and the United States is the commitment problem. The innovative organization needs a platform of committed owners prepared to delegate the scale and priorities of investment decision making to the managerial insiders similarly committed to the organization over time—but that is precisely what the Anglo-Saxon capital markets, as they have evolved over the last quarter of a century, do not do.

British and American companies do not in general have a multiplicity of small owners (a structure in which the influence of any one shareholder is tiny, offering collective stability) or a small core of committed owners, either of which might provide such a platform; instead, the bulk of their equity is owned by some twenty or thirty representatives of collective savers—pension funds and the like. No single pension fund or insurance company is large enough to reap the rewards of offering a committed platform to innovative companies; to do so risks suffering poor investment performance while others exploit more appealing short-term opportunities—and savers migrate to them because their marketing literature can boast that they have outperformed whatever share prices on average have done in the short term. So because the large financial institutions cannot be organized collectively, insisting that they must have the same rights to buy and sell as freely as any other shareholder, however small, and because they are at the same time very powerful, major companies have an unstable and demanding ownership base. In reality, of course, the principal investment institutions are too large to sell all their shares in the top 200 companies, because prices would collapse if they did so; but they reserve their right to do so, thus condemning the system to the worst of all possible worlds: the appearance but not the reality of liquidity. That appearance makes corporate organizations more peripatetic and short-termist in their business strategies in order to appease their short-termist owners. One result is the phenomenally high proportion of after-tax cashflow that companies pay out in dividends (an average of 50 percent in both Britain and the United States) or in buying back their own shares to support the price.

The markets' priorities cut to the quick of corporate decision making. In the United States, the story of Boeing and the rise and fall of the dot-coms are salutary enough; and Britain has its own share of disasters from applying the doctrine. The demise of GEC, one of Britain's leading manufacturing companies, as a result of the interplay of shareholder value and the financial markets' fads is one of the saddest. At the beginning of 1999 it sold its defense operations to raise a war chest to fund its transformation into what the financial markets at that time considered the fashion—a focused high-technology company. In order to justify the markets' expectations, it had to buy companies quickly rather than grow organically—and in April 1999 it splashed out $2.8 billion on buying the most fashionable company of all, an American producer of Internet switching equipment called Fore Systems. In May the chairman, George Simpson, told an investment conference that he would double GEC's value in three to five years, and in October the group was renamed Marconi.

The demands of the capital markets were overtly dictating Marconi's strategy, so that it was buying overpriced companies in the middle of the world's biggest financial bubble to assuage its shareholders' expectations. Research, creativity, and innovation were subordinated to one overarching aim: to double the stock price. As the dot-com and telecom bubble deflated, Marconi's orders fell—but worse, the companies it had bought proved worthless. In November 2001, two and half years after it was bought, Fore Systems was judged valueless and $2.8 billion was written off. By now Simpson and two other senior executives had left the company (with Simpson insisting on an extravagant golden parachute as a reward for his disastrous services), but the damage done was irreparable. By following the injunctions of maximizing shareholder value and obeying the markets' wishes, Marconi has cast its very future in doubt. In September 2002 it bowed to a bank-mandated restructuring that rendered its shares virtually worthless.

Marks & Spencer (M&S) is another sorry story. For decades the company had been a byword for value for money and quality in British retailing; it had a close relationship with its supply chain and state-of-the-art Main Street stores. The priority was the customer. But over the 1990s the gangrene of shareholder value began to infect this great British institution. The financial markets wanted ever higher margins and ever greater commitment to growth; M&S should do deals and it should squeeze its assets harder. Creativity and commitment to organic growth were downgraded; lifting the share price became the endgame. Instead of investing to be at the frontier of fashion, in 1997 the company paid Littlewoods £182 million for nineteen large center-city stores which would cost another £450 million to refurbish. The financial markets liked the signal of commitment to growth through deal making—but in fact it was symptomatic of a set of strategic priorities that would lay the company low.

Judi Bevan, author of *The Rise and Fall of Marks & Spencer*, writes that "a little at a time they [the executive directors] sacrificed the founding family principles of value, quality and service in the dash for profits."[18] Eventually the gradual loss of competitiveness and failure to invest in high-quality, fashionable products had their inevitable result: sales and profits fell. Three years of restructuring and shrinkage were to follow, involving the sale of the company's European and American operations. The new priorities were clear: the new executive chairman had a performance bonus closely linked to the share price, and the object was to shrink the company, selling sites at home and abroad, to raise £2 billion to give to shareholders. Twenty-five years of growth shuddered to a halt. If Marks & Spencer is now starting to recover, it is from a shrunken base and with its former commitment to creativity and quality much damaged. Shareholder value had again reduced a creative company to a dismal creature of profit maximization—paradoxically less capable of delivering high margins and profits than it had been when committed to the customer and a conception of quality. The fixation with increasing the share price enters the warp and woof of the organization. It becomes the fulcrum around which every facet of the company turns, dictating how budgets are set and negotiated, how performance plans are established, how the human relations functions are discharged, the priorities of research and development while setting demanding criteria for new investment with short payback times.

Corporate problems like these are never connected to the structure and culture of the capital markets by the conservative economic mainstream. McKinsey's report—and Stelzer's columns—are quintessential examples of this blindness, celebrating the "flexible" Anglo-Saxon capital markets as handmaidens of risk taking and enterprise, which reach their quintessential expression in the rise of venture capital. Yet, as O'Sullivan points out, there have been 3,500 venture-backed public offerings on the New York Stock Exchange since 1993, and even before the stock market fall in the spring of 2000 over half of them were trading below their offer price—an indication that many were essentially frivolous or brought to market too early. But on this, as on the structure and behavior of the financial system in general, there is a blind spot. Venture capitalists personify "enterprise"; they are part of a market-based financial system; therefore they are simply beyond reproach, and there can be no shortcomings in the way they function that they themselves would not recognize and correct. In McKinsey-land we must look to government and regulation for the sources of productivity weakness, not to the way the markets themselves are functioning—unless they are working "imperfectly," i.e., because of government and regulation. The European conception of organizations as having their own genetic codes out of which grow crucial social capabilities and needing to balance the interests of all their stakeholders in order to achieve high performance and innovation is not even on the radar.

Resurrecting the Public Realm and Discovering Europe

The conservative consensus spills over into the way public debate is conducted and defines what are considered to be the reasonable options of public policy. It has led the Conservative party to be characterized as hostile to society, disconnected from its own country. New Labour, for all its earnest desire to marry economic disciplines with genuine social progress, has more than half a foot in the same paradigm.

The Blair government certainly wants an improved range of social democratic outcomes, as do those who voted for it. It wants improved public services and more social cohesion. It wants less discrimination in every walk of life. It wants to promote a just capitalism in which companies take their obligations to their customers and workers more seriously while becoming more innovative and productive. It wants a stronger social safety net. More controversially, it also recognizes that Britain needs to be an active member of the European Union, because Britain as a European power needs to be part of an emerging continental market and party to the evolving European political conversation. None of these aims can be seriously doubted.

The problem is that it is attempting to achieve them while respecting the canons of American conservatism; for that is the route, it thinks, to relegitimizing the center-left while building a new coalition with the center. Thus it can make suitable obeisance to the new conservative common sense while trying to make stealthy social democratic advances. But there is more to it than that. Both Tony Blair and Gordon Brown have come to believe that there is enough that is correct about the conservative propositions to make it unnecessary to challenge them. So the political project at the heart of the third way is the attempt to marry two incompatible value systems—American conservatism and a modernized European social democracy. It is an exercise doomed to failure. Already there is a growing disconnection between the leadership of the Labour party and its natural constituency; without a change of course, the gap could become unbridgeable.

For the universe of ideas that supports notions of the enterprise culture cannot be made to serve a declared public interest or purpose; its very objective is to celebrate the primacy of markets and individualism over public endeavor and social goals. It is to substitute the private for the public. Business should be untrammeled and have no social claim or regulatory "burden" placed upon it. The third way reply does not dispute this point; rather, it argues that in practice business can be made to serve a public purpose, and that no reasonable person should object on principle to a service being owned publicly or privately. As long as the end result of public delivery is ensured, all that should matter is that the means are efficient and cost-effective.

It is a delusion. The advocacy and defense of the public realm is important in itself. This is an idea that should not be scrambled up and killed along with ideas of socialism and collectivism. It defines a universe of belonging, membership in which allows individuals to relate to society and society to them. It is this philosophy that opens up the notion that business is not solely about the exercise of property rights in the service of wealth creation; instead business has social capabilities and a social dimension that it must respect. It is through recognizing these facets that a different and richer conception of enterprise is opened up, one whose values connect to social democratic social goals. Put another way, this European conception of enterprise is underpinned by the same value system that underpins the establishment of the social contract—a value system epitomized by the Rawlsian idea of an infrastructure of justice.

This crucial idea of the public has been corrupted by the socialist legacy. Just as each act of nationalization was portrayed as another building block in the full-scale socialization of the means of production via "public" ownership, so each act of privatization is now hailed as a retreat from socialism and an advance towards full-blooded capitalism. This ideological discourse prevents straight thinking about the attributes some economic and social functions must have if we are to construct a just civil order.

The case for public education and health care clarifies the point. The universal provision of education to every child and access to health care of every citizen, irrespective of their capacity to pay, builds on the core Western belief that some institutions and processes in society must be universal in their scope—not as a precondition for socialism, but as part of the foundations of a humane civilization. European socialism did not choose to make this distinction, lumping together the establishment of universal education and health care with the public running of natural monopolies like water, gas, and electricity networks, and the nationalization of, say, coal, steel, and airline industries—all as uniform elements of the same socialist advance. They never were. Now that socialism is receding, American conservatism and the Washington consensus are trying to make the same claim in reverse. Just as socialism bundled a collection of disparate activities under one rubric, so privatization does the same; everything can be privatized. But it cannot. There are some activities that are irreducibly public in their scope and need to stay public.

This distinction is what is absent from New Labour's approach. It has accepted the proposition that publicly owned and run activity is necessarily inefficient, and that by moving to the McKinsey universe of free contracting and managerial direction incentivized by profits it will gain more value for every pound spent. It believes that, as long as the elected government of the day can specify the outcomes it wants, then it can preserve the public character of what is provided through regulation or clearly specified contracts.

In some areas, of course, this proposition holds. There is little public interest in the public ownership of a steel company. But this is not true in the building and sustaining of a national network—like rail or even broadband cable—where there are no immediate profits to be made and even long-run trading losses to be borne, but where the public interest demands that the network be universal in its reach, first-class in its quality, and equitable in the way it treats its users, who definitionally constitute the entire population. A national postal service must serve every household, wherever located; a national rail network must offer every citizen the ability to travel; a national broadband network must offer every user the same opportunity to be "wired." The privatization and fragmentation of British Rail and the inability to build a broadband cable network through private initiative both reveal the same truth. The character of some forms of enterprise requires public engagement, public direction, and even public ownership.

The case of the rail industry and the collapse of Railtrack (the name given British Rail after it was privatized) is important, for it shows that the formula of public regulation of a private company to achieve a public interest has failed. The narrow quest for operational efficiencies by thinning out layers of management, scaling back the workforce, lowering wages and eroding skills has hollowed out the rail infrastructure and made it less safe—witness the accidents at Paddington and Hatfield. The fragmentation of the industry into contracting parties—over twenty train-operating companies and Railtrack—raised costs as contractors sought to lift profit margins. On some estimates the cost of building and maintaining new track has trebled; the electrification and upgrade of the west coast line is costing £16 million per mile—three times as much as similar upgrades undertaken by British Rail.[19]

Railtrack, charged with investing in new rail infrastructure, never had a sufficiently large capital base to allow it to take on the billions of debt necessary to finance rail modernization. It needed continual government grants; yet after receiving them, its first obligation had to be to sustain its creditworthiness and stock market rating by paying dividends to its shareholders. It failed both as an innovative company and as a company discharging the public interest. Its collapse in September 2001 and replacement by a public interest company (Network Rail) with no obligation to pay dividends to shareholders was a seminal moment. By ensuring that the new company has the capacity to borrow and invest, and to direct the reintegration of the rail infrastructure with the train operating companies, the government is ensuring that the public interest is protected. This is not renationalization; it is securing the public realm and universality of provision in an economic activity where it would otherwise be lost.

A similar intervention is now required with the private finance initiative (PFI). This is an allegedly technical means of introducing private finance and management into the construction and maintenance of public assets—hospitals, prisons, and schools—in return for a fee paid over a thirty-year period. The argument is that the state gets better-managed assets that are funded off balance sheet; the means justify the end. But, as the left-of-center think tank the Institute for Public Policy Research pointed out in a critical report in 2001, *Building Better Partnerships*, the means *change* the end. The report usefully identifies three criteria that define "publicness," to which PFI contracts must, it argues, conform if they are not to change the character of the public service they are providing. They must be accountable to every citizen; they must protect social equity, so that they continue to maintain universality of access; and their improved efficiency must be won not at the expense of the terms and conditions of public sector workers, but through genuine organizational innovativeness brought by a private sector approach.[20] Judged on these criteria, very few PFI contracts in the NHS would have gone forward. They offered little or no genuine increased efficiency to compensate for increased financing costs—indeed, on some calculations construction costs were almost twice the original estimate.[21] Most hospitals were smaller than the publicly owned and funded hospitals they replaced, and tended to have none of the "expensive" attributes—like accident and emergency departments or beds for the long-term sick—of publicly run hospitals because those would menace the financial returns the PFI contractors sought. Organizational innovativeness has meant no more than brutal cost minimization. The means had changed the ends. In some areas of the public service, notably prison provision, standards had fallen so low that the PFI has produced improved outcomes. But this cannot be taken as the axiomatic, general truth to which the Washington consensus and its faithful followers in London lay claim.

Once policy makers enter the conservative paradigm, none of these subtleties is admissible. Rather like McKinsey recommending a relaxation of planning laws to boost productivity because it defines all problems in the terms of American conservatism, New Labour has trapped itself into conceptualizing the problem of public service delivery as how to introduce as much private enterprise as possible into the public sector while preserving its public character. But the real question is different. It should be how to organize the public sector so that it is organizationally creative, rigorously run, well led, and properly funded. The private sector might be an effective agent of change or a subcontractor to help achieve these ends, but it cannot and should not be expected to become a surrogate public sector. That is not what it is set up to do.

The same conflict infects New Labour's social policy. The great fight in the first half of the twentieth century was to win citizens a basic income so they could avoid destitution in the face of life's hazards—unemployment, illness, and disability—and the certainty of old age. This was portrayed as a social citizenship right to match the political rights so hard fought for over the previous century. The goal was to offer every citizen the opportunity to participate in the life of society, whatever his or her circumstances. This was described as the welfare state: the collective underwriting of risk to ensure that everyone could express their humanity.

Here again ascendant American conservatism has spread its baleful influence. The social contract should not, it insists, be expressed as a system of social insurance which brings entitlements to all citizens. Instead, entitlements should be conditional, means-tested and meager. In Britain the principle now spreads from disability benefits to pensions; do not expect a basic income from the state to support you without some form of means test to ensure you are deserving. The notion that as a citizen you have a right to participate in society through being offered a basic income is dead; it is too expensive for the Treasury, implies higher taxes, and might undermine your moral character. Where possible you should undertake your own provision in the private sector, which will necessarily be more efficient.

It is not. Take pensions. One of the proudest boasts of Britain's political class is that Britain, unlike mainland Europe, is not sitting on an expensive pension time bomb. Future pension funding is going to prove expensive if the retirement age remains the same as the population becomes proportionally older. Historically, Britain has shared the costs of provision among the state, the corporation, and the individual. As understanding has grown about future funding problems, both the government and companies have been withdrawing their support. Britain is avoiding the pension time bomb only because it has largely privatized the problem and is prepared to accept relative pensioner poverty.

The government is allowing the basic pension gradually to wither away, indexing it only to the increase in retail prices rather than to average earnings; all the government will agree to do is to provide a safety net for the poor in retirement, pitched at a level well below the standards of living available as a citizen's entitlement elsewhere in Europe. To ensure a decent retirement income each individual must save and invest through a company pension fund or private pension plan managed by an insurance company. The pensions thus provided depend on share prices remaining buoyant to drive up the value of accumulated savings, along with interest rates staying high so that the annuities bought with the investments provide a solid income. Neither precondition holds, so that if the current cohort of savers wants to achieve the same pension as those retiring today they will have to save twice as much.

But that is not the state's concern. People must look after themselves, even if the insurance company through which they might save—like Equitable Life—turns out not to be able to honor its promises. The Equitable cut its pension benefits by 16 percent for 900,000 savers as a result of a miscalculation it made in the mid-1980s; others will doubtless do the same as investment returns fall generally. The number of companies operating pension funds in which they promise to pay a pension linked to final salary has fallen by three-quarters in just seven years; they are too expensive given low interest rates and modest investment performance. This is a devastating collapse that will have a disastrous impact on the income of future British pensioners for which they are completely unprepared.[22]

Not only are companies closing their final salary pension plans; they are lowering their contributions to the replacement plans in which pensions are completely dependent on the performance of the stock market and interest rates. To compensate, individuals need to raise their own contributions to 10 percent or more of their salary if they want reasonable retirement incomes—equivalent to lifting the basic rate of income tax by 10 percent. If they are saving wholly by themselves, they should be putting aside at least £15 out of every £100 they earn for their entire working life—and even then their pension will be very modest and unpredictable, dependent on the vagaries of the stock market and interest rates.

Yet in the Panglossian world of the conservative, none of this should be happening. Only the state does not keep its promises; the private sector always does, and it is morally better for individuals to act for themselves rather than act collectively. New Labour is at least attempting some improvement in pension provisions by offering a minimum retirement income guarantee, so that those who have no savings or private pension at least do not have to rely on the now impossibly low state pension; yet this minimum guarantee, in proportion to average earnings, is still well below what is offered in mainland Europe. Worse, it penalizes those pensioners who, on low incomes, have saved all their lives but whose resulting private pension only brings them up to the guarantee level. They get nothing. But the state is not interested in fairness, or offering a square deal to its citizens; it wants to save money.

What would be fairer and more cost-effective, and offer a predictable pension, would be a nationally run social insurance system to coexist with private saving—exactly like the plan hammered out by Barbara Castle when she was secretary of state for Social Security in the mid-1970s. This was the use of the state to improve the condition of the people in a social contract—now deemed impossible, intellectually, ideologically, and financially. The British state has avoided the pension time bomb only by displacing risk, misery, and poverty onto the next generation of pensioners. If the Europeans have a problem, it is because they plan to treat their pensioners properly.

Yet Britons want to retain their social contract; they even want to improve it. If they understood the pensions issue, they would want a European-style pay-as-you-go state pension rather than the lottery they are offered. They want improved delivery of all public services, and they understand the limitations of asking the private sector to assume public responsibilities. They certainly want an improved public transportation system, and are beginning to ask hard questions about why Britain seems incapable of providing it. They are, in short, very European.

And, as the debate about raising British productivity and economic performance rages, it is worth noting that few European companies are suffering the calamities that have afflicted Marconi and Marks & Spencer. Europeans have economic and social structures that create more high-performance, world-class companies and many fewer disasters. Yet all this is only insecurely and uncertainly understood on either Downing Street or in the wider British business, economic, and financial establishment. The British campaign, almost laughable under the circumstances, is to persuade the mainland Europeans to emulate the British and recast their economies and societies along the lines preached by American conservatives so that Britain can live with EU membership more easily—and the EU can improve its economic and social performance.

To mock this stance is not to argue that every aspect of the European model works perfectly. Yet if Britain is to make reforms, they should conform to core European values and principles that, as I will show in the next chapter, work demonstrably better than our own. Only if this is grasped wholeheartedly can Britain make a success of its membership in the EU and of shaping its own economy and society in the way that our people and our history require. For we share our distinct values with our fellow Europeans.

The march of the American conservative right and the eclipse of American liberalism have helped to undermine Britain's own distinct conceptions of the public realm, citizenship, and the proper relationship between the market and society. It is time Britain recognized that Europe has something very important to offer—something much better than the United States. And if the British can make this recognition, so too should mainstream Americans.

8
Europe Works

British and American commentators have been administering last rites over the European economic and social model ever since British and U.S. unemployment began to fall in the early 1990s while Europe's stayed stubbornly high, falling only toward the end of the decade. European "stakeholder capitalism" is being gradually dismantled, runs the argument. The vital disciplines of the stock market are being gradually imposed through an enlargement of their role and adoption of the principle of maximizing shareholder value, while overexpensive, featherbedding welfare states are scaled back. The European model is being compelled to converge with the American model both because of the remorseless logic of having to match the latter's economic efficiency and because of pressure from global investors, notably pension funds, insisting that if European companies want access to capital on the same terms, then the rules that favor them in the United States and Britain will have to be reproduced in Europe. Above all, change is necessary to lower unemployment, the price Europeans pay for ignoring the injunctions of laissez-faire economics and persisting with their inflexible labor markets and rigged capital markets.

It is true that European companies today are taking the interests of shareholders more seriously than formerly, whether as a result of the Vienot report in France, arguing for more transparency and fewer defensive cross-shareholdings,[1] or of the new "Eichel law" in Germany, that will allow the disposal of cross-shareholdings without incurring capital gains tax. The British mobile phone firm Vodafone's successful hostile $200 billion takeover bid for Mannesman in 2000 was hailed as further evidence of the trend. Equally, budgetary pressure and persistent unemployment are forcing retrenchment of the welfare state, and most European countries are focusing on tax, benefits, and training policies that make work pay, closing down the scope for individual workers voluntarily to remain unemployed for sustained periods. American conservatives contentedly assure themselves they are winning the argument.

But what is actually impressive is less the unequivocal march toward the American model, and more the degree to which Europeans are updating the best of the old in new conditions and discarding only what is plainly redundant. The social contract conception remains at the heart of the European attitude towards employment regulation and the character of the welfare state. And while more care is being taken not to disadvantage shareholders in a globalizing capital market, European businesses still fight to retain the notion that the interests and capabilities of the entire business must come first, and that shareholders should not become an overprivileged sectional interest group. Moreover, as we will explore later in this chapter, high unemployment originates more in lack of overall demand than in the price of labor market regulation.

The value of shares quoted on European stock markets may have risen strongly over the 1980s and 1990s, with British and American pension funds and insurance companies proportionally increasing their ownership—but there is nothing like the same "market for corporate control" that exists in the United States and the UK. Nor is there likely to be; for what is striking is that European companies retain their commitment to organic growth rather than financial engineering along Anglo-Saxon lines. Over the 1990s there were only nine hostile takeovers in France, and seven in Germany; dividend distributions remain low; and comparatively little money is raised directly from the stock market. Mannesmann was uniquely exposed to takeover—it courted foreign ownership of its shares, so that 40 percent were held by overseas institutions; no other German company approaches such a high percentage.

Europe's economic and social model lives. Certainly it is under continuing pressure from both the capital markets and conservative propagandists, and part of Europe's business and financial elite is increasingly attracted by the glittering universe of American capitalism with its dazzling incomes for senior executives and glamorous deal making. Yet again, what is remarkable is how much stands in the face of pressure and temptation alike. For example, the aligning of the interests of executives and shareholders in share option plans, now developing in both France and Germany, is much more modest in scope—and the criteria for earning such benefits are much more long-term and demanding than in the United States. As America reappraises its approach to stock options and executive compensation, Europe's determination to stand by its model is likely to harden.

The distinctive European approach to capitalism is deeply embedded, and Europe's economic and social institutions and values are widely respected—even venerated. The various countries of Europe have outwardly different structures of capitalism, but what they hold in common is far greater than what divides them. And what they all have at their core is the high-investment, high-performance enterprise.

European Enterprise at Work

Volkswagen should be a basket case. It manufactures cars and trucks in high-cost Germany. It has a highly unionized workforce that works a 28.8-hour week for up to $35 an hour. Its largest shareholder is the state government of Lower Saxony, which owns 18.6 percent of the company's shares. It has a cumbersome supervisory board on which both the trade unions and the regional government are represented. Its directors have only a small number of share options, and its chief executive is paid under $1 million a year—a tiny fraction of the $32 million and $22 million made by his counterparts at Ford and General Motors. The total value of stock options available to every VW employee in 2000 in aggregate was $1.7 million; when Jacques Nasser ceased to work as CEO of Ford he alone had over $16 million of unexercised stock options. Worse, VW shareholders' voting rights are limited to 20 percent, so the company can neglect to promote shareholder value, allowing it to become sclerotic and uncompetitive. It is under no threat of takeover unless its system of voting rights is changed.

There is scarcely a canon in the conservative free-market rule book that Volkswagen does not offend. It was only in 2001 that it prepared accounts conforming to international standards, and although it acknowledged that it was going to change its focus from sales maximization to achieving the highest possible stock market value of the group, this was not done because it believed in the primacy of shareholder rights; rather, it was because in a world in which creditworthiness and even reputation are so closely linked to the markets' judgments, having a higher share price was better than having a low share price. It pays only 16 percent of its posttax earnings as dividends, retaining the rest to support its enormous investment in R&D, which at 4.8 percent of turnover is higher than Ford (4.0 percent) and General Motors (3.6 pe cent).[2]

Yet Volkswagen remains Europe's largest car maker and has increased its market share from 16 to 19 percent since 1993—largely at the expense of Ford and General Motors. Even in the United States its market share has jumped by 2 percent over the same period. It is the most internationalized car company in the world. It has revived the near-bankrupt Czech car manufacturer Skoda. Its Passats and Golfs, redesigned VW Beetle, and range of new cars are the envy of its rivals. Its engineering prowess and innovativeness are miles ahead of its American competitors: the VW Golf, Bora, New Beetle, Audi A3, Audi TT, Seat Toledo, and Skoda Octavia all have the same A4 platform, sharing a single chassis, engine, gearbox, power train, gearshift, and air-conditioning system—a degree of engineering excellence well ahead of its American competition.[3] According to the predictions of American conservatives, none of this should be happening. VW should be down and out.

Or take tire maker Michelin in France. This is a firm that, 112 years after it was formed, is still dominated by the family whose some 250 members own around a third of its stock; its current chief executive, Edouard Michelin, is the son of another Michelin, François. It has to deal with the communist trade union, the CGT, and to operate within the allegedly crippling confines of the thirty-five-hour week, recently introduced in France. Like Volkswagen, it pays its chief executive and directors a fraction of the salaries of their American competitors at Goodyear. And, like Volkswagen, it has not given top priority to the promotion of shareholder value; its declared aims are to be at the technological forefront of tire manufacture and to sustain its market position. Dividends were only 26 percent of depressed earnings in 2000, with the more typical ratio well below 20 percent. It invented the first car tire in 1895 and the first radial tire in 1946, and its latest contribution is the Pax—a tire that can function even when punctured. Michelin tires are used by five of the eleven Formula One Racing teams; when the Concorde needed a new foolproof tire after the disastrous crash in Paris in which all the crew and passengers died, it turned to Michelin to find an answer. Michelin spends 4.2 percent of sales on R&D compared with Goodyear's 2.9 percent.[4] What should be another basket case is the technological leader of world tire manufacture. Before Goodyear bought Sumitomo, it was also the world's largest tire manufacturer; it remains the largest in Europe. Yet according to conservative theorists it should be on the road to competitive extinction.

And then there is Finland's Nokia, the world's leading mobile phone company. This is another corporation that should not exist, and has dared to challenge the principles of capitalism as set out by the ideologues of the enterprise culture. Originally a wood-processing and rubber-boot company, Nokia started the 1990s worrying about how its toilet-paper sales would hold up in its main market—the former Soviet Union. High levels of Finnish taxation should have dampened this company's ambitions from the start, and if that didn't trap it, powerful trade unions should have finally sealed its fate. Nearly half of its 60,000 global labor force work in high-wage Finland, a country encumbered with monstrous charges—in conservative eyes—to finance its generous and incentive-depleting welfare state. Nor does it pay especially high executive salaries which, even with the addition of share-option plans, are severely reduced by penal Finnish tax rates on high earners. Chief executive Jorma Ollila was paid $1,250,000 before stock options in 2001; G. R. Wagoner Jr., his counterpart at Motorola, the number two in the mobile phone market, received over $2.5 million with some $9 million in unexercised stock options. Yet Nokia has managed to keep together the senior management team that over the past decade has directed the company's exponential growth.

Nokia's success is legendary. It has 35 percent of the world mobile phone market—more than twice its nearest rival Motorola—and its track record for innovation, commitment to design, and effective management of its 150 subcontractors is second to none. Dan Steinbock in *The Nokia*

Revolution quotes one key Nokia manager as saying: "Using traditional financial measures is liking driving a car by looking at the rearview mirror . . . for us there are three basic critical success factors: customer satisfaction, operations efficiency and people involvement."[5] Steinbock adds that at Nokia innovation is not thought of as the preserve of the R&D or product development departments; "instead, it has been thought of as something that can and should pertain to the entire value chain." Yet for an ideological commentator like Irwin Stelzer the company should have no right to trade at all, let alone successfully.

These three companies are representatives of three of the more distinct of Europe's economic and social models—the German social market model, the French statist model, and the Scandinavian social democratic model (all discussed in chapter 9). The cities in which they are headquartered, Wolfsburg, Clermont-Ferrand, and Helsinki, are recognizably German, French, and Finnish, and each company culture resolutely reflects its country of origin. Yet each is a global force with a superlative track record of technological and organizational creativity. And each challenges the precepts for successful enterprise as defined by American conservatism. They are largely insulated from takeover except on their own terms; their executive teams are not fully aligned with shareholders' interests; unions are powerful and workers are protected; taxes are high, and the work week is short and regulated. Nor are they alone. The same success story could have been told in relation to a leading German chemicals company (Bayer) or a French industrial gases company (Air Liquide); representatives abound across Europe—as they must, given the region's astonishing record in investment and productivity growth. Nothing should be less surprising given the buildup of European investment over the past thirty years; while the U.S. capital stock grew a mere 65 percent between 1965 and 1991, Italy's grew 130 percent, France's 150 percent and Germany's 175 percent.[6] On the basis of trends in investment over the past ten years, the differential will remain the same or widen. European capitalism has a vitality and dynamism wholly disallowed by the conservative consensus.

But Volkswagen, Michelin, and Nokia are not goody two-shoes. They are unambiguously capitalist. Michelin has halved its workforce in Clermont-Ferrand over the past fifteen years and has not hesitated to close factories or curtail production when necessary; when it announced 7,500 lay-offs after a profit increase in 1999 it was condemned by France's socialist prime minister, Lionel Jospin, for its capitalist insensitivity. Volkswagen has bargained toughly with its workforce to hire new workers on considerably poorer terms than its existing German employees in order to stay competitive, while Nokia will not be able to survive the downturn in mobile phone sales without layoffs and retrenchment. Each is mindful of the need to sustain profits and avoid losses. The notion that they are in any way "socialist" is risible.

Yet, as capitalist enterprises, they conduct themselves very differently from their American competitors, each embodying the European sensibility that its job is to remain faithful to the organization's fundamental mission—in these three cases, respectively to make the best cars, tires and mobile phones—and it is prosecuting that mission by integrating all their stakeholders into the whole that will enable their organizations to grow sustainably and make profits over time. Their shareholders are but one vital part of the organization—not the masters to whom every part of the company must be subservient—and, moreover, they and the directors have wider obligations to the society of which they are part. Although each company comes from a different society and culture, they all provide similar answers to the basic question whether property rights in a capitalist society should be exercised wholly self-interestedly and autonomously. The answer, in all three countries, is a decisive No. In each, laws of corporate association have developed, along with a network of supportive financial institutions, that permit the interests of the whole organization to come before the sole interests of the property holders—the shareholders.

Moreover, that formal requirement is supported by a corporate and managerial culture personified in each case by the chief executive and senior management team. Volkswagen's chief executive from 1993 to 2001, Ferdinand Piesch; Nokia's CEO from 1992 to the present day, Jorma Ollila; Michelin's Edouard Michelin—each is steeped in the organization he leads and in what is required to sustain its technological and market leadership. These are not chief executives on the U.S. model, holding office on average for four years or less, charged overtly above all to maximize shareholder value; these are chief executives who set out to husband their companies to a position of sustained market leadership over time, and who are buttressed in that objective by their countries' rules of corporate governance, legal structures, and banking systems. They want to make profits and can be as hard as nails; and the organizations they lead are as capable of cutting corners, manipulating markets, and lobbying for special favors as any other capitalist enterprise. That is the nature of the beast. But the structures and cultures in which they operate drive them toward business building rather than financial engineering. Robust and sometimes painful decisions are taken in the service of the organization and the communities in which it is embedded—not primarily in the interests of the shareholders.

The first precondition for this approach lies in the way shareholders interpret the rights attached to property ownership and how those are shaped by law. Essentially, in each of the three systems highlighted here, the institutional, legal, and cultural framework permits managers to put the needs of the organization—constrained, obviously, by the competitive exigencies of the marketplace—before the demands of any one stakeholder group, notably those of shareholders. This offers each enterprise a twofold advantage. First, it defines an overall ownership culture which new shareholders, including those of British and American pension funds, must accept in the act of buying shares. Dividend distributions, for example, are set in terms of the overall financial needs of the company rather than driven by the need to conform to shareholder priorities. The payout ratio of dividends to earnings for these three companies varies between a fifth and a third—around the European average, and a fraction of that among their American counterparts, where the average is close to 80 percent (see below). Corporate law erects legal obstacles to the process of hostile takeover bids; in Germany voting rights may be restricted, for example, and in France the freedom for holders of bearer shares to remain anonymous may make it impossible for a hostile bidder to assess the chances of success in a bid because he or she does not know the identity of the shareholders and whether they support the incumbent management. Again, French company law permits companies to reward loyal longstanding shareholders with a double vote, or to give the founding family or trust a golden share with overriding voting rights; more than two-thirds of the top 200 French companies allocate double votes to longstanding shareholders.[7] Without the support of the president director general (PDG), a successful hostile takeover is very difficult to mount.

Second, the existence of this institutional, cultural, and legal framework allows the organization to manage its shareholder structure to give it a stable platform on which it can rely in good times and bad. Both Volkswagen, with the stake held by Lower Saxony and the 20 percent limit on shareholder voting rights, and Michelin, taking advantage of the French corporate law that allows it to be established as a *compagnie générale des établissements*, with a third of the shares held by the family and also operating shareholder voting right restrictions, can thus ensure that a critical mass of shareholders will stay invested in the company for the long term. At different times in the 1990s the trading prospects of both Michelin and Volkswagen would have made them vulnerable to takeover had their corporate governance and share structure been organized along American lines; both retained their independence and have subsequently flourished. Until 1998 Nokia took advantage of Finnish company law that allows voting rights to be restricted to a privileged group of friendly shareholders; but with some 90 per cent of its nonvoting shares held by overseas investors and under pressure to cater to Wall Street's prejudices this became untenable, and now it has one class of shares with equal voting rights. However, the company's embeddedness in Finland, its unique managerial culture and track record, and its market leadership provide it with a strong bulwark against takeover. It is now big enough to argue that its own style gives shareholders the value they seek—but it needed Finnish protection to reach this position of strength.

The conservative consensus attacks this approach across the board. The first criticism is that, because being a shareholder in such an enterprise is unattractive compared to other investments, European companies will progressively suffer from a shortage of willing investors so they have to pay a premium to attract them. Their cost of capital will rise. Nor is it easy for them to engage in big international takeovers, because shareholders in target companies—especially in Britain and America—will prefer to sell to companies who take their obligations to shareholders more seriously. Worse still, the lack of threat of hostile takeover and complacency about the need to make profits will featherbed senior directors and managers.

They will not hunt aggressively for deals and efficiency in production. They will take the soft option in negotiations with powerful unions. They will be less hungry and enterprising.

This is a naive view about organizational productivity, as argued in chapters 5 and 7, and plainly ignorant about the sources and cost of external finance. Over the last two decades the American stock market has been a trivial source of capital for American enterprise. Between 1952 and 1995 in the United States, for example, 90 percent of capital expenditure in nonfinancial enterprises was financed internally by the companies themselves rather than raised through issuing shares. Between 1981 and 1996 U.S. nonfinancial enterprises actually bought $700 billion more in shares through stock buyback programs and takeovers than they issued to finance investment. And the stock market makes a huge claim on profits; between 1990 and 1995 firms paid out 78 percent of their after-tax profits in dividends.[8] Whatever else it does, promoting the interests of stock markets and shareholders does not deliver cheap and plentiful capital.

Indeed, as argued in chapter 4, it does the opposite. The paradox of creating a market in which the direction and management of companies can be contested through hostile takeover is that it creates an increasingly insupportable burden on companies. Internally generated funds are largely earmarked for shareholders as dividends or share buybacks. Payback on investment has to be fast. Overall investment levels have to be lower. When an economic downturn occurs or the company faces a competitive challenge, it has to place the shareholders' interests before the organization's—holding up dividends but cutting investment, for example. Neither Volkswagen nor Nokia nor Michelin could have established and maintained its technological and design leadership in an American context, any more than Boeing has managed to do.

For the stock market–shareholder value nexus raises the cost of capital and compels the company to make its top strategic objective keeping the share price as high as possible. Recall, too, the evidence marshaled in chapter 4 about the terrible record of failure following takeovers and mergers. One of the reasons plausibly advanced for Europe's high productivity is that the "market for corporate control" is so undeveloped. Thus the only reliable way to buy a company is to secure the agreement of its directors and senior managers—the precondition for the successful marriage of cultures that is difficult enough to achieve when integrating any two companies, and virtually impossible if one company has been the prey of the other in a hostile takeover. Restructuring is driven by economic need rather than deal makers' expectations of fast profits.

Independence from the stock market is not just about the ownership structure; it is about companies' capacity to look to the banking system for long-term finance. European companies, like their American counterparts, raise the vast bulk of finance for expansion through their own internally generated cashflow: over 80 percent of German investment is typically financed from internal funds. Supplementary long-term finance is raised from the banks, which in France, Germany, and Scandinavia have played a crucial role—augmented in the German case from the vast pool of savings built up as the in-house pension reserve, safeguarded from fraud or by the fate of Enron's pension fund by compulsory reinsurance with the great German reinsurance companies. These banks are prepared to offer long-term committed loans, financing gaps and allowing European enterprises to capitalize upon being relatively free from takeover and take a longer-term developmental approach to building their businesses.

European companies plainly watch their share price, but they do not see it as the key driver in determining their fortunes. For example, Volkswagen's memorandum setting out how it intends to organize its internal financial control system to maximize the Volkswagen share price is revealing. The company assumes that a 13-percent cost of equity—no more and no less—is reasonable, given shareholders' expectations, and says that in the future it will organize its pricing and investment strategy to offer this return—but adds, "It is not intended to adjust the cost of capital continuously to short-term fluctuations in the financial markets."[9] This is not the pursuit of shareholder value as understood in the United States. Volkswagen seeks, as an international company in an era of financial deregulation and globalization, to offer shareholders a better deal to reflect their growing power; but only as one group among many key stakeholders whose interests have to be balanced in the interests of the organization as a whole. They should expect 13 percent; no more, no less. The expectation in Britain, by contrast, is to earn 20 percent.

All three countries' banking systems were developed to support the growth of industry and commerce, and again, although the relationships are loosening, they still exist. France's big bank groupings have historically had a close relationship with the French state, and were even nationalized after World War II before being subsequently privatized in the 1980s and 1990s, while Germany developed a more complex relationship of public savings and investment banks at the regional or *Land* level, with an industrial refinancing arm—the Kreditanstalt für Wiederaufbau—at the national level. With a commercial arm that has built close relationships with its customers in order to develop confidence in their borrowing policies and supported the relationship by taking shares, Germany's banking system has been a ready supplier of long-term finance to business on a scale even greater than its counterpart in France. Despite all the talk of reform and a greater equity culture, only 18 percent of the liabilities of German companies is owed to shareholders today—exactly the same proportion as twenty years ago.[10] The Scandinavian countries' industrial banks follow the German model: for example, the Swedish government still has a 25 percent stake in MeritaNordbanken, the largest commercial bank, which was established in the nineteenth century explicitly to channel Swedish savings to industrial development, and still retains that culture.

All three banking systems strive to create long-term relationships with business borrowers in order to serve each client's credit needs as an organization; this provides a more reliable market for the bank, allowing it to build a portfolio of loans in which it has confidence, and provides a crucial financing ally for business. The more the company can borrow paying predictable interest rates and the less it has to rely on issuing shares where it has to pay a risk premium, the lower its overall cost of capital—and the more investment it can undertake. Moreover, if it has a platform of stable ownership it can take a strategic view of its direction, knowing that there will be a powerful payback from its investment in research and people alike. Together, these are the institutions and processes that support a culture of production and wealth creation, in sharp contrast to the American conception of wealth generation as primarily about deal making and pure buying and selling in markets. It is a profound dichotomy.

Airbus—a Case Study

Airbus represents perhaps the quintessential expression of European attitudes toward production and technology—and also the point at which the gulf between the European and American approaches is most public and uncomprehending. From the U.S. point of view this project is the creature of protracted government subsidy and protection—yet for Europeans it embodies their distinct approach to enterprise. In 1967 the French, German, and British governments committed themselves to a long-term vision of building an organization dedicated to civil aerospace production and technology, which Europe needed as a counterweight to the de facto monopoly supplier Boeing, and whose ownership structures and managerial culture were to be designed to serve the organization rather than maximize short-term profits. Now, in the first decade of the twenty-first century, the Europeans are reaping the fruits of a commitment sustained over more than thirty years.

To design, build, and develop a fleet of state-of-the-art civil aircraft was always going to be a long-term task. It would require shareholders prepared to defer their returns for perhaps decades. It would require, as the American aerospace industry had received through defense contracts and tax rebates from export rates, billions of dollars of grants to support the public interest in possessing an aircraft manufacturer that the markets could not create spontaneously themselves. The time horizons for the returns on equity investment and private bank debt are extraordinarily short-term compared to the time needed to develop an aircraft business. It was only the capacities of the European enterprise model that allowed Airbus to be contemplated for a moment—capacities that the British never understood, thus condemning them to the smallest role in the enterprise, one which even then they very nearly forfeited. In 1969 the British pulled out of the consortium, reentering only in 1978 when Airbus had successfully made its first American sale to Eastern Airlines; the ideological and political wobble reduced its stake from an equal third to only 20 percent. Yet even that minority holding has proved a good investment.

To get Airbus started required a corporate structure that would not enthrone the interests of private shareholders and which could mix flows of grants and loans freely in order to serve the needs of the organization. French corporate law provided the answer in the idea of a *groupe d'intérêt économique* (GIE), a form of incorporation whose overt purpose is to grow an organization rather than produce returns for shareholders—a constitutional impossibility in the United States. Ever since the establishment of Airbus the American criticism has been that massive subsidies, together with the French and German governments' insistence that Air France and Lufthansa, respectively, buy Airbus planes, have given the consortium a protected market. In the late 1980s the Gellman Research Associates report commissioned by the U.S. government alleged that since its establishment Airbus had received $13.1 billion in 1990 prices from its government shareholders and that it had repaid only $500 million of $25.8 billion of loans that it has raised over its life.

The numbers were probably exaggerated, even if correctly signaling the broad scale and nature of the support, and Airbus's deliberately opaque accounts did not permit an authoritative rebuttal. However, if Airbus has received a subsidy, so have Boeing and McDonnell Douglas. Between 1978 and 1988 the U.S. firms received over $10 billion in research grants from the Pentagon and a further $13 billion in indirect support. Boeing's defense contracts alone, with their guaranteed profit margins, were worth $40 billion over the 1980s. Without some form of government subsidy, aircraft production and development, which can take decades to become profitable and where upfront costs can run into billions, is impossible on either side of the Atlantic. The Americans chose to offer their subsidy through an ongoing relationship between defense contractor and government that they considered legitimate; what they consider illegitimate is to give a subsidy in such a way that a business plan that the markets would not sanction becomes operational.

Boeing's dependence on subsidy was thrown into sharp relief by the success of its lobbying efforts after September 11 and the consequent sharp fall in demand for civilian airliners. Its Washington office, headed up by Rudy F. de Leon, former undersecretary of defense under Clinton, went into overdrive. Congress agreed to a $20 billion deal, leasing 100 new widebodied unsalable 767s to the U.S. Air Force; there will be a major military aircraft renewal program after the campaign in Afghanistan; Boeing is pressing for corporate tax rebates; and new R&D work is being undertaken on military prototypes, in particular unmanned aircraft. Boeing is as much a client of government as Airbus, if not more so.

At the heart of the dispute are the twin issues of time horizons and the character of corporate sustainability. Airbus, after thirty years, has dropped its GIE status and become a single corporation with publicly quoted shares. It prepares accounts to international standards and makes a profit. Its family of civilian aircraft is technologically advanced and, as Ivan Pitt and John Norsworthy say, offers airlines around the world "lower operating costs, a new generation of technology, spacious cabins and onboard avionics."[11] By providing competition, in future it will prevent Boeing from charging the same monopoly prices for new aircraft that it set on the jumbo, the 747, throughout the 1970s, 1980s, and 1990s. Its capacity to operate independently of the time horizons of the capital markets means that it can find the $12 billion it needs to build the A380, the superjumbo, offering airlines and passengers technological possibilities for cheap air travel that would otherwise not exist. It has enriched the technological depth of the European aircraft industry. U.S. suppliers also benefit; Airbus spends $5 billion a year with American subcontractors.

In production and design style Airbus is fundamentally different from Boeing. The U.S. company, as described in chapter 4, has been unable to husband its workforce, design capacity, and production infrastructure before the demands of Wall Street. It suffers from production bottlenecks as a result of reducing its overhead to provide the required short-term returns. It has had to reduce risk, contracting out production to other suppliers and thus weakening its central productive capacity; the long-distance version of the 777, for example, part of which was built in Japan, went into service late because of difficulties in coordinating the size of the plane with the necessary jet engines—and as a result lost further ground to Airbus's A330 and now A340. Meanwhile Airbus, because it has the necessary financial muscle, can retain control of the central production process and collaborates around a central purpose to gain knowledge, skills, and expertise. This, it believes, is the key to its success. Like Volkswagen, Nokia, and Michelin, it is dedicated to production and engineering excellence, and its wider constitutional structures support this mission.

In order to achieve its success it has had to take a thirty-year rather

than a three-year view of profitability; and that in turn has meant a declaration of independence from the criteria for liquidity and profitability
set by the capital markets. It has had to put the interests of building
planes, fighting for orders, and pleasing customers before the demand for
dividends. In the conservative discourse this subsidized aircraft manufacturer, free from the disciplines of the financial markets, should be a
failure, along with Nokia, Volkswagen, and Michelin. On the contrary,
Airbus is the most successful aircraft manufacturer in the world. Europeans can be proud, and look their tormentors in the eye. Their system
works.

So What about European Unemployment?

The overwhelming blight on Europe's record, undermining its self-
confidence and seeming to validate the conservative critique, is its indifferent performance over the 1990s on increasing employment and
reducing unemployment. But, as mentioned in chapter 7, in the late 1990s
job creation in France, Italy, and Germany began to contrast favorably
with trends in both Britain and the United States, disproving the notion
that there is something intrinsic about the European labor market that
condemns it to never-ending high unemployment. It is wrong to concep-
tualize joblessness as resulting purely from the Europeans' mistaken desire
to extend ideas of the social contract to the labor market, burdening it with
charges and regulations so that it cannot sustain high employment. The
OECD, for example, finds that the degree of European employment protection "has little or no effect on overall unemployment" and, to the degree
that it has any impact, affects the demographic distribution of work rather
than its overall level.[12] Another study finds that the nonemployment rate for
men age twenty-five to fifty-four over the period 1988–95 was 11.9 percent
in the United States (excluding the very high U.S. incarceration rate in
prison) and averaged 11.7 percent in Germany, Italy, and France.[13] Where
the United States has scored over Europe has been in the creation of jobs
for women; but, as argued earlier (see chapter 5), that has more to do with
the feminist revolution coming earlier to the United States than Europe, so
that women's desire and willingness to work, along with society's struc-

tures and attitudes, are more advanced. Moreover, many American women have gone to work because of household need, and strong consumer demand has created the opportunities.

None of the conservative explanations for unemployment holds water. For example, the leading German economist Fritz Scharpf, in the definitive study on the relationship between the welfare state and unemployment, proves that unemployment is unconnected to the level of social spending.[14] While it may be true that the United States and Japan have achieved high employment with low social spending, it is also true that the Scandinavian countries have achieved high employment with high social spending and generous levels of income support for the unemployed. More significantly, if the sectors of the economy that are exposed to international competition are isolated, his study still shows zero correlation between the level of social spending and unemployment. In fact, in those sectors, the United States has the same employment rate as France, and a lower employment rate than Austria and Germany! Therefore, the size of a welfare state and generosity of unemployment benefits have no impact at all on employment, and the lack of international competitiveness is not the cause of European unemployment.[15] If anything, writes Scharpf, "the countries with the highest levels of employment in the internationally exposed sectors of the economy are characterized by stakeholder-oriented forms of corporate governance and by cooperative industrial relations that differ significantly from American (and British) forms of shareholder-oriented corporate governance and deregulated labor markets."[16]

Next there is the commonplace assumption by many American critics that the pattern of demand in the new knowledge economy favors skilled rather than unskilled workers, that the burden of regulation and strong unions borne by Europe has prevented its unskilled workers from pricing themselves into low-paying jobs—and that this is the chief cause of high unemployment. Scharpf refutes this thesis, too—and so does almost every scholar who examines the figures closely. Professor Stephen Nickell of the London School of Economics, a member of the Bank of England's Monetary Policy Committee, finds in an important paper that European unemployment afflicts unskilled and skilled workers to almost the same degree—and that Germany in particular does not suffer from especially high unemployment among its unskilled workers.[17] (He also points out that Germany's strong system of education and training means that even workers in the "unskilled" category are grounded in basic skills that make them eminently employable.) Nickell's finding is confirmed by John Schmitt and Lawrence Mishel, who report that unemployment rates for poorly educated adults at the margins of the labor force are only marginally higher in France and Germany than they are in the United States. But this is precisely the category for whom any form of employment protection should—if the conservatives are right—weaken their employment prospects still further. The ratio of the college-educated unemployed to those with no qualification is, as reported in chapter 4, high in the United States compared with Europe, again suggesting that the European labor market works quite well in pricing unskilled workers into jobs.[18]

One more piece of proof. The claimed "flexibility" of the U.S. labor market implies that job turnover rates should be higher, and that this helps to generate jobs; in fact, they are lower than in highly protected Italy and the same as those in France. The lowest job turnover rates are in Britain, whose unemployment record is the best among the big four European economies.[19]

The only impact welfare seems to have on differential unemployment and employment rates relates to the strictness with which access to unemployment benefits and income support is associated with a demand that applicants undertake training, look for work actively, and/or participate in government work programs. Thus unemployment has fallen rapidly in France, Sweden, and Finland, where over 10 percent of the labor force has entered active work programs since 1998,[20] and remained low in Denmark and the Netherlands, which accompany generous unemployment benefits with a strict requirement that the unemployed search for work. But, as important, these trends are independent of the overall level of labor market regulation, extent of unionization, and generosity of welfare payments.

The lazy charge that European unemployment is the fault of unions, regulation, and social requirements does not bear serious scrutiny. Job creation has system-wide roots, and the role of demand is at least as important as the character of the labor market—or so conclude Scharpf, Nickell, and Schmitt and Mishel. The more telling characteristic of both the United States and Britain is that both economies and labor markets have benefited from a sustained rise in personal consumption, which would not have been possible without financial systems that permit consumers to assume enormous amounts of personal and mortgage debt. In effect, the American and British economies have enjoyed the benefits of a long-term, privatized reflation.

Over the five years up to 2000, for example, private consumption in real terms rose by 4.5 percent per annum in the United States and by 3.9 percent per annum in the UK, compared to 1.7 percent per annum in Germany and 2 percent per annum in France—and this in turn has helped support a burgeoning service sector in both Britain and America, with the accompanying job creation.[21] Relatively depressed growth in private consumption in France and Germany has not been offset by buoyant public consumption; in Germany, public consumption has grown by 0.5 percent per annum in the five years to 2000 and in France by only 1.8 percent per annum. In Britain and America, by contrast, it has grown by a useful 1.6 percent per annum in real terms—underwriting the growth in private spending so that total spending has grown handsomely over the five-year period.[22]

The combination of financial market deregulation and a financial system organized to funnel credit to consumers has been the critical component in generating this demand growth, which France and Germany have been able neither to reproduce nor to compensate for by an orthodox Keynesian public sector–led reflation. Both countries have been compelled by their obligations to the Maastricht Treaty creating a European monetary union to keep their economies on a tight rein in the preliminary to and launch of Europe's single currency; and on top of this, Germany has been transferring some 4.5 percent of GDP every year during the 1990s to the former East Germany,[23] forcing it to take even more of a hair-shirt budgetary approach. In a climate of economic austerity in which no risks could be taken with inflation lest it imperil the chance of creating and then joining the single currency, neither country was able to initiate a major program of financial deregulation—with the accompanying chance of a credit and consumer boom—even had it wanted to.

The policy task is self-evident. It is to guard what is good while lifting the growth of public and private demand to American and British levels; if that can be done, together with bringing a greater supply of women into the labor market, there is no reason why the European economy should not experience similar rates of growth and job creation to those America has achieved over the past twenty years.

In any case, Europeans have viewed their financial systems in a different light—as having a primary role in the long-term development of their economies, rather than as marketing money to generate personal consumption. They may need to modify this approach, as I have suggested; but they should not simply discard it, for the character of the financial system is fundamental to how property rights are exercised, and that in turn is fundamental to the creativity and productivity of their corporate sectors. The European system—the cluster of approaches to property, equality and the social contract, and the public realm—works as an integrated whole. It offers high productivity, quality workers, organizational creativity, and high social protection. Nor does it have to pay for these advantages with high unemployment, as the conservative consensus insists; rather, unemployment is the short-term by-product of the shocks that the European economy, and especially the German economy, have suffered and the constraints that have been placed on the growth of consumption. It can be ameliorated by greater demand and by adopting more activist policies toward getting the unemployed to search for work—while preserving the scope and generosity of Europe's welfare state. Europe's future, if it guards what is best about its model, is bright.

9
Siblings under the Skin

Europe is a collection of countries replete with ancient enmities, united by no common language or culture. If the United States, built on immigration from Europe and with English as a lingua franca, can organize only a limited cultural fusion around the lowest common denominator principles of liberty and free markets, and has had little success in sustaining a consensus to provide a continent-wide social contract or public realm, then what chance has the continent from which its founders came? So runs the daily cry of Britain's army of Euroskeptics. What unity of economic and social purpose is possible that might underwrite its new single currency, the euro? What European public is conceivable in which European political institutions might be rooted and by which they can be held to account? The only Europe that is sustainable, runs this skeptical argument, is a Europe that has no more ambition than to trade with itself peaceably while guaranteeing capitalism and democracy; one that makes no incursions on the sovereignty, institutional structures, and cultures of its member states.

It is an argument all the more powerful because it seems grounded in European reality. Even if EU members succeed in achieving similar inflation, interest rates, and fiscal policies to qualify for entry into the euro, this is only surface convergence, for which in any case a high price has been paid by some in lost output and unemployment. The underlying economic and social structures of the EU states still vary hugely. There is an academic industry devoted to classifying and reclassifying European countries into any number of models, depending on the character and relationships of their trade unions, companies, welfare systems, labor markets, regulatory regimes, financial markets, and governments—fortifying those who can see only differences and obstacles to the European project. Moreover, each of these elements hangs together with all the others as part of an interdependent national whole; weaken any one to serve the cause of building Europe, goes the argument, and you do so at your peril.

There is, though, another argument. In the first place, the big economic indicators of Europe's performance are much closer than commonly realized; the differences in inflation, interest rates, and budget deficits are now minimal for countries in the single-currency area.[1] Patterns of taxation and public spending are also converging toward similar levels. This is not surface convergence. Moreover, this parallel economic performance is matched by common values and purposes that lie beneath the apparently irreconcilably different matrices of institutions and systems. Those clusters of values around property, the social contract, equality, and the public realm surface and resurface across the continent. Europe does have an approach to capitalism that is distinct from that of the United States, and although there are different variants across Europe, more unites than differentiates them.

By now it should be clear how this European brand of capitalism manifests itself at the level of the company. But the same value system extends beyond the corporate environment to constitute the platform for building a society-wide contract in which risks are collectively shared; incomes for the unemployed, sick, and retired are pitched generously enough to allow them fully to participate in society; and powerful education and training systems attempt to give each individual the opportunity to maximize his or her individual potential. The reason why Europe compares so favorably to the United States with respect to social and income mobility is that every European state sets out to offer equality of opportunity to all its people; the American neglect of the bottom 50 percent in the name of individualism is not reproduced in Europe. And this social capability is supported by a conception of the public realm whose underwriting of public science, public transportation, public art, public networks, public health, public broadcasting, public knowledge, and the wider public interest gives European civilization its unique character while offering many of its enterprises competitive advantage. These are the structures upon which European companies base their innovativeness and creativity, and which have allowed them the extraordinary rates of investment and productivity growth that have enabled them to begin to overtake their U.S. counterparts. Each variant of European capitalism may have elected for different means; but the ends they want to achieve are undergirded by the same values. There may be different varieties of European capitalism, but they are siblings under the skin. Far from its being impossible to build a European Union with a common public and common values that could hold its institutions to account, the avenue is open to Europeans if they choose to take it. But first we need to understand just how much Europe holds in common.

What the European Models Hold in Common

The most famous of the European models is "Rhineland capitalism" and its associated social-market economy, which prevails in Germany, Austria, and the Netherlands, extending in part to Belgium. This is the universe of the decentralized state, consensual labor relations, and the stakeholder company that overtly sets out to establish itself as a freestanding, associative organization rather than the creature of its shareholders. Profits are reinvested in the enterprise and dividends are proportionately low. A company's shares tend to be owned by other companies, banks, and insurance companies that have trading relationships with the business and are well disposed toward it rather than regarding a rising share price and swelling dividends as the supremely important objectives of their shareholding. The system of corporate governance provides for representatives of the shareholding groups to join representatives of the workforce and unions on supervisory boards that set the overall strategic direction of the company. It is difficult to mount a hostile bid successfully without the agreement of the supervisory board. Article 76 of German company law requires managers to run their business in the interests of the entire organization and prohibits the supervisory board from detailed intervention.

Despite globalization, the fulcrum of German industrial relations and wage setting remains the agreements and deals reached between industry-wide trade associations and industry-wide unions—more than two-thirds of wage agreements formally or informally are set by collective wage agreements in this way[2]—but the unions behave as responsible business partners because as stakeholders they are integral members of the organization. The reputation that the overall system has for constructing high-performance, cooperative workplaces is so good that it is very hard for companies to undermine and break up the unions without occasioning a public relations disaster. In 1995, for example, the metal industry employers' association, Gesamtmetall, tried to face down the industry-wide union, IG Metall (the second largest union in the world), to achieve job flexibility, but the consequent strike so threatened the image of constructive cooperation that individual firms broke ranks to show solidarity with their workers. Gesamtmetall backed down.[3]

The crucial intermediary is the works council, which by law has to be represented in corporate decision making—but which is, conversely, prohibited from initiating strike action.[4] Thus the council is deliberately set up to be the intermediate, neutral forum where union and employer can work out their relationships and manage tensions without the risk of precipitating industrial conflict—an agency for constructive conversation and communication within the organization. It was Volkswagen's work council that suggested a pay cut and the twenty-eight-hour week to the management in response to its threat to lay off 30,000 out of a 140,000-strong labor force in the mid-1990s; and the works council again that was central to Volkswagen's recent ability to hire new workers at lower wage rates than the existing workforce. The system is central to Germany's ability to arrive at cooperative solutions to competitive pressures.

German workers have high levels of education and training—a commitment that has its roots in the medieval guilds—so that workforce and employer alike have an investment in long-term organizational growth. Companies voluntarily participate in a national training system, which offers apprenticeships of at least three years in 370 accredited training courses—and the training system is integrated into the educational system, so that students move seamlessly from schools into training colleges or company-based apprenticeship systems.[5] Sixty percent of German teenagers are engaged in some form of vocational training, which carries little of the social stigma it still bears in Britain and America, where it is seen as a second-class option for those unable to pursue formal academic qualifications. Readers will recall that in the United States 46 percent of high school graduates receive no form of educational or vocational quali- fication (see chapter 5).

This combination of high skills, high investment, and commitment to long-term organic business growth is at the heart of the German produc- tivity miracle, endowing the German economy with its capacity to build companies, large and small, that are extraordinarily adept at diversifying and upgrading production while maintaining high quality. American con- servative critics portray the expensive system of training, lack of threat of takeover, and high union involvement in management as inhibitions on productivity, but German defenders of the system reject such arguments. The leading German economist Wolfgang Streeck, for example, argues that the combination of high costs and what American conservatives would describe as an excess of skills forces German companies to be more cre- ative and compete on their capacity to be innovative in their product ranges—and that high skills and capability to invest become instruments of competitiveness. "Excess skills make possible an organization of work capa- ble of flexibly restructuring itself in response to fast-changing, highly uncer- tain environmental conditions."[6] By operating in an environment in which economic and social obligations are intertwined, the firm paradoxically finds itself more competitive than if it aimed only for economic benefits.

This stress on the importance of the social spills over into the generous German welfare state. Employers' and employees' social security contribu- tions together tend to be very high, and are clearly differentiated from the tax system as a system of social insurance.[7] Benefits, however, reflect vary- ing contributions, a demand made by postwar Christian Democrats as the price of their support for the system; as a result there is a wide range of ben- efit levels, especially in pensions, rather than equal entitlements for every citizen. The middle class thus have as much of an incentive to belong to the social insurance system as the poor. The society-wide social contract and its explicit reflection in business organization could hardly be more evi- dent—and the result is a high-wage, high-productivity, production-ori- ented economy characterized by a commitment to quality and technology.

The conventional account is that this social-market economy is on the ropes in the face of the encroaching influence of the stock market and its priorities. Share prices on the German stock market have more than quintupled over the last two decades, and three financial market promotion laws have sought to make trading in shares easier and cheaper—culminating in the recent decision to make the disposal of large strategic cross-shareholdings (where friendly companies invest in each other's shares) free of capital gains tax. Companies are taking more interest in their share prices and their shareholders' views, introducing investor relation departments; directors' remuneration rose by 66 percent between 1996 and 1999 as performance-related pay kicked in.[8] These developments, together with the announcement by the leading car manufacturer DaimlerChrysler that its prime objective is now the pursuit of shareholder value, and the transformation of the giants of German banking, notably Deutsche Bank, into global actors, are meant to sound the death knell for the traditional system of finance and corporate governance. And, as this is the linchpin of German social-market Rhineland capitalism, offering the stable ownership and financing that underpin the whole fabric of long-term planning, industrial relations, and workforce development, the whole edifice is said by its critics to be about to fall.

However, the continuities in the picture are more striking than the differences. Martin Hopner at Cologne's Max Planck Institute, in the most exhaustive survey of how German corporate governance is changing, concludes that far from abandoning its traditional model, Germany is rather combining it with elements of the Anglo-Saxon model.[9] Only 26 percent of German shares are held in dispersed ownership, he writes, and while shareholder value is admired in Germany its injunctions are not followed; the fact that executive pay is rising and more foreign institutions own German shares does not mean that Germany has a market for corporate control, or that the legitimacy of trade union associations and works councils has been reduced. Indeed, paradoxically, it is trade unions and external investors in alliance that are pressing for more transparency of accounting standards.

German banking, too, should be seen in this way—as combining its traditional German approach with the new opportunities offered by globalization. As Richard Deeg argues, German banking has always been profoundly segmented into local, regional, national, and international operating units, both by regulation and by the desire of the German banking community to build strong business relationships—which requires being embedded in local and regional business.[10] The segmentation remains, but it has become more marked. The international arm of German banking has become more globalized and more strongly oriented toward the capital market, while the local and regional segments of German banking have continued to play their role as relationship bankers to German business. The institutional matrix of savings banks, cooperative banks, the regional *Landesbanken* and the industrial lending banks are all still pumping out long-term bank loans to businesses they know intimately, just as they always have.

Thus, although German banks have been unwinding their single large shareholdings, so that today there are only two bank shareholdings exceeding 25 percent in the top fifty companies, that pattern has been replaced by one of a number of banks with smaller shareholdings. Companies, especially in Germany's highly competitive small and medium-sized business sector, still look first to the public savings and cooperative banks for finance rather than the stock market. Bank debt still constitutes some three-fifths of the capital employed in German business, and equity remains at just under 20 percent, as it was twenty years ago.[11] As a result, businesses that in the United States and Britain would feel they had to have a stock market quotation can in Germany remain controlled by the founding family or its network and be supported by the local and regional banking system; there are 650 public limited companies in Germany, compared to over 2,000 in Britain and 7,000 in the United States—but business overall has higher rates of productivity, innovation, and investment in Germany than in either of the other two. The banking system created by state and national government to support German business remains as important as ever, even though its international operations have changed their character; and even that change has been embraced only in order to serve German business better. Thus the heart of the stakeholder enterprise and social market economy remains intact—supported by a powerful consensus that it should remain so.

So attractive is this model that it is overtly copied by the postcommunist societies in eastern Europe. They have tried to sustain the same stability of private ownership through German-style cross-shareholdings and investment funds owned by banks.[12] They have constructed banking systems—underwritten by the government—to supply long-term loan finance to enterprise as cheaply as possible. Hungary's Underwriting Company, for example, guarantees long-term loans exactly as Germany's industrial refinancing arm did after World War II. The welfare system is necessarily less generous, but it remains universalist in its ambition; education and health care are seen as public goods to be provided by the state.

The second variant is that practiced by the social democratic Scandinavian countries. These are more overtly collectivist and egalitarian, and the influence of Christian Democracy, especially in its concern to match social benefits with social contributions, is less strongly felt. Union membership rates are very high, ranging from 70 percent of the workforce in Norway to over 95 percent of the workforce in Finland.[13] Welfare is based on universal entitlements and is very egalitarian; there is virtually no means testing, even though the welfare system is substantially funded by taxation rather than social security contributions. Income tax, as a percentage of gross wages, is the highest in Europe; social security contributions are no more than average.[14] The state actively sponsors training, job mobility, and job search, while paying high levels of unemployment benefit. There is also a powerful commitment to support the family, with long periods of maternity and paternity leave. Besides the generous welfare state, there is high-quality provision of public health and education, important sources of employment in their own right.

These are important differences; but the outcomes are very similar. Benefits are as high as in social-market Europe—unemployment benefits vary from 58 percent of average earnings in Finland to 90 percent in Denmark—and the plans are combined with training programs.[15] There is huge investment in human capital. And companies, although not organized along formal stakeholder lines, have the same commitment to sustaining associative organizations through integrating and balancing the demands of unions and shareholders. Hostile takeovers are made very difficult by companies being allowed to allocate voting rights to friendly shareholders, so that in Sweden, for example, one share can carry as many as 1,000 votes.[16] Dividend distributions are low, and bank financing is preferred to stock market financing; the banking system still has a high degree of state involvement to ensure support for business. National trade unions reach accommodations with national employers' associations. Wages are high, but so are productivity levels, buoyed by high levels of investment and social peace. Regulation is extensive. The state plays a more active role in the name of the collective social will, but the character of the resulting capitalism is very similar to that in social-market Europe.

Then there is Catholic southern Europe, where the legacy of fascism and military dictatorship still casts a long shadow—Italy, Greece, Spain, and Portugal have all had direct experience of one or the other, some of both. These are more corporatist countries, where relationships between big business and the state remain close. Organized labor is more overtly political, oppositional, and distrustful of private enterprise, but equally is less powerful; union membership ranges from only 11 percent of the workforce in Greece to 26 percent in Portugal. The social contract is still discernible, however. Employment protection is the highest in Europe, maintained at these levels to minimize worker discontent and head off grievances that might spark trade union recruitment;[17] and pains have been taken to build a welfare state that will offer care from cradle to grave, although there is not the ideological coherence that defines the welfare systems of social-market and Scandinavian Europe. Provision in the south tends to consist of a mishmash of universal payments, especially pensions, together with more means-tested, targeted, and conditional benefits.

Capitalist firms in this model have the same organizational template as the two north European models, although this owes much more to the role of family and state than to a compact between unions and shareholders. Family enterprise remains immensely important; this is especially so in the dynamic small- and medium-sized business sector, but even leading firms like Italy's Fiat can still be dominated by the founding family. Over three-quarters of the top thirty Italian firms listed on the Milan stock exchange are each controlled by one shareholder with a majority stake, usually the founding family.[18] Where the family interest is absent, direct state ownership and regulation achieve similar results. Again, the stock market is less important than banks in financing enterprise, and the state is ready to step in to cushion and manage industrial change. Economic development can be uneven, with substantial disparity, for example, between the south of Italy and the north, and markets tend to be regulated to favor particular interests and client groups. The state—in all cases a post-1945 creation—has much less legitimacy than in the north, and the traditions of social citizenship and political participation that inform northern Europe are much less firmly embedded, but southern Europe has found its way to a capitalism and social contract that perform in similar ways.

The final two models are each represented by a single country: France and Britain. Both are long-standing nation-states with powerful central governments and traditions of weak regional autonomy; but their approaches to economic and social organization could hardly be more different. France, with its Napoleonic code and tradition of state support for industry that goes back to Colbert, remains dirigiste and statist despite recent "liberalization"—but over and above that it has elements that resonate with the southern, social-market and Scandinavian models alike. It has a generous universal welfare system paid for by social security contributions along social-market principles; and it has a profound commitment to public health and education along Scandinavian lines. The proportion of students qualifying for tertiary education has risen from 28 percent in 1980 to nearly two-thirds today.[19]

However, the close relationship of its large corporations to the state, even though loosened by fifteen years of privatization, and the adversarial and politicized trade union movement are more southern European in character. Union membership, at 9 percent, is the lowest in Europe; but French companies, like their northern European counterparts, accept that employee-employer agreements should apply to all their workers, so that collective bargaining agreements cover more than three-quarters of the workforce. Employment protection legislation is stronger than that of every other European country outside southern Europe.[20] The French, like other Europeans, have drawn up a recognizable social contract. And if the state owns less than it once did, it remains a powerful regulator and driver of French economic and social life; any company, for example, considering significant layoffs has to produce a social plan explaining how it will help those laid off to reattach themselves to the labor market. In addition, the government has been among the most interventionist in Europe, supporting early retirement programs for those over 55, and more recently promising to create up to three-quarters of a million jobs for young people.

The configuration of elements may be different, but the end result is a degree of protection and welfare for French employees similar to those in Scandinavia and social-market Europe.

As in Germany, there has been a significant transformation of the economic model over the past two decades. For some, the retreat of the traditional state influence in planning, the financial system, and direct ownership of industry is evidence that France is in the throes of becoming fully Anglo-Saxonized or modernized (the two terms are seen as interchangeable by French business); others see as much continuity as change.[21] At first sight the scale of change is certainly extraordinary. The privatization of the banking system and the scrapping of the entire mechanism that allowed the government to direct loans and credit to favored companies has implied a massively significant move to a more market-based financial system. The sell-off of state-owned business, along with the phasing out of state subsidies to the business sector, have removed another traditional state instrument of economic direction. Foreigners now own some 40 percent of the equity of the top 100 French companies,[22] and as we have seen there have been moves to match the corporate governance rules of Britain and America.

Again as in Germany, however, the movement toward a more market-based financial system has not meant the surrender of the core, long-termist, business-building attributes of French enterprise, which remains recognizably stakeholder in character even if the means by which it pursues these ends are very different. French company law states, echoing German company law, that management should pursue the company's social interest (*intérêt sociale de l'entreprise*) or social capability; in other words, the shareholder interest is only one of several that need to be balanced to serve the organization as a whole.[23] The president director general (PDG) is formally entrusted with enormous executive power to prosecute and represent the interests of the entire organization, and although the old system of *bancassurance* in which financial holding companies held friendly cross-shareholdings is rapidly unwinding, French PDGs can accord differential voting rights to their shareholders depending on their longevity and loyalty so that they can always secure a majority of friendly votes in any hostile takeover bid. As noted in chapter 8, shareholding in France, as in Germany, tends to be concentrated, with the majority of shares being owned by a few groups or individuals, typically including the founding family; on average, 48.2 percent of the shares of the 416 largest French companies are held by the five largest shareholders, all of whom will have a long-term relationship with the company.[24] They will have elected in the PDG, who can thus expect their support. In short, if the supervisory board is the gatekeeper to controlling a business in social-market Europe, the PDG plays a similar role in France.

This allows French businesses to take a similar broad view, encompassing the whole associative organization, of its long-term needs as its German counterparts. Like them, French companies tend to look to the banking system rather than the stock market for financing; dividends are low, and the accent is on retaining profits to invest in research and development. French output per man-hour, like that of the former West Germany, now exceeds that in the United States—and French capitalism, while remaining distinctive, is converging toward the European norm.

And then there is Britain. This is Europe's outlier—the economy and society regarded as nearest in Europe to the American model. At one level this is self-evidently true: no other European economy has financial markets as powerful and international as those of the City of London, nor a business environment—supported by a web of company law and institutional practice—dominated by the notion that the sole obligation of companies, policed by the savings institutions and investment banks, is to maximize shareholder value. Hostile takeover is easier and more prevalent than anywhere else; in Britain bank support for business tends to be contractual rather than relational, and lending is very short-term. Employment protection is the weakest in Europe,[25] and business regulation and all forms of taxation are fiercely resisted by the business establishment as a "burden." The cultural aversion—embedded in the state and business community alike—to intervening in the operation of the market has been reinforced by the recent intellectual and political ascendancy of conservatism, in particular under the Thatcher and Major governments.

The consensus view is that this "Anglo-Saxon" structure has brought the British economy many benefits, notably the lion's share of inward investment flowing into Europe, on which Britain is uniquely reliant; but the bitter truth is that on almost every measure of true competitiveness (productivity, investment, innovativeness, research and development, market share, new patents) Britain lags behind both Europe and the United States. The reliance on inward investment for so much growth and innovation is in one sense a sign of economic weakness. Britain has been fortunate that since the pound's forced exit from the European exchange rate mechanism in 1992 the management of the economy has been benign, and since 1997 positively good. The independent Bank of England established by Chancellor of the Exchequer Gordon Brown in that year has proved adept at setting interest rates judiciously to meet its target for inflation, while the framework of rules for setting public spending, taxation, and borrowing has proved robust and effective, and the economy has enjoyed nearly a decade of sustained growth. But this has not compensated for the deep-seated structural weaknesses in its approach to capitalism that continue to plague its performance.

Britain's difficulty is that despite sharing with the United States a common language and many common approaches to finance and corporate governance, the same values that underpin European capitalism are embedded in Britain. The doctrine of shareholder value is more controversial in Britain than it is in the United States for this very reason. Despite more than twenty years of being lectured by the political class on the need to celebrate business and enterprise and give thanks for having capitalism, Britain remains firmly European in insisting that business has no right to insist on special privileges, and that it should rather earn the right to trade in British society through the integrity of its commercial relationships and the quality of its service. Britain has had four codes of corporate governance over the past decade—the Cadbury, Greenbury, Hampel, and Turnbull reports. These are not isolated, unconnected attempts to assuage the concerns of a temporarily aroused public that business should respond to its wish to see more ethical behavior. Rather, they are a response to a persistent and growing demand for better standards, more rigor in the transparency of decision making and clear rules for conduct at the highest level in companies. The business community and business associations have needed to show that they are prepared to consider change as the decade has unfolded, exposing successive shortcomings in the way companies are run, notably over the setting of executive pay. British business has urgently needed both a code of practice and a narrative to fend off the accusation that its practitioners behave little better than cowboys.

The rise in executive pay, though trivial by American standards, brings stormier criticism every year, and British institutional investors are compelled by public opinion to intervene—or at least be seen as intervening—to make sure that executives and directors do not pay themselves overextravagantly. Their interventions may be feeble, but that in turn creates more criticism. Unlike American business, British companies operate in an environment heavily influenced—as in the rest of Europe—by the legacy of feudalism and notions of the common good, expressed alike in one-nation Toryism and socialism. To hold property, including corporate equity, is a privilege that comes with attendant reciprocal responsibilities. Capital gains tax and planning laws carry more legitimacy in Britain than they ever could in the United States. But instead of understanding this and turning the culture to the service of building a more long-termist, innovative capitalism, Britain is still seduced by the possibility of becoming more like America as the route to capitalist success—unwilling to accept the reality of its core European beliefs or recognize how rich the rewards of the European capitalist tradition have been in promoting productivity and innovation. The British are so fixated on what happens across the Atlantic that they cannot see the merits of what is happening across the Channel, and how it might be adapted to deliver the productivity growth that business, government, and society want and need. Instead, Britain sticks stubbornly to an organization of capitalism that is at odds with its fundamental values and which works poorly even in its original American context—let alone a British European one. For there is much less that is American in Britain's success than the United States likes to boast—its achievements have been won by a more European approach to capitalism, whether or not it understands this itself; and even if Britain wanted to reproduce the mores and attitudes of the United States, as a deeply European country it simply could not.

Where Britain is unambiguously European is over the idea of the social contract. The British variant may be increasingly flyblown, but it exists nonetheless—and the population remains fiercely attached to it, to the despair of the political class. The provision of health care free at the point of use by a tax-financed, publicly owned National Health Service is a political imperative no politician can escape. Although the welfare system is by European standards mean and limited in its scope, it remains the lineal descendant of Beveridge's system of social insurance and impossible to abandon. Support for health and education spending remains high, with 63 percent of respondents in the latest social attitudes survey reporting they would increase taxes to spend more on education, health, and social benefits,[26] and trade union membership still encompasses a third of the working population. The axiomatic assumption that Britain is more American than European, and that it could not hope to sit easily within the European Union and its economic and social model, is misplaced. In trying to Americanize itself, Britain has lost its way. It is through the rediscovery of what it holds in common with Europe that it can heal its psychosis—looking to America while being European: a dislocation that enfeebles its effort to build a creative capitalism and a just society. Britain needs to rediscover and reassert the European value system at its core.

Europe's welfare states, trade unions, labor market regulations, and belief in the husbanded or stakeholder enterprise—along with the role played by government—are not economic and social aberrations. They arise from its feudal, Christian past, its tortured experience of industrialization and urbanization, and the searing clash between fascism and communism as attempts to establish a universalist response to the moral crisis posed by the inequities of income, wealth, and power created by capitalism. Europe's economic and social model is everywhere the result of the reconciliation of these tensions, and Europe's social democratic and liberal parties on the left and Christian Democratic parties on the right have become the twin custodians of core European values and the European settlement. They define Europeanness. They are nonnegotiable European realities.

Thus the attempt to build an ever closer union in Europe is less farfetched than it might seem. The builders of Europe should be more confident, less in awe of the boasts of conservative America, and less ready to accept that their continent is plagued by irreconcilable differences. For even the pro-European consensus accepts that if Europe wants to build a single market and single society, then its only route is to copy America as far as it can. The EU has allowed itself to define its task as "liberalizing" and "deregulating"—what Fritz Scharpf describes as "negative integration"—in accordance with the consensus view that there is little to be done in Europe except build a single market because its varying economic and social models are impossible to integrate. In today's conservative climate, this is the new common sense.

Indeed, the pro-European consensus insists that if Europe wants to exhibit the same alleged economic and social dynamism as America, then it should go further still down the negative integration route. Its various economic and social models, with their "burdensome" rules that protect trade unions and shield companies from takeover, should be dismantled to reproduce America in Europe; taxes and social charges that limit the rewards to risk taking and undermine the so-called enterprise culture should be lowered; and so on and so on—by now the reader should be familiar with the dreary litany. This, it is said, will produce the win-win outcome of unleashing economic dynamism and promoting integration simultaneously. It may turn the EU institutions into agencies that are hostile to key European values, losing legitimacy and support in the process—but this is the only realistic option.

It is not, of course. The choices Europe has made are more than reasonable. They produce efficient outcomes, embody profound economic and social priorities that have a great deal in common with one another, and are currently modifying themselves to the forces of globalization rather than capitulating in wholesale abandonment of their core values and principles. There is thus is a different approach to building Europe. It starts with the same shared commitment to democracy, human rights, and market capitalism. From that foundation the EU could go further and assert that the European model is distinct and valuable, and that it wants to set out to help rather than hinder European states as they try to reform their systems—rather than abandon them—in the face of globalization. It would underline that Europe's commitment to the social, far from being a source of inefficiency, is a source of competitive advantage, and while it should be modernized to reflect global economic changes it should not be abandoned. In short, Europe should work to build itself up—to integrate positively—around a much more self-confident belief in the merits of its distinct approach to capitalism and the social contract.

The Social Contract Works . . .

Even if core European beliefs did lead to the inefficiencies portrayed by conservative critics, they would still be defensible. Europe's social contract produces valuable social outcomes—a reality frequently neglected within the barrage of criticism.

This is important. As we have seen, each European economic and social model is characterized by a combination of income redistribution, social insurance, means-tested social benefits, and provision of public health and education that make taxes and social security contributions higher than in the United States—and a combination of employment protection, labor market regulation, and higher trade union representation that buttresses the rights and powers of Europe's workers more than those of their counterparts in the United States. As demonstrated in the previous chapter, these mechanisms do not create higher unemployment, nor have they damaged Europe's powerful record on enterprise and productivity. What they have done is to produce an array of social outcomes which on every important measure are significantly better than in the United States.

In the first place, it is worth recalling some of the findings set out in chapter 5. The widespread view in America, shared by many in Europe, is that this immigrant society, where millions came to better themselves, is much more socially mobile and less class-bound than any in Europe. This was not supported by any evidence even in the immediate postwar period, and more recent surveys of income and social mobility have shown that it is no better than that in Europe—and at its worst significantly poorer. The grip of the rich on the upper echelons of the education system has grown, while the lack of skills and education among the bottom 50 percent of the U.S. population is increasingly trapping them in low-wage, low-skill jobs from which their rate of exit is much worse than in Europe. For all its record of employment generation, it is the United States that is the more sclerotic society in terms of measured mobility.

Moreover, the United States is much more unequal, and notwithstanding its higher overall per capita incomes, its poor are absolutely worse off than their counterparts in Europe. Capitalist economies generate inequality; typically, if there are no interventions and social transfers, between 20 and 30 percent of the population will have incomes that are at least 50 percent lower than the median disposable personal income, the definition of poverty used by the OECD and the EU. The issue is how societies should respond to alleviate this situation. The American approach is minimalist, except only in provision for its elderly. As the economist Timothy Smeeding has shown, the U.S. welfare system, even before its scaling back during the Clinton years, raised the incomes of the poor to reduce the proportion of adults in poverty only moderately, from 26.7 to 19.1 percent.[27] In Germany, France, and Italy social transfers are dramatically more effective; using the same benchmark, only 7.6, 7.5, and 6.5 percent of their adult populations, respectively, live in poverty. And while 24.9 percent of American children live in poverty, the proportions in Germany, France, and Italy are 8.6, 7.4, and 10.5 percent, respectively. Whatever other boasts it may make, the United States can hardly claim to be compassionate or more efficient than Europe in its attitude to the relief of poverty.

Britain, as the Anglo-Saxon representative in Europe, should be expected to produce similar results to the United States. It is true that with 14.6 percent of its adult population and some 18.5 percent of its children living in poverty, its social outcomes lie somewhere between those of mainland Europe and the United States. However, because the British starting point is the most dire on either side of the Atlantic—29.2 percent of its population live in poverty before any intervention or social transfer—the proportional impact of its social security system in reducing poverty is much closer to Europe than to America.

Here again, what stands out are not the differences with mainland Europe, but the similarities. The key benchmark for adults of working age is what happens when they are made unemployed. Britain's system is built around means-tested and qualified benefits rather than a comprehensive and universal system of social insurance; but if as a result unemployment benefits are wretched by European standards, this is partially compensated for by generous contributions to help with rental payments (housing benefits). The so-called replacement ratio—the aggregate support provided by the government to unemployed workers, expressed as a proportion of their former earnings—is 64 percent for a British couple on average earnings with two children, within shouting distance of the 74 percent ratio in France and Germany.[28] And, as workers' incomes fall to two-thirds of average earnings, the British system of means testing offers a robust safety net (rather than social insurance) that produces outcomes that compare reasonably with other European countries—and contrast sharply with what happens in the United States. The replacement ratio for a couple with two children on this lower income rises to 83 percent, higher than Germany's 74 percent and in the same area as France (86 percent), the Netherlands (90 percent), and Sweden (90 percent). This is why the British system, even though allegedly much closer to the American approach, is nearly as effective as the European in alleviating poverty. The U.S. replacement ratio for a couple with two children on two-thirds of average earnings is 51 percent—much lower than any European country except Italy and Greece—which is why the United States is so ineffective at reducing poverty. The conservative theory is that this makes its unemployed more keen to find work. But again, to recall Fritz Scharpf's findings outlined in the previous chapter, there is no relationship between the replacement ratio and the generosity of the welfare state and unemployment. The Netherlands and Denmark, for example, have higher proportions of their workforces in employment than the United States, but also greatly higher replacement ratios, taxation, and social spending.

All Western countries act aggressively to limit poverty among the elderly—those over sixty-five. The U.S. social security system lowers the proportion of the elderly living in poverty from 58.7 percent before payments to 19.6 percent after payments—an intervention that reduces the prevalence of poverty by a cool two-thirds. But even here the Europeans outperform the United States. Germany, France, and Italy all spend more than 10 percent of their national income on pensions, twice as much as the United States and the UK. As a result it is hardly surprising that only a tiny proportion of their elderly live in poverty—7.7, 4.8, and 4.4 percent, respectively—and that they all lower pensioner poverty by around 90 percent through state intervention. The country with the highest proportion of pensioner poverty is Britain, where a whopping 23.9 per cent of the elderly live below the poverty line. Britain may be able to boast that of all five countries it is the only one in which spending on the elderly will be lower in 2050 than in 2001, so that it has no impending budgetary crisis; but the other side of the coin is that its elderly are in the most acute financial circumstances. There is no such thing as a free lunch.

Once more, all is not as it seems. While the United States is debating the privatization of its social security system to compel individuals to save and invest on their own account for retirement, Britain's Labour government is working within its own means-tested conception of the social contract to offer pensioners a minimum retirement income guarantee over and above the British basic state pension. Poor pensioners, if they have no other form of income, qualify for this guaranteed retirement income, which is 25 percent higher than the state pension. This measure may not be part of a Scandinavian or social-market-Europe system of social insurance, working instead within the British means-tested social safety-net tradition, with all the disadvantages cataloged in chapter 7; but it does nonetheless represent an attempt to address pensioner poverty within a social-contract framework. In any case, with France, Germany, and Italy all trimming pension benefits and extending minimum contribution periods because of budgetary pressure,[29] there is some sign of convergence—but the social-contract approach for all stands. As the privatization of pensions proves to have greater and greater shortcomings, the British reaction will not mirror that of the U.S. administration; for public pressure will demand an improvement in government-provided pensions and a strengthening of the social-contract framework.

European electorates are profoundly committed to publicly led social benefits and institutions, which they recognize directly improve their lives and living standards. The most obvious of these, apart from various forms of income support, is health care. Germany led the way with the introduction of compulsory health insurance for industrial workers in 1883, and fifteen years later France had established a system of near-comprehensive insurance—both predating the rise of socialism. Britain's system of health insurance followed in 1911, but eligibility was confined to the employed. Thus before World War I Europe's big three states had already put in place one of the building blocks of the social contract in health—but built around the insurance principle.

Since then there has been a divergence of how health care is financed; but each European country has become committed to making health care available to every citizen free at the point of use (although some require small nominal payments from citizens, with the poor protected by means-tested assistance if they cannot pay) and provided on the basis of medical need. France, Germany, and the Netherlands have built on their original foundations and made health insurance compulsory and comprehensive, while Britain, Spain, Italy, and the Scandinavian countries have developed health systems financed by general taxation. But whether tax- or insurance-based, all the systems are unambiguously public creations. Health insurance funds are not privately run by profit-making companies quoted on stock markets, but have overtly social aims and have been established explicitly as non–profit-making bodies to provide the public goal of universal health insurance. French employees, for example, insure through the Caisse National d'Assurances Maladies des Travailleurs Salariés and mutual insurance companies, while in Germany, with its social-market tradition, the task is left to closely regulated mutual insurance companies supplemented by sickness funds, whose boards—like those of its companies—include both worker and employer representatives. Their tariffs are negotiated with government, and the terms on which they do business with hospitals, clinics, and doctors are also closely regulated. As the economist Richard Freeman comments in his account of European health systems, "social insurance systems are clearly not public systems in the way that national health systems are, but nor can they be said to be 'private.' Finance and delivery are organizationally separate but publicly mandated: these are public systems with prices, not private systems with elements of regulation."[30]

The American system, based on private insurance with profit-making insurance companies and supplemented by Medicare for the old (which still needs private supplementary medical insurance to pay surgeons' and doctors' fees!) along with Medicaid for the "categorically needy" on or below the federal poverty line, rests on very different philosophical foundations. This is not a social contract by which access to health care is guaranteed whatever your income; the United States is prepared to allow 16 percent of its population—some 43 million people—to live without any form of health insurance. A quarter of those earning less than $25,000 have no insurance, while only 8 percent of those earning more than $75,000 are without insurance.[31] This is the social expression of a market society in which the same patterns of inequality of income are allowed right at the center of one of every human being's most important aspirations—the right to health, even to life.

The U.S. system is not only socially unjust but also calamitously economically inefficient. Despite around 14 percent of GDP being spent on health, American life expectancy is lower than in the four big European countries—and markedly lower for men. Male life expectancy in France is 74.2 years, in Germany 73.6, in Italy 74.9, and in Britain 74.2: all are higher than in the United States, where it is 72.7.[32] Infant mortality is lower in Europe. Eight babies under a year old die for every 1,000 births in the United States—significantly more than in France (4.9), Germany (5.3), the UK (6.0), and Italy (6.2).[33]

What inflates American health expenditure is the inevitable desire of the privately insured to pay whatever is needed to restore themselves to health—and the medical profession's readiness, given that there is no budget constraint, to offer whatever they can to their patients. For the better off, the system provides very high-quality health care indeed, dragging up certain average health outcomes. American survival rates for breast and lung cancer, for example, are better than in the UK, and only 10 percent of patients wait more than a month for nonemergency surgery, compared with over half in Britain.[34] However, American performance is not especially better than that of mainland Europe, where expenditure runs at two-thirds of American levels. And as dissatisfaction mounts in Britain about the low level of health expenditure and indifferent health outcomes, the United States is explicitly not the model held up for public admiration. New Labour is pledged to lift public health expenditure to the European average by 2005 and has dared to raise taxes to achieve its aim, to its shock winning popular support. Even the Conservative party openly cites the social-insurance model of France, Germany, and the Netherlands as being more likely to increase the resources devoted to health, deliberately avoiding the political mistake of copying the U.S. model. Britain, its political parties are finding, is very much a European country with European attitudes. America might surprise itself by rediscovering its European roots.

. . . and a Vibrant Public Realm Supports a Vibrant Economy and Society

Nor is belief in public agency confined only to creating and sustaining a social contract. It is, as argued in chapter 2, part of a much wider value system that sees the public realm as a means of establishing, expressing, and working toward common economic and social goals that cannot be achieved by individual interests but are nonetheless intrinsic to any society's well-being. The universe of political debate and government action, critical to a democratic society, is but a subset of the wider public realm and dependent upon it for its vitality. Citizenship is not just about the exercise of votes or the right to live under the impartiality of the law; it is about participation in the totality of public choices, economic, social, and cultural, that confront any community. The public realm is where communal choices are examined from the point of view not of individual but of public advantage—and where political options are framed, as far as possible, impartially and disinterestedly. This in turn requires a public space in which information can be publicly and freely gathered, exchanged, and disseminated—through channels ranging from newspapers to scientific debate—which is thus the precondition for a vibrant culture of citizenship. Broadcasting, scientific research, the process for making public appointments—all are parts of a sphere of attempted impartiality dedicated to serving the common good. This sphere becomes the basis for public initiative to create opportunities through government action that could not be created by private economic and social actors alone. The public is larger than the narrowly political, and it both demands and accords the widest definition of citizenship—economic, political, and social.

The concern to uphold this broad conception of citizenship rights to serve a common interest runs through European civilization like a golden thread. Thus there is a public interest in every citizen being well educated, because the social whole benefits from high average levels of educational attainment. There is a public interest in every citizen having access to good health care, not least because infectious disease knows no boundaries. There is a public interest in every citizen having access to impartial news and information, without which there is no chance of participating in public debate on some broadly equivalent basis of knowledge. There is a public advantage in the dissemination of scientific knowledge so that its veracity can be tested and so that it is universally available as a basis for material advance for all. Every citizen should have access to a telephone network. And so on.

These notions of the public good entail profound economic and social choices that are distinct in character from those made by the United States. They are, as we have seen, the moral underpinning of universal health care provision and measures for poverty alleviation more comprehensive than those attempted by the United States—but they also extend to economic initiatives such as establishing the Airbus consortium or ensuring that the banking system provides long-term credit flows. When European states are sufficiently farsighted this readiness to establish common public rules can have not just useful social results but rich economic paybacks too. When, for example, Finland, Norway, Denmark, and Sweden came together in 1983 to form the Scandinavian mobile telephone network, they paved the way for the European standard bandwidth that Nokia and Ericsson so successfully exploited in the mobile phone business—and which is now set to become the global standard. Rather than allow market forces to establish a common bandwidth, the route the Americans have followed, the Nordic countries acted to produce the win-win outcome of rapid mobile phone development for consumers—and industrial success for mobile phone producers.

This idea of the public and the legitimacy it accords to the state is analytically distinct from socialism—although European socialism has drawn upon it to justify its philosophy, and, as argued earlier, by conflating socialist and collectivist aims with public interest aims has helped to discredit both. Plainly there are occasions when the collective and the public are the same; for example, clean air and drinkable water can be regarded as both public and collective interests. Collective ownership of a particular industry may not be in the public interest. In other circumstances, it may be necessary to establish public ownership of, say, a rail system, in order for it to be run effectively or indeed at all; but the public for whom this transportation is created includes the wide array of private and individual interests that constitute society—not an egalitarian collective. Collectivism and the public realm are not interchangeable concepts.

This confusion stands as a barrier to American understanding of what is going on when Europeans justify government initiative with reference to conceptions of the general or public interest which Americans too readily interpret as socialist. For while socialism as a philosophy demands that the interests of private capital be subordinated to some expression of an egalitarian collective or community, the public interest is an idea that coexists with markets and private property—and indeed can be put to their service. Thus the 1957 Treaty of Rome provides for a liberal, market-based European economy that entrenches private property rights, free trade, competition, and openness, but also specifies the duty of the European Economic Community (as it was then) to protect the general interest. It is not that the United States does not have a public-interest tradition itself—Madison argued that the federal system of government was designed to uphold the public interest, and the consistent appeals to bipartisanship are an appeal to this tradition—it is that it has become so degraded by lobbying, pork-barrel politics, lack of control of campaign finance, and the ideology of individualism that it has lost any relationship to the core principle.

This is most obvious in the two civilizations' respective approaches to information and ideas, always present over the past fifty years but becoming more important as ICT and the "knowledge economy" become driving forces of economic and social progress. In the infancy of the ICT age every European country acted to ensure that a national public broadcasting organization was established, bound by law to disseminate politically balanced news and information—a determination reinforced by the disastrous experience of communist and fascist control of television and radio. It is a tradition that has continued. The quintessential expression of this European conception of public service broadcasting is Britain's BBC, obliged constitutionally to attempt impartiality in its coverage of news and current affairs, but beyond that to entertain, inform, and explain to every citizen. The Netherlands ensures that broadcasting time is allocated to all social and political groups proportionate to their size in a patchwork quilt of religious and political channels, while Germany's public broadcaster, the ARD, has a complex system of rules ensuring that senior appointments exactly reflect the balance of political forces in Germany. France's TFI and Italy's RAI are under the same obligation to attempt impartiality and public service broadcasting. In the hurly-burly of real politics, parties and governments jockey for advantage while the public broadcasters themselves, under proliferating competition from television delivered terrestrially, by cable, and by satellite, have had to popularize their schedules—but the underlying mission survives even in Italy, where the politicization is most acute. There is a public interest in ensuring that each citizen has the opportunity to be informed and entertained by a broadcaster with that mission, rather than profit maximization, at its heart.

European governments and the EU are aggressive in their regulation of broadcasting content. The public interest demands that advertising not be openly misleading. Racist expression is banned. There has to be clear separation between programs and any sponsorship. There are guidelines about how much content can be foreign-made—entrenched in article 4 of the 1989 EU broadcasting directive—and broadcasters should allocate 10 percent of their budgets to support program makers "independent of broadcasters."[35] While American broadcasters plead the First Amendment's commitment to absolute free speech, making public interest regulation almost impossible, Europe acts to ensure that television and radio conform to public interest criteria. In particular, there are tough laws on media ownership and cross-ownership; Germany prohibits the granting of national broadcasting licenses to any group in which one individual has more than a 50 percent interest, while France forbids any company or individual to control more than 30 percent of total newspaper circulation. Even Britain, which has been ineffective in preventing the concentration of newspaper ownership, only allows newspaper groups with less than 20 percent of national circulation to control TV stations with up to 15 percent of the market. Even though rules on foreign ownership have been relaxed, rigorous rules on the content of schedules will be maintained or even strengthened.

The thinness of American conceptions of the public interest has been accentuated by the ICT revolution. The tradition that information is essentially an economic commodity in which corporations trade, and that attempts to assert a public interest are essentially statist, has been deployed to full effect by the corporations of the New Economy to privatize the access to information that in Europe is regarded as a public good. As a result of intense lobbying by the United States's giant media and ICT companies, in 1998 the United States passed the Digital Millennium Copyright Act, making it a criminal offense either to break a copy-protection mechanism or to circumvent any control designed to prevent access to information—in essence a giant step toward privatizing the Internet. But by the same token, U.S. legislation protecting individuals with respect to how information about them might be traded and used without their knowledge is extraordinarily weak—so that insurance companies and credit rating agencies can swap data they have collected without any obligation to tell the individual concerned. There is deemed to be no public interest either in maximizing access to potentially public knowledge and information or in offering individuals privacy.

The Europeans, by contrast, have attempted—albeit weakly—to protect a conception of the public interest. The EU's copyright directive attempts to balance the proper desire to secure intellectual property rights with reasonable exemptions for what might be copied. While the United States bans the breaking of any encryption code in any circumstances, the EU permits reproduction and the breaking of codes if there is a presumption that this might advance the public interest. The 1998 EU data protection directive, moreover, details exactly what companies can and cannot do with data in their possession; in particular, they cannot pass it on to a third party without the consent of the individual or company concerned. Nor can companies gather any information about individuals' sexual behavior, race, religion, or health without their express consent. To add insult to injury from an American perspective, the directive prevents companies from transferring data and information to countries where there is "an inadequate level of protection"—which under current law includes the United States. American Airlines lost a lawsuit in which they tried to defend transferring information about their Swedish customers to the United States.

The same concern to advance—or at least protect—the public interest has informed the EU's approach to telecom liberalization, in contrast to what has happened in the United States. Readers will recall that it was under intense U.S. pressure that the EU established an internal market for telecommunications in the late 1980s and early 1990s, importantly specifying that public telecommunications contracts should be subject to competitive tender. This opened up the European equipment market to American manufacturers while giving private companies the right to built telecommunications networks. While the U.S. 1996 Telecommunications Act paid due lip service to the principle of universal telephone provision, it set in motion such powerful forces balkanizing the U.S. telephone system with such weak regulation that the declaration made little practical sense. By contrast, the 1993 EU green paper declared that telecommunications are a matter of citizenship. Telecom operators should accordingly provide public phone boxes and directory assistance services; and the need for universal provision meant that even if some services were unprofitable they should be paid for by all service operators. The aim, it said, "should be to provide consumers and businesses with a diverse offering of quality telecommunications at competitive prices whilst guaranteeing universal access to basic telecommunications services for all citizens."[36]

American critics regard this concern as antediluvian, costly, and an inhibition of liberty. Yet it is the Scandinavian countries that are in the vanguard of developing the New Economy, aided by the public realm concern to implement a system of broadband cable with universal reach, mirroring their establishment of a universal bandwidth for mobile phones. As the telecom bubble bursts, leaving in its wake a trail of bankrupt companies and incomplete networks, it is plain that the preoccupation with promoting private interests in the hope that the public interest would spontaneously emerge (as Adam Smith predicted) has proved a false compass. And if democracy and the good society are underpinned by the maximum access to information, its privatization in the United States will in the long run surely undermine the vitality of its civilization.

Europeans, in keeping with their values, have fought to keep the remarkable findings of the human genome project in the public domain for the benefit of all humankind; the United States, in keeping with its values, is prepared to permit their privatization. If this clash over the importance of protecting a public realm is at bottom a moral argument, the Europeans win hands down. The promotion of the corporate bottom line cannot be allowed to dictate the codes and values by which we live—in the United States any more than in Europe. It is time to draw a line in the sand; and for that we need a European Union with a clearer sense of what it can and should be doing—supported by members who understand that alone they have little chance of sustaining the values and principles they hold so dear.

This must be at the heart of the European task; a clear articulation of those values will be needed to underpin integration. But the United States, I submit, should not be Europe's critic and enemy. The present U.S. position is not what most Americans—the quiet liberal majority—want. They should start to reassert themselves. Interdependence, the social contract, an enlightened view of enterprise, and a revived public realm are goals Americans also should cherish. The question, rather, is how and when.

Conclusion

As the twenty-first century begins, the United States holds a unique position. Accounting for 40 percent of the world's defense spending, no country has ever been so militarily dominant. Able to exert its will as no other state before, it possesses a vigorous capitalism, dominating the two sectors that drive globalization—information and communication technology and finance. It has a profound commitment to freedom, democracy, and the rule of law. It remains a magnet for immigrants, surely testimony to the attractiveness of its society and values. American popular culture is embraced worldwide; few countries want to be excluded from the American sphere however much they may criticize it.

Yet for all that, the country feels vulnerable, insecure, and uncertain. It is at war with radical Islamic terrorism. Without wholesale acceptance by the Islamic world—at least of the rule of law, and, at best, of the principle of democracy—and without a durable peace settlement in the Middle East, it is hard to see how the threat will be completely eliminated. Moreover, such a prospect is beyond America's sole capacity to achieve. The rest of the world insists that any legitimate aggression against sovereign states should take place within the framework of agreed international law and UN process. Preemptive U.S. intervention and military activism against states suspected of harboring terrorists or creating weapons of mass destruction means that the United States overtly and unilaterally sets the terms of international law in a manner that the rest of the world considers illegitimate—and thus undermines the action itself. Durable political settlements can only be organized within a framework of legitimacy.

Nor is legitimacy a mere legal construct. Legitimacy needs to be earned in its widest sense. It not only means observing the processes of multilateral law but putting pressure on Israel as much as on the Palestinians to reach a peace agreement, regime building in Afghanistan and other bankrupt states, constructing a fair trade, aid, and debt relief system, and broadening multilateralism. It also means accepting the irksome and even Lilliputian constraints of the international community. The conservative temptation to go it alone, however superficially seductive, is not an option. Acting alone may bring short-term gains, but in the long term, as a country that believes in the rule of law, the United States needs to make law not war.

At the same time confidence in the American economic model has waned. The New Economy has been gravely damaged by corporate fraud, plummeting stock prices on Wall Street, and the growing recognition that highly borrowed consumers cannot continue to drive American growth. American society, with its gated communities at the top and trailer parks at the bottom, is pockmarked by inequality and selfishness. There is a sense of foreboding about the future. Concern arises that important American values—duty, integrity, responsibility, and kindness—are being buried by an avalanche of commerciality and unrelieved self-interest. Opportunity and mobility, two of the country's greatest assets, are under assault as the rich tighten their grip on the instruments of economic and social advance, most notably education. America's political institutions, its social contract, and its framework of corporate and financial regulation have not yet fashioned a response. The country seeks and deserves better.

And better it will get, if America can rise above the conservative discourse that has dominated its national conversation for the last twenty years. There are two essential preconditions for change. First, America must become more self-knowing and modest—proud of its extensive achievements, certainly, but much more willing to face its shortcomings and admit the strengths of others. Pride in country is a noble emotion, but excessive patriotism, in the famous British aphorism, is the last refuge of the scoundrel. Too much scoundrel-like thinking has been allowed to become part of the accepted American consensus under the sobriquet that anything other than conservative thought is somehow "un-American."

The second precondition is a readiness to accept—alongside the rugged values of independence, individualism, and self-reliance—another set of values, centered on human interdependence. Conservatives want to write off interdependence as the creed of Europeans, Arabs, American liberals, and women. In their eyes interdependence caters to appeasers, wimps, welfarists, and socialists; to conservative minds it signifies soft options abroad and economic inefficiency at home.

If this book achieves one thing, I hope it shows that interdependence deserves to prevail. Only then can the United States, by reviving its social contract, regain the security and respect it craves from other countries and offer to its own citizens a genuine twenty-first-century version of the American dream.

The Challenge Abroad

A conservative approach to ordering the world is self-defeating, and would be even if the United States was the acme of economic, social, and moral virtue. Lying behind this approach is the exercise of brutish power and the demand that others submit to a superior force. As such, it is inherently pregnant with tension and ultimately unsustainable. This is problematic enough in America's relations within the industrialized West and Asia, but in the context of a complex militant Islamist terrorism and those who incubate it, such a stance ensures enduring enmity—and risk of another September 11.

Much brave talk of a new multilateralism followed the terrorist atrocities, but the hard truth is that the U.S. predisposition to unilateralism has been reinforced. America secured regime change in Afghanistan with little cost in terms of American lives and needed no help from any ally; indeed European offers were spurned because, had Europe been included, American freedom of action might have been modified. As a result, a precarious international effort to rebuild Afghanistan is not nearly as mobilized and engaged as it might have been. The same conservatives are inclined to support preemptive action against any other state suspected of harboring terrorist cells—President Bush's infamous "axis of evil"—and are hardening support for a militaristic Israel. America, in the view of its partners and allies, can no longer be relied upon to uphold international law or sustain the coalition that was painstakingly built after September 11. "It is the mission that defines the coalition," as Defense Secretary Donald Rumsfeld has repeatedly declared, "not the coalition that defines the mission."[1] In other words, the United States will set the strategic goal and execute it alone if necessary, a predisposition that undermines even those occasions when it does act multilaterally, as in the UN resolution over Iraq. Multilateralism must be authentic, rather than a tactic to serve unilateralism.

It has escaped nobody's attention that beyond terrorism and the Middle East, the United States's quest to impose world security arrangements around its own self-interest is quickening. Notice has been served on Russia: the United States seeks to install its own missile defense system against attack from rogue states and therefore it will no longer abide by the antiballistic missile treaty. The same unilateral attitude encompasses climate-change talks, agreements on chemical weapons, and the right to arrest and try those suspected of terrorism under military law, whether they live within the United States or have been extradited from abroad. Those looking to the United States to lead toward a new liberal framework of trade, aid, and debt relief to provide some succor to the less developed world can think again. At the Johannesburg Summit on poverty and development, the United States blocked almost every serious initiative. At this juncture, as at other times in its history, the United States is looking inward.

In economic terms this is especially hazardous. The rest of the world has, in effect, been required to accept globalization almost entirely on American conservative terms and around American conservative preoccupations. Yet economic interdependence inevitably follows globalization. Shockwaves from the collapse of Enron and WorldCom, history's largest bankruptcies, have spread far beyond the United States, as did the bubble and bust in dot-com and telecom shares. Largely owing to financial and telecom deregulation, pushed hard by the United States, the bubble and bust swamped all the leading stock markets. Estimated losses total up to $1 trillion in bankruptcies, write-offs, and telecom stock-price collapses worldwide.

For the first time since the 1974 oil shock, the world faces a prolonged period of below-average growth, and we do not have strong enough institutions or processes to attempt any global policy response. The IMF remains a satrapy of the U.S. Treasury. There is no international system of financial regulation, notwithstanding the fragilities of hedge funds and the domino impact of any financial institution's bankruptcy given today's integrated financial markets. The Group of Eight industrialized nations remains a talk shop only, with no systems for economic coordination. The United States repudiates suggestions for improvement as an infringement of its economic sovereignty. It continues to press for the "liberalization" of national regulatory structures. The world is required to build a market in which American transnationals and investment banks can run free, where capital can flow without hindrance to the United States to finance what for any other country would be an unsustainable trade deficit and buildup of private-sector debt.

Hopes in early 2002 that the dynamic U.S. economy would leap back into life, courtesy of cheaper oil and very low interest rates, have dissipated. In their place is a new realism, born from weakness in the stock market and distrust of American corporations. The likelihood of a quick return to 1990s growth is limited by a huge debt overhang and trade deficit, along with the United States's constant dependence on foreign capital. The financial system has taken a major hit, and U.S. consumers and businesses alike are chronically indebted. As it becomes clear that the United States is probably now unable to grow at exceptional rates, foreign capital inflows and the buoyancy of Wall Street will be undermined. The United States will be forced to adjust its ambitions and living standards, and it will resist. As a sign of the times, it has unilaterally imposed whopping tariffs to save its beleaguered but uncompetitive steel industry, in abuse of world trade rules. More such tariffs are likely to follow on agricultural products and semiconductors, with officials warning that America is no longer prepared to be "a market of last resort."[2] The EU is willing to fight fire with fire, disputing what it sees as one rule for the United States and another for the rest of the world. If the economy underperforms or foreigners stop buying America's financial assets, the U.S. proclivity for protecting itself and twisting the arms of its trading partners will grow more pronounced.

American electors are expected to endorse this fragile and insecure success at home, and others are expected to copy it abroad. If the American way was as successful as conservative propagandists claim, this might be rational—but the consistent argument of this book is that American capitalism is weaker than acknowledged, and that American society is seriously disfigured by the way its economy is structured and managed. This has been disguised so far but can be disguised no more. Ordinary Americans have forgiven the social consequences of its economic structures, for they have believed in the myth of the country's exceptional social mobility, along with their profound cultural attachment to a very particular idea of liberty. But as the economic tide recedes, this could waver. Recent domestic polls show enormous distrust of corporate America. Nor will the citizenry willingly turn a blind eye on the deformation of democracy by the forces of rapacious inequality—notably, the impact of cash on American politics. If this is the mood in America, it may lead to a harder examination of the claims made over the last decade.

Time for American Modesty

Insistence that the American model is best has squelched all arguments to the contrary. The consensus in the United States and European Union, at least until recently, holds that the route to economic success lies in "flexible" labor markets, financial markets ready to take "risks," corporate governance processes that maximize "wealth creation," and minimal regulation, taxation, and welfare. Accordingly, the European approach is definitionally wrong and must be changed, a proposition now accepted by many Europeans. This book argues that this blanket condemnation was and is mistaken.

Start with labor markets. For all its vaunted flexibility, the American labor market works fitfully, and European markets work better than most have imagined. American workers have trouble moving out of low-paid jobs, turnover rates are not especially high, and unemployment in low-skilled jobs relative to high-skilled jobs is higher than in "regulated" Europe. Much of America's success in job creation derives from immigrant and female laborers willing to work for low wages in the expanding service and security sectors. These are, of course, driven by buoyant, credit-driven spending. Light labor-market regulation did not obstruct this development and even enabled it; but it did not cause it.

Were the dot-com and telecom bubbles worth the financial deregulation that spawned them? Credulous European leaders at the Lisbon and Stockholm summits said that Europe should find ways to generate a similarly vigorous venture capital industry. They cannot have known that only a fraction of the thousands of initial public offerings financed by American venture capital over the 1990s are still trading above their offer price; many have gone bust. A number of commercial and investment banks that issued IPOs are now under inquiry by Congress and/or the Securities and Exchange Commission (SEC) and/or New York State's attorney general.

Some steps have been taken toward the European model. In compliance with the Sarbanes-Oxley Act, passed in summer 2002, American chief executives must sign off on their accounts on pain of potential imprisonment if falsification is found. This is a useful confirmation of what was already the law. But America needs to go much further, taking a long, cool look at its very foundations of enterprise. Great companies, as this book has argued, are great organizations with their own genetic code and purpose; they are not webs of contracts to be traded as disposable commodities in the name of "shareholder value." Europeans have put in place stronger safeguards to prevent the self-interested cronyism of American boards. Such caution no longer appears sclerotic. It appears wise and so does their caution in making takeover and merger too easy. Restructuring is a part of creative destruction in any capitalist system; when this idea, however, degenerates into an obsession with financial engineering, deal making, and financial manipulation, the results are wealth destroying rather than wealth creating.

Regulation, taxation, public provision, and welfare are attacked for their alleged economic ill-effects, and European examples are wheeled out to support the ideological cant. But we now know that this criticism cannot be supported. The benefits conferred by high-quality universal education and health care are rarely acknowledged. The gains from guaranteeing income for the marginalized and weak, which the welfare system provides, are equally underacknowledged. At heart, conservative American theory rests on a half-baked moral stance—that any idea of a social contract lying behind these European structures offends America's belief in individualism, liberty, and self-reliance.

Herein lies the rub. European civilization stands on values its leaders could not give up even if they wanted to, and to which America is linked by history, family, language, and institutions. Their roots lie deep and define what it means to be a European. They believe that the wealthy and propertied have obligations to their society, obligations that cannot be discharged by charity alone. This idea goes back to early Christendom, as does the notion that a settled people must form a social contract to entrench their association. It follows that a public realm should permit the articulation of what we hold in common. When turned into structures and policies, these principles produce the high-quality social outcomes that set Europe apart from the United States. They have also begun to give Europe an edge in productivity and innovation, albeit obscured by the unsustainable 1990s U.S. boom.

European history has had its peaks and troughs. This continent invented capitalism, democracy, and human rights, but it has also been soaked in war, dark ideology, and blood. Since 1945, it has rediscovered its better traditions and has better delivered democracy, human rights, the rule of law, and productive capitalism. To be sure, unemployment endures, caused chiefly by lack of demand across Europe that will remain depressed until the new single currency, the euro, is bedded down and a more confident, coherent system is established to coordinate monetary and fiscal policy. Meanwhile, the EU cannot have the same indifference to stimulating demand as America does. Europe has its share of political scandals. But, Italy apart, these scandals do not define its democratic systems. In none of them can office be so systematically bought—or democratic debate so explicitly defined—by those with money, as in the United States. Europeans have much to be proud of, and much to offer. It is time for America to look across the Atlantic and not mock what it sees, but to recognize that it shares European values. American reassertion of its Europeanness is long overdue.

Europe's Gathering Challenge

Europe's creation of the euro is an epic event, a tangible signal of willingness to express its interdependence, pool sovereignty, and exploit the gains that come from acting together. The euro should cement Europe's single market and by eliminating exchange-rate risk, allow European business to operate on a continental scale like its counterparts in the United States. But the euro does even more. It gives Europe a world currency—the only conceivable challenger to the dollar, with all that implies. Expansion will be possible under a monetary umbrella that insists on compliance with European regulations and approaches. Financial institutions and transnational companies must comply with American rules to win the benefits of a New York Stock Exchange listing. The European Union can play the same card. It can insist that globalization assumes a European dimension. That dimension casts a wide net: company law, financial regulation, workplace information and consultation, environmental standards, profit disclosure, transparency over accounts, and taxation. The United States will face a coequal economic partner across the Atlantic—and an equally confident but strikingly different economic and social model. In response, the United States will need to choose between interdependence and unilateralism.

The European Union will grow, probably soon admitting up to another eight countries in eastern Europe (excluding Bulgaria and Romania, who are expected to join later). It can become the exemplar of what a peaceful multilateral system of governance can achieve. The EU's cross-border initiatives demonstrate that multilateralism does work and can provide a vital bulwark of democracy, markets, social justice, and human rights. The European Court of Human Rights, along with Europe's commitment to an International Criminal Court, point the way. But above all, the EU offers a forum where Europe's nation-states can broker their differences and adopt common economic, social, and foreign policy positions. It is a novel development in world terms.

The world needs to build on this example, with the United States and the EU working in tandem, brokering a common vision. For example, the global economy needs a genuine supranational financial institution that monitors economic performance and supplies hard currency in times of difficulty. Instead it has the IMF. Argentina's economy collapsed, and it defaulted on its debt in December 2001. The IMF—and not for the first time—was forced into an absurd posture by its American masters; it should have intervened earlier and more generously. Argentina should have imposed capital controls and devalued the peso previously, rather than imposing a four-year recession on itself, but that option lay outside the orthodoxy promoted by Washington. The IMF needs more financial resources and a wholesale recasting of its economic thinking. The EU could provide the finance and insist that the Fund's approach change. It could, in extremis, reconstitute the IMF around the euro as an alternative world reserve currency. Perhaps this threat, above any other, might persuade the United States to take a more liberal stance.

The U.S. laxity on regulation of international financial institutions, accounting standards, and tax havens can no longer be abided. It gives a green light to feral capitalism, organized crime, and international terrorism. Trying to make U.S. accounting standards a global one is now risible. Likewise, the reluctant endorsement of the OECD's drive to improve disclosure standards in tax havens is inadequate. The globe needs a World Financial Authority that will oversee the balance sheets of international financial institutions, regulate international financial markets, set common accounting standards, and police tax havens. If the United States refuses to accept any infringement of its sovereignty, then the EU should go ahead and establish the authority anyway, in the expectation that one day the United States will join.

There needs also to be a recasting of relationships between the industrialized West and the less developed world. The EU already gives more than three-fifths of the world's aid, but on trade its record is poor. It remains too protectionist. The EU needs to rethink its attitude toward agriculture; instead of protecting domestic production of commodity foods, it should move into higher value-added production and open up its markets to producers in the less developed world. This, combined with a generosity toward Third World health expenditure and a reframing of the international financial and trade system, would raise living standards and prospects of the world's poorer populations. Again, in the face of U.S. reluctance the EU should blaze the trail.

According to the World Health Organization, some 640 million people in Third World countries have a life expectancy of 51 years of age, compared to that of 78 in richer countries. For every 1,000 live births, 159 of their children die; only 6 die in richer countries. Another 1.8 billion of the world's people live in countries where the figures are nearly this bad. If the richer countries allocated just 0.1 percent of their collective GDP in grants and offered between $15 and $20 per head for basic health spending in the less developed world, 8 million lives would be saved, as per the WHO.[3] That and the general overall improvement in life expectancy would raise the less developed world's income by $360 billion annually. It would be the biggest bang for our collective buck yet conceived.

George W. Bush's United States lifts only a grudging finger. From a conservative perspective, the WHO initiative—and other international initiatives—suffers from two colossal defects. It is predicated on public action to produce a global public good, and it involves a redistribution of income from rich to poor. It seems that the United States is reluctant to make common cause with its allies in a supranational initiative. So America stays aloof.

Consider also the case for a World Competition Authority, to police the immense concentrations of private corporate power now emerging. The International Criminal Court has already been mentioned, as has the UN Framework Convention on Climate Change. We need an international agreement on genetically modified food, child labor, space, piracy at sea, land mines, chemical weapons, the environment—the list goes on. In some of these areas the United States might get exactly the regime it wants; in others it will have to give ground—but the trade-off is always the same. Acting alone in any of these areas is an option available to the United States, but such autonomy will delegitimize the action. For any state that believes in the rule of law, legitimacy is the gold standard, a matter of self-interest as much as realpolitik. The United States must act multilaterally, and its necessary partner is the EU.

The same rules apply to security. There needs to be a credible deterrent to war. If war occurs, we need a credible means of brokering, and then policing, a settlement between the combatants. We also need a credible system for the inspection of weapons of mass destruction. Since the end of the Cold War, flagrant human rights abuses are no longer acceptable. The Indonesian, Serbian, and Iraqi subjugations of the Timorese, Kosovans, and Kurds, respectively, have been judged to violate human rights, and the international community responded with military interventions. Now Americans have eliminated terrorist bases within Afghanistan. The threats and disturbances will not go away, and the United States is faced with a choice. Does it want to shoulder the responsibility, cost, and risks of involvement alone? Or does it want to build a clear, internationally agreed-on system of rules? Any transgression of those rules would trigger an equally clear international response from, say, a standing supranational, highly mobile military force. Of course, the American military would necessarily be this force's most significant, and thus most influential, component. But that does not remove the case for collaboration. Quite simply, it is not in the U.S. or global interest for America to become the sole arbiter of world order, even if it has the power to do so.

Yet conservatives are right—such multilateral proposals do trigger major issues of sovereignty. How are decisions made and accountability assigned within such global initiatives? Are they intergovernmental collaborations, in which sovereignty rests with nation-states, or are they the forerunners of genuinely global institutions?

There's only one answer to this question, and it's not pleasing to conservative America. Already over the Kyoto climate accords and the International Criminal Court, the EU is going ahead, because it knows the globe cannot function without such agreements. In the decades to come, the world will develop other global institutions to discharge a multiplicity of global responsibilities. The UN, portrayed by conservative America as a nest of pink liberals and do-gooders, is actually an institutional arrangement upon which the globe must build. The U.S. position on Iraq was immeasurably strengthened by the UN resolution. It must be strengthened, and its processes made accountable and democratized. Here the EU has become both an inspiration and an exemplar. As a multilateral institution itself, it can do nothing other than back multilateralism.

The EU is ambitious, but also still young and burdened with problems. How much interdependence should it express? Is it a confederation of sovereign states or a federal supranational body? These questions are familiar to any student of American history. The EU's decision-making procedures tend to be administrative or by executive fiat; there is too little accountability, transparency, and democracy. And as yet there is no European public with a sense of "Europeanness" in which to ground its democracy. At present the EU is a series of national democracies. This union of 350 million people spends some $130 billion a year on defense, compared to the United States's $300 billion; until that gap is closed, the EU will lack overseas strength to underpin the international legal framework it supports.

It would all be so much better if the United States rejoined the world on new terms. From the viewpoint of this European, we badly need the better America—the liberal, outward-looking, and generous United States that won World War II and constructed a liberal world order that has sustained us to this day. Yet it is today's United States that places this valued world order at risk and menaces the world's capacity to recognize its interdependence. Even a U.S. president whose heart was in the right place, Bill Clinton, was forced by the current dynamic of U.S. politics into unwelcome postures. The United States should make common cause with the EU and reclaim its proudest legacy, that it underwrote democracy and international law by respecting multilateral processes. In this, George W. Bush's America cannot be consistently trusted—a dereliction that threatens to divide the West as never before.

Interdependence at Home and Abroad—Hard Liberalism as the Next American Frontier

The situation is not hopeless. Important, if limited, initiatives have been made to clean up business (the Sarbanes-Oxley Act) and politics (the McCain-Feingold Act), signs of a new public mood. In the new ideopolises, a new liberalism is developing that wants a revived and modernized social contract. That contract centers on the belief that government must invest in education, health, and transportation; it must protect equal rights and provide support for the disadvantaged. Public service and the role of government are no longer being decried with the same venom. The self-sacrifice and sense of duty of New York's firefighters on September 11, for example, could not be bought by any private enterprise. New Yorkers and the liberal East and West Coasts, along with the liberal Great Lakes region, understand this, and there are echoes even in the conservative heartland. An older, less brash civic America stands in the wings, ready to support a hard liberalism.

Three domestic battles must be won. The first is to attack the Wall Street view of wealth creation as short-term financial engineering. It should be seen as a social and organizational act as much as one of heroic individualism. The United States also needs to revisit its concept of the corporation. James Collins and Jerry Porras, in *Built to Last*, one of the great business books of the last ten years, show how the best visionary companies in the United States see profit not as their overriding purpose but as the oxygen that allows them to live and so deliver their higher, organizational raison d'être. Yet American company law, corporate governance, and financial systems now militate against companies acting in accordance with this objective. The United States needs more patient long-term investors; company boards should be balanced between executive and nonexecutive directors and act as stewards of the company's integrity, rather than as cronies of the CEO. Independent audits must give a true and fair view (as in Europe) of the integrity of the accounts. Stock options should be accounted for as a form of remuneration rather than regarded as a free, costless gift to executives. A good start has been made. The United States needs to take the constitution of its corporations as seriously as it takes its political constitution. It should legislate how they are governed.

Beyond this there needs to be a root-and-branch overhaul of the financial system. The separation between investment and commercial banking needs to be restored; state banks need to be better protected from takeover as vital components of a decentralized banking system. The Federal Reserve and the SEC need to take a robust approach to all forms of margin trading and be much readier to clamp down than they were during the 1990s bubble. Antimonopoly provisions in assessing the go-ahead for mergers and takeovers need to be vastly reinforced, and the lax accounting rules that allow takeover expenses to be hidden must be tightened. The SEC needs the resources and finance to enable it to complete its cycles of inspection every three years rather than every six, as at present. Obligations to inform and consult regularly with representatives of the workforce should be imposed. In short, the United States needs to equip itself with a regulatory environment in which entrepreneurs can build great companies rather than becoming financial chips in a crazed, short-term casino.

The second domestic battle is for the United States to offer a robust social contract, one in which the bottom 50 percent of Americans are offered a fair chance and protected against life's unavoidable hazards; inequality, hardship, and falling social mobility should not be countenanced in a country as rich in money and ideals as the United States. Here the proposition is the simple Rawlsian idea detailed in chapter 2. The United States should create an infrastructure of justice so that every citizen has a chance and is seen to have had one. America must be fair. There needs to be a sustained attempt to ensure high-quality education for the bottom 50 percent, and, as important, access to training. It boggles the mind that nearly half of America's eighteen-year-olds have no formal educational or training qualification. No wonder so many are trapped at the bottom. Grants to support students from low-income families attending college need to be restored to what they were twenty years ago. It is also a standing reproach to any concept of fairness that over forty million Americans have no access to medical care and are uninsured. Medicare must be universalized. Prisoners should be thought of as potential citizens; rehabilitation in the long run is cheaper and more moral than incarceration and permanent felon status.

Moreover, America's system of assistance to the old, disabled, and unemployed is too harsh. Half of Americans rely on Social Security for their pension; unemployment benefit is time limited. The campaign to lessen this assistance and to privatize Social Security must be confronted head on. It is a barbaric notion that poor citizens in retirement should rely wholly on what trivial sums they have personally saved and on the performance of the stock market. The rich should not be relieved of an obligation to contribute tax to support the pensions of those poorer. Without social-contract taxation, many Americans will live in penury and insecurity in their later years. Even if low-tax societies were universally more "moral" and more "economically efficient," this would be a contestable proposition.

Such social reforms would require higher taxation, although at levels short of those in Europe. This is a tough challenge for hard liberals; a notion that taxation is coercive and illegitimate runs deep in American culture. Yet the argument must be made. Taxation is the down payment for membership in civic society. It must not be unnecessarily high, but those who boast of avoiding and evading tax need to be seen for what they are— civic outlaws. The rash of gated communities and growth of private schools with private curricula are not simple expressions of individual choice; they are a form of civic secession that threatens the integrity of American life.

This leads directly to the third crucial battle: a struggle to relegitimize the public realm and see to it that America, above all else, lives up to its own criteria of democracy. That a successful bid for elected office depends on one's wealth is a travesty. The McCain-Feingold reform of campaign finance was a significant advance, attacking some of the wilder uses of soft money. But unless the United States caps election expenditure, its democracy will be little more than a procedural shell, its political discourse auctioned to corporate interests and the rich. This is not just about fairness. It is about setting new ground rules in order to create a forum for genuine political exchange and possibility of public action, thus breathing life into citizenship and civic participation. Perhaps that new wind can rattle the cynicism and disenchantment so entrenched in American's public realm.

In our new century, the fight for security, prosperity, and justice can no longer be won on any single nation's ground. It is international. It requires agreement on values and a political narrative. It requires courage and leadership. Europeans, however imperfectly, recognize these realities and will shoulder as much as they can alone—but the incompleteness of the EU's political architecture and the still unresolved question of how much should be carried on at EU or at nation-state level limits its effectiveness. If we, as a world, are really to make progress, we need America back as part of this multilateralist project. And Americans need to come back—in their own interest, and in the interest of us all. Pray God they will.

Notes

1: The Reckoning

1 Paul Kennedy of Yale University wrote in the *Financial Times* on February 2, 2002, that nothing in world history paralleled this degree of disparity of power.

2 Dominique Moïsi, deputy director of the French Institute for International Relations, is quoted in the *International Herald Tribune* (Feb. 4, 2002) as saying that Donald Rumsfeld's America now threatens NATO's cohesion as de Gaulle did in the 1960s.

3 The Conference Board 2002. Figures for the former West Germany from Adair Turner, *Just Capital: The Liberal Economy* (Macmillan, 2001).

4 *Business Week* (April 9, 2001) describes Exxon's "culture of radical cost reduction"; for a description of GE's strategy see Alan Kennedy's account in *The End of Shareholder Value: The Real Effects of the Shareholder Value Phenomenon and the Crisis it is Bringing to Business* (Orion Business, 2000).

5 "Rich Bosses Start to Feel the Squeeze," *Financial Times*, Sept. 14, 2002.

6 See Richard Freeman, *The U.S. Economic Model at Y2K: Lodestar for Advanced Capitalism*, working paper 7757 (National Bureau for Economic Research, June 2000), Exhibit 4.

7 Robert Frank, in Juliet Schor (ed.), *Do Americans Shop Too Much?* (Beacon, 2000).

8 See Wynne Godley and Alex Izuricta, *The Developing US Recession and Guidelines for Policy*, Levy Economics Foundation, Oct. 2001.

9 The Q ratio of stock market value of companies to their net worth reached 1.92 in the first quarter of 2000, 50 percent higher than the previous peaks in 1929 and 1969.

10 U.S. Federal Reserve, Flow of Funds Table L107.

11 See "Is the U.S. Trade Deficit Sustainable?" Washington, D.C., Institute for International Economics, 1999.

12 William Frey et al., *America by the Numbers* (New Press, 2001), p. 172.

13 Ibid., p. 138.

Notes

14 A good account is Robert Parry's "So Did Bush Steal the White House?" www.consortiumnews.com, Nov. 27, 2001.
15 Vincent Bugliosi, *The Betrayal of America* (Nation Books, 2001).
16 ABC News national survey, 1994; ACLU/BRS national surveys, 2001.

2: Custodians of the Light

1 Locke, John, *Two Treatises of Government*, ed. Peter Laslett (Cambridge University Press, 1988), II para. 34, p. 301.
2 Ibid., para. 96, p. 331.
3 Ibid., para. 27, p. 288.
4 Leslie J. Macfarlane, *Socialism, Social Ownership and Social Justice* (Macmillan, 1998), p. 26.
5 Quoted in Macfarlane, *Socialism*, pp. 26–27.
6 For example, Germany's Brother Arnold, a dissident Dominican monk, and France's Jean de Roquetaille, a radical Franciscan monk, both urged uprisings of the suffering peasantry against their duplicitous, oppressive betters—ranging from loose-living clergy to swindling merchants—to anticipate Christ's second coming. See Macfarlane, *Socialism*, op. cit.
7 Leo Strauss, *Natural Rights and History* (Chicago University Press, 1953), pp. 242–43.
8 "We the People of the United States, in Order to form a more perfect Union, establish Justice, insure domestic Tranquility, provide for the common defense, promote the general Welfare, and secure the Blessings of Liberty to ourselves and our Posterity, do ordain and establish this Constitution for the United States of America." From the Avalon Project at Yale Law School; see www.yale.edu/avalon/constpap.htm.
9 See Madison's notes of the Constitutional Convention in the Avalon Project at the Yale Law School at www.yale.edu/avalon/constpap.htm.
10 Leo Pfeffer, *This Honorable Court: A History of the United States Supreme Court* (Beacon Press, 1965).
11 For a discussion of this movement see Paul Misner, *Social Catholicism in Europe: From the Onset of Industrialisation to the First World War* (Darton, Longman & Todd, 1991).
12 Bernstein criticized Kautsky's vulgar theory of capitalist collapse. Capitalism was immensely adaptable, he argued. The socialist task was rather to embark on a never-ending process of capitalist reform, the explicit reasoning behind the Erfurt program. See Donald Sassoon, *One Hundred Years of Socialism: The West European Left in the Twentieth Century* (I. B. Tauris, 1996).
13 Quoted in Mark Mazower, *Dark Continent* (Penguin, 1998), p. 133.
14 Ibid., p. 135.
15 See Seymour Martin Lipset and Gary Marks, *It Didn't Happen Here* (W. W. Norton, 2000), table 8.5, p. 289.
16 Alberto Alesina, Rafael di Tella and Robert MacCulloch, "Inequality and Happiness: Are Europeans and Americans Different?" (Feb. 2001).
17 See his great work *The Division of Labor*: Emile Durkheim, *De la division du travail social* (Félix Alcan, 1893).
18 Philip Collins, "A Story of Justice," *Prospect*, May 2001.
19 Alexis de Tocqueville, *Democracy in America* (Cambridge, 1864), p. 244.
20 Daniel Lazare, "America the Undemocratic," *New Left Review*, Dec. 1998.

21 Ibid., p. 29.
22 See Michael Sandel, *Democracy's Discontent: America in Search of a Public Philosophy* (Harvard University Press, 1996).
23 De Toqueville, *Democracy in America*, pp. 183–84.
24 Richard John Neuhass, quoted by Wilfred McClay in the *New York Review of Books*, Oct. 1996.
25 See Michael Shudson, "Was There Ever a Public Sphere? If So, When? Reflections on the American Case," in *The Power of News* (Harvard University Press, 1995).
26 Kant, "An Answer to the Question: What is Enlightenment," *Political Writings*, ed. Hans Riess, trans. H. B. Nisbett (Cambridge University Press, 1970).
27 Hannah Arendt, *The Human Condition* (University of Chicago Press, 1958).

3: Waging War without Blood: The Collapse of American Liberalism

1 Milton Himmelfarb, quoted in Nina Easton, *The Gang of Five* (Simon & Schuster, 2000), p. 42.
2 See, e.g., Peter Diamond, "A Model of Price Adjustment," *Journal of Economic Theory*, no. 3 (1971).
3 See D. F. Hendry and N. R. Ericsson, "An Econometric Analysis of UK Money Demand in *Monetary Trends in the United States and the United Kingdom*," by Milton Friedman and Anna J. Schwartz, *American Economic Review* (1991), pp. 8–38. The authors were able to publish this challenge to Friedman and Schwartz only after lengthy negotiations.
4 Ruy Teixeira and Joel Rogers, *America's Forgotten Majority: Why the White Working Class Still Matters* (Basic Books, 2000).
5 David Reynolds, *One World Divisible* (W. W. Norton, 2000), p. 166.
6 See Robert Skidelsky, *John Maynard Keynes: Fighting for Britain* (Macmillan, 2000).
7 Between 1965 and 1971, the *Wall Street Journal* published an average of 20.7 editorials each year criticizing the size or role of government. In the next six years, 1971–76, the average jumped to 43.8 such editorials a year. Meanwhile the number of stories about government actually declined by about 2 percent each year. See Dick W. Olufs III, *The Making of Telecommunications Policy* (Lynne Rienner, 1999), p. 108.
8 Sidney Blumenthal, *The Rise of the Counterestablishment* (Harper & Row, 1988), pp. 51–58.
9 Davidson, *Under Fire*.
10 Jeffrey H. Birnbaum, *The Money Men: How the Media Undermine American Democracy* (Crown, 2000), p. 35.
11 Robert Dallek, *Ronald Reagan: The Politics of Symbolism* (Harvard University Press, 1994), p. 125.
12 Quoted in Thomas Byrne Edsall, *Chain Reaction: The Impact of Race, Rights and Taxes on American Politics* (W. W. Norton, 1991).
13 Paul Krugman, *Peddling Prosperity* (Norton, 1994), p. 135.
14 The classic text was Paul Kennedy's *The Rise and Fall of the Great Powers* (Random House, 1987).
15 Kenneth J. Heineman, *God Is a Conservative* (New York University Press, 1998), p. 208.
16 See William Berman, *America's Right Turn from Nixon to Clinton* (Johns Hopkins University Press, 1998).

17 Education spending fell by 9.2 percent, science by 19.1 percent, and transportation by 11 percent. See Robert Pollin, "Anatomy of Clintonomics," *New Left Review*, June 2000, p. 25.

18 See John B. Judis, *The Paradox of American Democracy: Elites, Special Interest and the Betrayal of Public Trust* (Random House, 2000), p. 204.

19 Quoted in Easton, *Gang of Five*, p. 308.

20 See David Brock, *Blinded by the Right* (Crown Publishing, 2002).

21 Teixeira and Rogers, *America's Forgotten Majority*, p. 51.

22 See Teixeira and Rogers, *America's Forgotten Majority*.

4: Greed Isn't Good for You

1 See Mary O'Sullivan, *Contests for Corporate Control: Corporate Governance and Economic Performance in the United States and Germany* (Oxford University Press, 2000), pp. 123–30.

2 Ibid., p. 156.

3 Lawrence Mishel, Jared Bernstein and John Schmitt, *The State of Working America* (Cornell University Press, 2001), p. 8.

4 Mark Zepengauer and Arthur Naiman, *Take the Risk of Welfare* (Odonion, 1996).

5 Alan Greenspan was on the record arguing for the abolition of Glass–Steagall as a priority for the Federal Reserve Board as early 1987; see Leonard Seabrooke, *US Power in International Finance: The Victory of Dividends* (Palgrave, 2001).

6 Gary A. Dymski, *The Bank Merger Wave: The Economic Causes and Social Consequences of Financial Consolidation* (M. E. Sharpe, 1999).

7 See David C. Mowery (ed.), *US Industry in 2000: Studies in Competitive Performance* (National Academy Press, 1999).

8 *Business Week*, Nov. 20, 2000.

9 Robert Monks, *The New Global Investors* (Capstone, 2001), p. 69.

10 Stephen Nickell, *The Performance of Companies* (Blackwell, 1995), p. 23.

11 *Business Week*, April 7, 1998.

12 Matthew Lynn, *Birds of Prey: The War Between Boeing and Airbus* (Four Walls Eight Windows, 1997), p. 217.

13 From W. Lazonick, "Creating and Extracting Value," in Michael A. Bernstein and David E. Adler (eds.), *Understanding American Economic Decline* (Cambridge University Press, 1994).

14 O'Sullivan, *Contests for Corporate Control*, p. 196.

15 Quoted ibid., p. 194.

16 G. Baker and G. Smith, *The New Financial Capitalists* (Cambridge University Press, 1998).

17 M. Jensen, "The Modern Industrial Revolution: Exit and the Failure of Internal Control Systems," *Journal of Finance* 48, no. 9 (July 1993), pp. 831–80.

18 See Scott Klinger of United for a Fair Economy, "The Bigger They Come, The Harder They Fall," April 6, 2001, on www.ufenet.org. In six out of seven one-year periods between 1993 and 2000 at least half the ten companies with the most highly paid CEOs underperformed the S&P 500 in the following year; in four of the five years the underperformance over the following three years ranged between 57 and 66 percent.

19 O'Sullivan, *Contests for Corporate Control*, pp. 170–71.

20   M. Jensen and R. Ruback, "The Market for Corporate Control: The Scientific Evidence," *Journal of Financial Economics* (1983), no. 11, pp. 5–50.

21   Matthias M. Bekier, Anna J. Bogardus and Tim Oldham, "Is the Belief that Mergers Drive Revenue Growth an Illusion?" *McKinsey Quarterly* (2001), no. 4.

22   KPMG, *Unlocking Shareholder Value, the Key to Success,* Jan. 2001.

23   Arthur Levitt said: "While the problem of earnings management is not new, it has risen in a market unforgiving of companies that miss Wall Street's consensus estimates." Quoted in O'Sullivan, *Contests for Corporate Control,* pp. 203–4.

24   See David Mowery, "Overview," in Mowery (ed.), *U.S. Industry in 2000.*

25   Harvard Business School Time Horizons Project, referred to in ch. 1 above, p. 19.

26   Mary O'Mahoney, *Britain's Productivity Performance, 1990–1996* (NIESR, 1999).

27   See Julian Callow, "Minding the Gap, CSFB (Europe Ltd., Sept. 6, 2001), fig. 6. The U.S. productivity gap calculated on net GPD to adjust for the EU's more conservative depreciation policies in national accounts is only marginally higher between 1995 and 2000—some 0.3 percent per annum.

28   See the discussion in David Coates, *Models of Capitalism: Growth and Stagnation in the Modern Era* (Polity, 2000), pp. 149–57, in which he variously cites Abramovitz, Lazonick, von Tunzelman, et al.

29   See Mowery (ed.), *U.S. Industry in 2000,* p. 8.

30   See Z. Griliches, "R&D and Productivity," in collected papers (University of Chicago, 1998); Ci Jones and J. C. Williams, "Measuring the Social Return to R&D," *Quarterly Journal of Economics* (Nov. 1998).

31   Michael E. Porter and Debra van Opstal, *U.S. Competitiveness 2001* (U.S. Council on Competitiveness, 2001).

32   Mandel, *The Coming Internet Depression,* p. 36.

33   Robert J. Gordon, "Does the 'New Economy' Measure up to the Great Inventions of the Past?" *Journal of Economic Perspectives* (2000).

34   William W. Lewis, Vincent Palmode, Badouin Regout, and Allen Webb, "What's Right with the U.S. Economy," *McKinsey Quarterly,* 2002, no. 1.

35   David Miles, in "Testing for Short-Termism in the UK Stock Market," *Economic Journal* (Nov. 1993), showed that profits expected in five years' time are undervalued by 40 percent.

36   In June 2001 Suria wrote in a research report for Lehman that Amazon "showed the financial characteristics that have driven innumerable retailers to disaster throughout history."

37   Quoted in Kennedy, *The End of Shareholder Value,* p. 65.

38   Quoted in *Business Week,* June 24, 2002, p. 164.

5: To Those Who Have Shall Be Given

1   Mishel et al., *The State of Working America,* p. 293.

2   Freeman, *U.S. Economic Model,* Exhibit 4.

3   Milton Friedman, *Capitalism and Freedom* (Chicago University Press, 1962).

4   Mishel et al., *The State of Working America,* table 7.16, p. 395.

5   The Policy Information Center, the Educational Testing Service Network, www.ets.org.

6   James Coleman found this figure in 1965 in *The Equality of Educational Opportunity;*

it was confirmed in 1997 by Harold Wenglinsky in *When Money Matters: How Educational Expenditures Improve Student Performance and How They Don't* (Princeton University Press, 1997).

7 Robert Hauser et al., "Occupation Status, Education and Social Mobility in the Meritocracy," in Kenneth Arrow, Samuel Bowles and Steven Durlauf (eds.), *Meritocracy and Economic Inequality* (Princeton University Press, 2000), p. 183.

8 Policy Information Center.

9 *Business Week*, Aug. 27, 2001, p. 75.

10 Quoted ibid.

11 OECD, *Education at a Glance: OECD Indicators* (OECD, 2000).

12 Robert H. Frank and Philip J. Cook, *The Winner-Take-All Society* (Free Press, 1995).

13 Robert Reich, *The Future of Success* (Knopf, 2001), pp. 145–57.

14 See Robert H. Frank, *Luxury Fever* (Free Press, 1999).

15 Ibid., pp. 14–32.

16 See Edward J. Blakely and Mary Gail Snyder, *Fortress America: Gated Communities in the United States* (Brookings Institution Press, 1997).

17 Ibid., p. 2.

18 See Patrick M. Garry, *A Nation of Adversaries: How the Litigation Explosion is Reshaping America* (Plenum Press, 1997).

19 See Martin Kettle in the *Guardian*, April 5, 2001, reporting the *Washington Post*'s lawyer's instruction to a reporter never to apologize again after a car accident in Kansas in which he said sorry.

20 Robert D. Putnam, *Bowling Alone* (Simon & Shuster, 2000), p. 42.

21 S. Knack and P. Keefern, "Does Social Capital Have an Economic Pay-off?" *Quarterly Journal of Economics*, 1997, 4, pp. 1251–88.

22 *Payne* v. *Western & Atlantic Railroad* (1884).

23 David H. Autor, *Outsourcing at Will: Unjust Dismissal Doctrine and the Growth of Temporary Help Employment*, NBER working paper 7557 (Feb. 2000).

24 Richard Sennett, *The Corrosion of Character* (W. W. Norton, 1998), p. 50.

25 OECD *Employment Outlook*, July 1999.

26 Mishel et al., *State of Working America*, pp. 316–17.

27 Michael Zweig, *The Working Class Majority: America's Best Kept Secret*, (Cornell University Press, 2000), p. 45.

28 Barbara Ehrenreich, *Nickel and Dimed* (Metropolitan Books, 2001), p. 214.

29 The 1996 Personal Responsibility and Work Opportunity Reconciliation Act abolished the New Deal Aid to Families with Dependent Children and replaced it with Temporary Assistance to Needy Families, setting a federal limit of five years over which benefits can be claimed; states may if they wish choose a shorter period. Virginia, for example, gives claimants only ninety days to find work before benefits cease.

30 *The Economist*, Aug. 25, 2001.

31 *Business Week*, Nov. 19, 2001, p. 10.

32 Mishel et al., *State of Working America*, p. 386.

33 OECD *Employment Outlook* 2000, ch. 2, "Earnings Mobility: Taking a Longer View."

34 Aarberge, Rolf et. al, "Income Inequality and Income Mobility in the Scandinavian Countries Compared to the United States" (1996), paper presented at the NEF workshop on income distribution, Sept. 26–27, 1996, Aarhus, Denmark; R. V.

Burkhauser and J. G. Poupore, "A Cross-National Comparison of Permanent Inequality in the United States and Germany during the 1980s," *Review of Economics and Statistics*, vol. 79, no. 1 (1997), pp. 10–17.

35 Robert Erikson and John Goldthorpe, "Are American Rates of Social Mobility Exceptionally High?" *European Sociological Review* (May 1985).

36 Mishel et al., *State of Working America*, p. 404.

37 See Economic Policy Institute, *Hardship in America* (Washington: 2001).

38 Elizabeth Drew, *The Corruption of American Politics: What Went Wrong and Why* (Overlook Press, 2000).

39 Birnbaum, *The Money Men*, pp. 65–66.

40 All figures from Frank, *Luxury Fever*, pp. 56–61.

41 Carla Brooks Johnston, *Screened Out: How the Media Control Us and What We Can Do About It* (M. E. Sharpe, 2000).

42 Ibid.

43 Quoted in Bartholomew H. Sparrow, *Uncertain Guardians: The News Media as a Political Institution* (Johns Hopkins University Press, 1999).

44 See Katherine Beckett and Theodore Sasson, *The Politics of Injustice* (Pine Forge Press, 2000).

45 Chrysler refused to advertise on ABC's *Ellen* in 1997 when the title heroine came out as a lesbian.

46 See James Fallows, *Breaking the News: The Real Story of Political Power in America* (Crown, 2000).

47 Sparrow, *Uncertain Guardians*.

48 *The Elements of Journalism: What Newspeople Should Know and the Public Should Expect* Bill Kovach and Tom Rosenstiel (Three Rivers Press, 2001), pp. 70–72.

49 Richard Cohen, "The Corporate Takeover of News," in Erik Barnouw et al. (eds.), *Conglomerates and the Media* (New Press, 1997), p. 32.

50 Margaret Crawford, "The World in a Shopping Mall," in Michael Sorkin (ed.), *Variations on a Theme Park* (Hill & Wang, 2000).

51 Ibid.

6: The Globalization of Conservatism

1 Richard Grasso, chair of the New York Stock Exchange, in 1997, quoted in Seabrooke, *U.S. Power in International Finance*; David Rothkopf, Clinton's former deputy under-secretary of commerce, "In Praise of Cultural Imperialism," *Foreign Policy*, no. 107 (Summer 1997).

2 *The Times*, Sept. 12, 2001, p. 2.

3 Robert Wade, "Inequality of World Incomes: What Should Be Done," www.opendemocracy.com.

4 See Anthony Giddens's 1999 Reith lecture series, "Runaway World."

5 *International Herald Tribune*, Feb., 23–24, 2002

6 Reynolds, *One World Divisible*, p. 404.

7 Andrew Walter, *World Power and World Money* (Harvester Wheatsheaf, 1993), p. 179.

8 David Held et al., *Global Transformations* (Polity, 1999), p. 211.

9 Nicholas Guyatt, *Another American Century? The United States and the World after 2000* (Zed, 2000), p. 8.

10 See Seabrooke, *U.S. Power in International Finance*.

11 Ibid.

12 Quoted in Barry Eichengreen, *Globalizing Capital* (Princeton University Press, 1996), p. 152.

13 See William Darity and Bobbie Horn, *The Loan Pushers* (Ballinger, 1988).

14 William R. Cline, *International Debt: Systemic Risk and Policy Response* (Institute for International Economics, 1984) pp. 23–26.

15 Seabrooke, *U.S. Power in International Finance*, p. 165.

16 Paul Blustein, "The Chastening: Inside the Crisis that Rocked the Global Financial System and Chastened the IMF," *Public Affairs* (2001).

17 Sachs is quoted as saying, 'Instead of dousing the fire the IMF in effect screamed 'fire in the theater' ": John Eatwell and Lance Taylor, *Global Finance at Risk* (New Press, 2000), p. 170.

18 World Bank, *Trade and Industrialization Report 1987*, quoted by Robert Wade in *New Left Review*, June 1996.

19 Reported Jan. 19, 2000, on the Internet service Business Line, www.indiaserver.com/businessline.

20 Joseph Stiglitz, "What I Learned at the World Economic Crisis," *New Republic*, April 17, 2000.

21 See Peter Gowan, *The Global Gamble: Washington's Faustian Bid for World Dominance* (Verso, 1999).

22 Reported Jan. 19, 2000, on the Internet service Business Line, www.indiaserver.com/businessline.

23 Reynolds, *One World Divisible*, p. 517.

24 FCC heads Fowler and Brenner argued in 1982 that the "perception of broadcasters as community trustees should be replaced by a view of broadcasters as marketplace."

25 The long-distance team included former Senate Republican leader Howard Baker and Marlin Fitzwater, President Bush's press officer, while the representatives of the regional companies (RBOCs) included Roy Neel, former deputy chief of staff under Clinton.

26 Dan Roberts, "Glorious Hopes on a Trillion-Dollar Scrapheap," *Financial Times*, Sept. 5, 2001.

7: Britain in the American Bear Hug

1 *Wall Street Journal*, June 19, 2001.

2 See Dominic Hobhouse and Alan Duncan, *Saturn's Children: How the State Devours Liberty and Prosperity* (Sinclair-Stevenson, 1995).

3 Ronald Inglehart, Miguel Basaney and Alejandro Moreno, *Human Values and Beliefs: A Cross-Cultural Sourcebook. Political, Religious, Sexual and Economic Norms in 43 Countries: Findings from the 1990–93 World Value Survey* (University of Michigan Press, 1998).

4 Roger Jowell et al., *British Social Attitudes; the 16th Report. Who Shares New Labour Values?* (National Centre for Social Research, 1999).

5 Quoted in David Dolowitz, *Learning from America: Policy Transfer and the Development of the British Workfare State* (Sussex Academic Press, 1998).

6   Ibid., p. 57.

7   Nuffield Trust, *Reflections on the Management of the NHS* (Nuffield Trust, 1985).

8   Peter Dixon of Commerzbank finds a negative correlation between tax borders and competitiveness. See "Taxing Questions of Growth," David Smith, *Sunday Times*, March 3, 2002.

9   HM Treasury, *The Myners Report* (2001), table 1.1, p. 27.

10 E. Philip Davis and Benn Steil, *Institutional Investors* (MIT Press, 2001).

11 Professor David Storey, head of the small business research center at the Warwick Business School, quoted in the *Sunday Times*, July 2, 2000: "If you look at start-up rates, attitudes to enterprise and provision of venture capital, there is no doubt that America wins hands down. We [Britain] are closer to America than most of the rest of Europe but we have a long way to go."

12 All figures derived from OECD *Economic Outlook*, December 2001. The UK's GDP growth between 1999 and 2003 is projected at 2.3 percent and employment growth at 0.8 percent. For France, the comparable figures are 2.6 and 1.6 percent, for Italy 2.1 and 1.3 percent, and for Germany 1.9 and 0.6 percent.

13 The 2001 Capex Scoreboard, DTI Innovation Unit, 2001.

14 Adair Turner, *Just Capital*, table 4.4, p. 117.

15 These comments are all derived from Stelzer's *Sunday Times* columns in the first eight months of 2001, notably those of Feb. 25, July 1, and Aug. 5. Occasionally his relentless anti-Europeanism and pro-Americanism lifts, but only when the U.S. government—as in contesting the EU's pro-competition ruling against GE's bid for Honeywell—falls from grace by not sticking to its usual pro-competition guns (see his column of June 24, 2001).

16 See Andy Thornley, *Urban Planning under Thatcherism: The Challenge of the Market* (Routledge, 1991).

17 OECD *Economic Outlook*, June 2001, p. 213.

18 Judi Bevan, *The Rise and Fall of Marks & Spencer* (Profile, 2001), p. 177.

19 See Roger Ford in *Modern Railways*, June 2001. Ford calculates that Railtrack's track maintenance costs have risen by 35 percent since 1997 and that major electrification projects have cost three times as much.

20 Institute for Public Policy Research, *Building Better Partnerships* (IPPR, 2001), p. 32.

21 The GMB union calculates that the cost of building the first fourteen private-sector financed NHS hospitals will be at least £1.3 billion—almost double the original £766 million estimate. See *Sunday Times*, Aug. 5, 2001.

22 In 1995 the government actuaries' department identified 38,000 active final salary plans; industry specialist Stewart Ritchie of Scottish Equitable estimates the 2002 figure at 10,000. The trend is confirmed by the National Association of Pension Funds; see Nicholas Timmins, *Financial Times*, Feb. 11, 2002.

8: Europe Works

1   The 1995 Vienot report, modeled on the UK's Cadbury report calling for codified and improved corporate governance, set out a voluntary code in which French companies were to become more Anglo-Saxon in their attitudes toward accounting, cross-share-holding, treatment of minority shareholders, presence of nonexecutive directors and separation of powers between the chairman and chief executive.

Notes

2   DTI, 11th annual R&D scoreboard, Sept. 27, 2001.

3   Ludiger Pries, *Accelerating from a Multinational to a Transnational Carmaker: The Volks-wagen Consortium in the 1990s* (Institute of Sociology, University of Erlangen-Nurnberg, 1999).

4   DTI, 11th annual R&D scoreboard.

5   Dan Steinbock, *The Nokia Revolution: The Story of an Extraordinary Company that Transformed an Industry* (Amacom, 2001), p. 128.

6   Francesco Daveri and Guido Tabellini, *Unemployment, Growth and Taxation in Industrial Countries* (Centre for Economic Policy Research, 1997).

7   Davis Global Investors' Report, cited in *L'Expansion*, July 10, 1997: "La France améliore son gouvernement d'entreprise. Capitalistes, encore un effort."

8   All figures from Doug Henwood, *Wall Street: How It Works and For Whom* (Verso, 1997).

9   Volkswagen, "Financial control system" (2001), p. 5.

10 Richard Deeg, *Finance Capitalism Unveiled: Banks and the German Political Economy* (University of Michigan Press, 1999).

11 Ivan L. Pitt and John R. Norsworthy, *Economics of the U.S. Commercial Airline Industry: Productivity, Technology and Deregulation* (Kluwer Academic, 1999), p. 23.

12 See OECD *Employment Outlook,* July 2000, p. 50.

13 Robert Buchele and Jens Christiansen, "Do Employment and Income Security Cause Unemployment? A Comparative Study of the US and the E-4," *Cambridge Journal of Economics* (1998), 22. "Nonemployment" includes the unemployed and so-called inactive workers who are not in receipt of formal unemployment benefit but are receiving other forms of income support, e.g., incapacity benefits.

14 Fritz Scharpf, *Governing in Europe: Effective and Democratic?* (European University Institute, 1999).

15 Ibid., pp. 128–29.

16 Ibid., p. 130.

17 Stephen Nickell, "The Distribution of Wages and Unemployment Across Skill Groups," in Michael Landesmann and Karl Pichelman (eds.), *Unemployment in Europe* (Macmillan, 2000).

18 See Schmitt and Mishel, chapter 5.

19 Robert Buchele and Jens Christiansen find that job turnover rates in France were 27.6 percent, in Italy and the U.S. 23.7 percent, in Germany 16.5 percent, and the UK 14.4 percent. See their "Do Employment and Income Security Cause Unemployment?"

20 Peter Taylor-Gooby (ed.), *Welfare States under Pressure* (Sage, 2002).

21 Figures computed from OECD *Economic Outlook,* June 2001.

22 Ibid.

23 *OECD Economic Surveys—Germany* (OECD, May 2001).

9: Siblings under the Skin

1   See *OECD Economic Survey of the Euro Area* (OECD, 2001), figures 4 and 12 and table 11. The dispersion of interest rates and inflation has fallen dramatically, while members of the euro area have nearly identical budgetary stances.

2 The OECD 2001 country survey for Germany says that 44 percent of wage agreements are set collectively and a further 20 percent voluntarily follow the collective agreement. See *OECD Economic Surveys—Germany* (OECD, May 2001).

3 This story is told in Kathleen Thelen, "Why German Employers Cannot Bring Themselves to Dismantle the German Model," in Torben Iversen et al. (eds.), *Unions, Employers and Central Banks* (Cambridge University Press, 2000).

4 O'Sullivan, *Contests for Corporate Control*, p. 246.

5 See Ian Finlay, Stuart Niven and Stephanie Young (eds.), *Changing Vocational Education and Training: An International Comparative Perspective* (Routledge, 1998).

6 Wolfgang Streeck, "Beneficial Constraints on the Economic Limits of Rational Voluntarism," in J. Rogers Hollingsworth and Robert Boyer (eds.), *Contemporary Capitalism: The Embeddedness of Institutions* (Cambridge University Press, 1997), p. 205.

7 Combined employer and employee social security contributions are for Austria 38 percent of labor costs, for the Netherlands 37 percent, and for Germany and Belgium 34 percent: OECD, *Taxing Wages in OECD Countries, 1998–99*.

8 See Martin Hopner, *Corporate Governance in Transition: Ten Empirical Findings on Shareholder Value and Industrial Relations in Germany*, discussion paper 01/05 (Max Planck Institute, 2001).

9 Ibid.

10 Deeg, *Finance Capitalism Unveiled*.

11 Ibid.

12 For a useful description of East European capitalism, see Lawrence Peter King, *The Basic Features of Postcommunist Capitalism in Eastern Europe: Firms in Hungary, the Czech Republic and Slovakia* (Praeger, 2001).

13 Trade union coverage of the workforce is 95.6 percent for Finland, 89.9 percent for Denmark, 86.4 percent for Sweden, and 71.3 percent for Norway. See TUC Task Force on Promoting Trade Unionism, *Reaching the Missing Millions* (TUC, Aug. 2001), p. 17.

14 Income tax as a proportion of gross wages runs at 34 percent in Denmark, 28 percent in Finland, 27 percent in Sweden, and 22 percent in Norway, compared with 21 percent in Germany, 11 percent in Austria, and 7 percent in the Netherlands. Social security contributions, however, are lower than those in Germany, the Netherlands, and Austria by a very considerable margin. See OECD, *Taxing Wages*.

15 Pal Eitrheim and Stein Kuhnle, *The Scandinavian Model: Trends and Perspectives*, EU working paper 99/7 (1999).

16 *Sweden: a Guide to Financial Management in a Global Economy* (Economist Intelligence Unit, 2001).

17 The OECD, in "Employment Protection and Labour Market Performance," gives employment protection rankings of 3.7 to Portugal, 3.5 to Greece, 3.4 to Italy, and 3.1 to Spain. By contrast, Britain ranks at 0.9. See OECD *Employment Outlook 2000*.

18 Arthur R. Pinto and Gustavo Visentini (eds.), *The Legal Basis of Corporate Governance in Publicly Held Corporations: A Comparative Approach* (Kluwer Law International, 1998).

19 Peter Hall, "The Evolution of Economic Policy," in A. Guyomarch, H. Machin, P. Hall and J. Hayward (eds.), *Developments in French Politics 2* (Palgrave, 2001).

20 France's index number is 2.8: OECD *Employment Outlook 2000*.

21 Charles Grant, in his pamphlet *EU 2010: An Optimistic Vision for the Future* (Centre for

Notes

European Policy Reform, 2001), looks forward to a 2010 when "globalisation is forcing even the French to liberalise their economy." (p. 4).

22 Hall, "Evolution of Economic Policy."
23 *OECD Economic Surveys—France* (OECD, 1997).
24 Pinto and Visentini, *The Legal Basis of Corporate Governance.*
25 Britain's index number is 0.9; see note 17 above.
26 *British Social Attitudes; the 16th Report.*
27 Timothy Smeeding, *Financial Poverty in Developed Countries: The Evidence from the Luxembourg Income Study* (UNDP, 1997).
28 All replacement ratios from OECD, *Benefit Systems and Work Incentives* (OECD, 1999).
29 Taylor-Gooby, *Welfare States under Pressure*, ch. 8.
30 Richard Freeman, *The Politics of Health in Europe* (Manchester University Press, 2000), p. 60.
31 Frey et al., *America by the Numbers.*
32 OECD, *Health Data 1999: A Comparative Analysis of 29 Countries* (OECD).
33 Ibid.
34 Commonwealth Fund, *International Health Policy Survey* (1998).
35 See Emmanuel Paraschos, *Media Law and Regulation in the European Union: National, Transnational and U.S. Perspectives* (Iowa State University Press, 1998).
36 Alain Supiot, quoted in Mark Freedland and Silvan Sciarra (eds.), *Public Services and Citizenship in EU Law* (Clarendon, 1998), p. 139.

Conclusion

1 Quoted in *Financial Times*, Dec. 19, 2001.
2 Grant Aldonas, U.S. undersecretary of commerce for international trade, quoted in the *Financial Times*, March 13, 2002.
3 Commission on Economic Development and Health, World Health Organization, Dec. 2001.

References

Aarberge, Rolf, et al., "Income Inequality and Income Mobility in the Scandinavian Countries Compared to the United States" (1996), paper presented at the NEF workshop on income distribution, Sept. 26–27, 1996, Aarhus, Denmark

Albert, Michel, *Capitalism Against Capitalism* (Whurr, 1993)

Alesina, Alberto, di Tella, Rafael, and MacCulloch, Robert, "Inequality and Happiness: Are Europeans Different?" (Feb. 2001)

Arendt, Hannah, *The Human Condition* (University of Chicago Press, 1958)

Arestis, Philip (ed.), *Employment, Economic Growth and the Tyranny of the Market* (Edward Elgar, 1996)

Arestis, Philip (ed.), *Keynes, Money and the Open Economy* (Edward Elgar, 1996)

Arestis, Philip, and Marshall, Mike (eds.) *The Political Economy of Full Employment* (Edward Elgar, 1995)

Aristotle, *Politics*, trans. C. D. C. Reeve (Hackett, 1998)

Augar, Philip, *The Death of Gentlemanly Capitalism* (Penguin, 2001)

Autor, David H., *Outsourcing at Will: Unjust Dismissal Doctrine and the Growth of Temporary Help Employment*, NBER working paper 7557 (Feb. 2000)

Baker, G., and Smith, G., *The New Financial Capitalists* (Cambridge University Press, 1998)

Balanya, Belen, et al., *Europe Inc* (Pluto, 2000)

Barber, Benjamin R., "How to Make Society More Civil and Democracy Strong," in Anthony Giddens (ed.), *The Global Third Way Debate* (Polity, 2001)

Barnouw, Erik, et al., *Conglomerates and the Media* (New Press, 1997)

Barry, Brian, *Culture and Equality: An Egalitarian Critique of Multiculturalism* (Polity, 2001)

Bauman, Zygmunt, *Globalization: The Human Consequences* (Polity, 1998)

Baun, Michael J., "'The Maastricht Treaty as High Politics: Germany, France, and European Integration," *Political Science Quarterly* (Winter 1996)

Beck, Wolfgang, van der Maesen, Laurent, and Walker, Alan (eds.), *The Social Quality of Europe* (Kluwer Law International, 1997)

References

Beckett, Katherine, and Sasson, Theodore, *The Politics of Injustice* (Pine Forge Press, 2000)

Bedau, Hugo Adam, *The Death Penalty in America: Current Controversies* (Oxford University Press, 1997)

Begg, David (ed.) *EMU Prospects and Challenges* (Oxford University Press, 1998)

Bekier, Matthias M., Bogardus, Anna J., and Oldham, Tim, "Is the Belief that Mergers Drive Revenue Growth an Illusion?" *McKinsey Quarterly* (2001), no. 4

Berman, Morris, *The Twilight of American Culture* (W. W. Norton, 2000)

Berman, William C., *America's Right Turn from Nixon to Clinton* (Johns Hopkins University Press, 1998)

Bernstein, Michael A., and Adler, David E. (eds.), *Understanding American Economic Decline* (Cambridge University Press, 1994)

Bevan, Judi, *The Rise and Fall of Marks & Spencer* (Profile, 2001)

Birnbaum, Jeffrey H., *The Money Men: How the Media Undermine American Democracy* (Crown, 1996)

Bitsch, Marie-Thérèse, *Histoire de la construction Européenne*, 2nd ed. (Editions Complexe, 1999)

Blakely, Edward J., and Snyder, Mary Gail, *Fortress America: Gated Communities in the United States* (Brookings Institution Press, 1997)

Bluestone, Barry, and Harrison, Bennett, *Growing Prosperity* (Houghton Mifflin, 2000)

Blumenthal, Sidney, *The Rise of the Counterestablishment* (Harper & Row, 1988)

Blustein, Paul, "The Chastening: Inside the Crisis that Rocked the Global Financial System and Chastened the IMF," *Public Affairs* (2001)

Bossuat, G., and Wilkens, A. (eds.), *Jean Monnet. L'Europe et les chemins de la Paix*, proceedings of a colloquium organized by Paris 1 University and the Historical German Institute, Paris, May 1997 (Publications de la Sorbonne, 1999)

Bowman, Scott R., *The Modern Corporation and American Political Thought: Law, Power and Ideology* (Pennsylvania State University, 1996)

Brock, David, *Blinded by the Right* (Crown Publishing, 2002)

Brown, Kenneth M., *Downsizing Science—Will the United States Pay a Price?* (AEI Press, 1998)

Buchele, Robert, and Christiansen, Jens, "Do Employment and Income Security Cause Unemployment? A Comparative Study of the US and the E-4," *Cambridge Journal of Economics*, vol. 22 (1998)

Bugliosi, Vincent, *The Betrayal of America* (Nation Books, 2001)

Burkhauser, R. V., and Poupore, J. G., "A Cross-National Comparison of Permanent Inequality in the United States and Germany during the 1980s," *Review of Economics and Statistics*, vol. 79, no. 1 (1997), pp. 10–17

Calhoun, Craig (ed.) *Habermas and the Public Sphere* (MIT Press, 1992)

Callinicos, Alex, *Against the Third Way* (Polity, 2001)

Carter, Dan T., *From George Wallace to Newt Gingrich—Race in the Conservative Counterrevolution, 1963–94* (Louisiana State University Press, 1996)

Charkham, Jonathan, *Keeping Good Company: A Study of Corporate Governance in Five Countries* (Clarendon Press, 1994)

Clayton, Richard, and Pontusson, Jonas, *New Politics of the Welfare State Revisited: Welfare Reform, Public Sector Restructuring and Inegalitarian Trends in Advanced Capitalist Societies* (European University Institute, 1998)

Cline, William R., *International Debt: Systemic Risk and Policy Response* (Institute for International Economics, 1984)

Coates, David, *Models of Capitalism: Growth and Stagnation in the Modern Era* (Polity, 2000)

Cobham, David, and Zis, George (eds.), *From EMS to EMU* (Macmillan, 2000)

Cockett, Richard, *Thinking the Unthinkable: Think Tanks and the Economic Counter-Revolution, 1931–83* (HarperCollins, 1994)

Cohen, G. A., *If You're an Egalitarian, How Come You're So Rich?* (Harvard University Press, 2000)

Coleman, James, *The Equality of Educational Opportunity* (U.S. Government Printing Office, 1996)

Collins, D., "Social Policy," in J. Lodge (ed.), *Institutions and Policies of the European Community* (Pinter, 1983)

Collins, James C., and Porras, Jerry I., *Built to Last: Success Habits of Visionary Companies* (Century, 1994)

Commonwealth Fund, *International Health Policy Survey* (Commonwealth Fund, 1998)

Comor, Edward A., *Communication, Commerce and Power: The Political Economy of America and the Direct Broadcasting Satellite 1960–2000* (Macmillan, 1998)

Cook, Adell, *Between Two Absolutes: Public Opinion and the Politics of Abortion* (Westview, 1992)

Council on Competitiveness, *U.S. Competitiveness 2001* (Council on Competitiveness, 2001)

Cox, Ronald W., and Skidmore-Hess, Daniel, *U.S. Politics and the Global Economy: Corporate Power, Conservative Shift* (Lynne Rienner, 1999)

Cram, Laura, "The Commission as a Multi-organisation: Social Policy and IT Policy in the EU," *Journal of European Public Policy*, vol. 1, no. 2 (1994)

Critchlow, Donald, *Intended Consequences* (Oxford University Press, 1999)

Cummings, Stephen D., *The Dixification of America* (Praeger, 1998)

Curtin, Deirdre M., *Postnational Democracy: The European Union in Search of a Political Philosophy* (Kluwer Law International, 1997)

Dallek, Robert, *Ronald Reagan: The Politics of Symbolism* (Harvard University Press, 1994)

Darity, William, and Horn, Bobbie, *The Loan Pushers* (Ballinger, 1988)

Daveri, Francesco, and Tabellini, Guido, *Unemployment, Growth and Taxation in Industrial Countries* (Centre for Economic Policy Research, 1997)

Davidson, Osha Gray, *Under Fire: The NRA and the Battle for Gun Control* (University of Iowa Press, 1998)

Davis, E. Philip, and Steil, Benn, *Institutional Investors* (MIT Press, 2001)

Deeg, Richard, *Finance Capitalism Unveiled: Banks and the German Political Economy* (University of Michigan Press, 1999)

Dehousse, Renaud, "Integration vs Regulation? On the Dynamics of Regulation in the European Community," *Journal of Common Market Studies*, vol. 30, no. 4 (1992)

DeMartino, George F., *Global Economy, Global Justice: Theoretical Objections and Policy Alternatives to Neoliberalism* (Routledge, 2000)

Denham, Andrew, *Think Tanks of the New Right* (Dartmouth, 1996)

Diamond, Peter, "A Model of Price Adjustment," *Journal of Economic Theory*, no. 3 (1971)

Dolowitz, David, *Learning from America: Policy Transfer and the Development of the British Workfare State* (Sussex Academic Press, 1998)

Dolowitz, David, et al., *Policy Transfer and British Social Policy: Learning from the USA?* (Open University Press, 2000)

Dore, Ronald, *Stock Market Capitalism: Welfare Capitalism, Japan and Germany vs. the Anglo-Saxons* (Oxford University Press, 2000)

References

Drew, Elizabeth, *The Corruption of American Politics: What Went Wrong and Why* (Overlook Press, 2000)

Drew, Elizabeth, *Whatever It Takes* (Penguin, 1997)

Drury, Shadia B., *Leo Strauss and the American Right* (Macmillan, 1997)

Durkheim, Emile, *De la division du travail social*, 5th ed. (Félix Alcan, 1926; first publ. 1893)

Dworkin, Ronald, "Does Equality Matter?" in Anthony Giddens (ed.), *The Global Third Way Debate* (Polity, 2001)

Dymski, Gary A., *The Bank Merger Wave: The Economic Causes and Social Consequences of Financial Consolidation* (M. E. Sharpe, 1999)

Easton, Nina J., *Gang of Five* (Simon & Schuster, 2000)

Eatwell, John, and Taylor, Lance, *Global Finance at Risk* (New Press, 2000)

Economic Policy Institute, *Hardship in America* (2001)

Economist Intelligence Unit, *Sweden: a Guide to Financial Management in a Global Economy* (EIU, 2001)

Edsall, Thomas Byrne, *Chain Reaction: The Impact of Race, Rights and Taxes on American Politics* (Norton, 1991)

Ehrenreich, Barbara, *Nickel and Dimed* (Metropolitan Books, 2001)

Ehrman, John, *The Rise of Neoconservatism: Intellectuals and Foreign Affairs* (Yale University Press, 1995)

Eichengreen, Barry, *Globalizing Capital* (Princeton, 1996)

Eitrheim, Pal, and Kuhnle, Stein, *The Scandinavian Model: Trends and Perspectives*, EU working paper 99/7 (1999)

Enthoven, Alain, *Reflections on the Management of the NHS* (Nuffield Trust, 1985)

Erikson, Robert, and Goldthorpe, John, "Are American Rates of Social Mobility Exceptionally High?" *European Sociological Review* (May 1985)

Esping-Andersen, Gosta, *The Three Political Economies of the Welfare State* (European University Institute, 1988)

Esping-Andersen, Gosta, "A Welfare State for the Twenty-first Century," in Anthony Giddens (ed.), *The Global Third Way Debate* (Polity, 2001)

European Commission, *One Market, One Money: European Economy*, 44 (Luxembourg, Oct. 1990)

European Commission, *RTD Strategies of the Top 500 European Industrial Companies and their Participation in the Framework Programme and EUREKA*, report 17244 (European Commission, 1996)

Fairris, David, *Shopfloor Matters: Labor–Management Relations in Twentieth-Century American Manufacturing* (Routledge, 1997)

Fallows, James, *Breaking the News: The Real Story of Political Power in America* (Crown, 2000)

Ferrera, Maurizio, Hemerijck, Anton, and Rhodes, Martin, "The Future of Social Europe: Recasting Work and Welfare in the New Economy," in Anthony Giddens (ed.), *The Global Third Way Debate* (Polity, 2001)

Finlay, Ian, Niven, Stuart, and Young, Stephanie (eds.), *Changing Vocational Education and Training: An International Comparative Perspective* (Routledge, 1998)

Fischer, Andrew, Jordan, Thomas, and Lack, Caeser, *Giving Up the Swiss Franc: Some Considerations on Seigniorage under EMU*, CEPR discussion paper DP 3156 (Dec. 2001)

Fligstein, Neil, and Mara-Drita, Iona, "How to Make a Market: Reflections on the Attempt to Create a Single Market in the European Union," *American Journal of Sociology* (July 1996)

Forder, James, and Chris Huhne, *Both Sides of the Coin* (Penguin, 2001)

Frank, Robert H. *Luxury Fever* (Free Press, 1999)

Frank, Robert H., and Cook, Philip J., *The Winner-Take-All Society* (Free Press, 1995)

Frank, Thomas, *One Market Under God* (Secker & Warburg, 2001)

Freedland, Mark, and Sciarra, Silvan (eds.) *Public Services and Citizenship in EU Law* (Clarendon, 1998)

Freeman, Richard, *The Politics of Health in Europe* (Manchester University Press, 2000)

Freeman, Richard, *The U.S. Economic Model at Y2K: Lodestar for Advanced Capitalism*, working paper 7757 (National Bureau for Economic Research, June 2000)

Frey, William, Abresch, Bill, and Yesting, Jonathan, *America by the Numbers* (New Press, 2001)

Friedman, Milton, *Capitalism and Freedom* (Chicago University Press, 1962)

Gabe, Jonathan, *The Americanization of British Health Care* (Royal Holloway, 1997)

Gabel, Matthew J., *Interests and Integration: Market Liberalization, Public Opinion and European Union* (University of Michigan Press, 1998)

Garry, Patrick M., *A Nation of Adversaries: How the Litigation Explosion is Reshaping America* (Plenum, 1997)

Gates, Jeff, *The Ownership Solution: Toward a Shared Capitalism for the Twenty-first Century* (Allen Lane, 1998)

Gibson, James William, *Warrior Dreams: Violence and Manhood in Post-Vietnam America* (Hill & Wang, 1994)

Giddens, Anthony, "The Question of Inequality," in Anthony Giddens (ed.), *The Global Third Way Debate* (Polity, 2001)

Giddens, Anthony (ed.), *The Global Third Way Debate* (Polity, 2001)

Glassman, Ronald M., *Caring Capitalism: A New Middle-class Base for the Welfare State* (Macmillan, 2000)

Godley, Wynne, and Izuricta, Alex, *The Developing U.S. Recession and Guidelines for Policy*, Levy Economics Foundation, Oct. 2001

Gordon, Robert J., "Does the 'New Economy' Measure Up to the Great Inventions of the Past?", draft paper for *Journal of Economic Perspectives* (2000)

Gowan, Peter, *The Global Gamble: Washington's Faustian Bid for World Dominance* (Verso, 1999)

Grant, Charles, *EU 2010: An Optimistic Vision for the Future* (Centre for European Policy Reform, 2001)

Grant, Charles, *The House that Jacques Built* (Nicholas Brealey, 1994)

Grantham, Dewey W., *The South in Modern America: A Region at Odds* (HarperPerennial Library, 1995)

Gray, John, *False Dawn: The Delusions of Global Capitalism* (Granta, 1998)

Greider, William, *One World Ready or Not: The Manic Logic of Global Capitalism* (Simon & Schuster, 1997)

Greven, Michael T., "Can the European Union Finally become a Democracy?" in Michael T. Greven and Louis W. Pauly (eds.), *Democracy Beyond the State: The European Dilemma and the Emerging Global Order* (Rowman and Littlefield, 2000)

Greven, Michael, and Pauly, Louis W. (eds.), *Democracy beyond the State? The European Dilemma and the Emerging Global Order* (Rowman and Littlefield, 2000)

Griliches, Z., "R&D and Productivity," in collected papers (University of Chicago, 1998)

Guyatt, Nicholas, *Another American Century? The United States and the World after 2000* (Zed, 2000)

References

Habermas, Jürgen, "The European Nation-State and the Pressures of Globalization," *New Left Review*, May–June 1999

Habermas, Jürgen, *The Structural Transformation of the Public Sphere* (Polity, 1985)

Habermas, Jürgen, "Why Europe Needs a Constitution," *New Left Review*, Sept.–Oct. 2001

Hall, Peter, "The Evolution of Economic Policy," in A. Guyomarch, H. Machin, P. Hall and J. Hayward (eds.), *Developments in French Politics 2* (Palgrave, 2001)

Hall, Peter, and David Soskice, *Varieties of Capitalism: The Institutional Foundations of Comparative Advantage* (Oxford University Press (2001)

Hanley, D. L. (ed.), *Christian Democracy in Europe: A Comparative Perspective* (Pinter, 1993)

Hauser, Robert, et al., "Occupation Status, Education and Social Mobility in the Meritocracy," in Kenneth Arrow, Samuel Bowles and Steven Durlauf (eds.), *Meritocracy and Economic Inequality* (Princeton University Press, 2000)

Hayward, Jack (ed.), *The Crisis of Representation in Europe* (Frank Cass, 1995)

Heineman, Kenneth J., *God Is a Conservative* (New York University Press, 1998)

Held, David, et al., *Global Transformations* (Polity, 1999)

Hendry, D. F., and Ericsson, N. R., "An Econometric Analysis of UK Money Demand in *Monetary Trends in the United States and the United Kingdom* by Milton Friedman and Anna J. Schwartz," *American Economic Review* (1991), pp. 8–38

Henwood, Doug, *Wall Street: How It Works and for Whom* (Verso, 1997)

Héritier, Adrienne, "Policy-Making by Subterfuge: Interest Accommodation, Innovation and Substitute Democratic Legitimation in Europe," *Journal of European Public Policy*, vol. 4, no. 2 (1997)

Herman, Edward S., and McChesney, Robert W., *The Global Media: The New Missionaries of Global Capitalism* (Cassell, 1997)

Hernson, Paul S. (ed.), *The Clinton Presidency: The First Term* (Macmillan, 1999)

Herzenberg, Stephen A., et al., *New Rules for a New Economy: Employment and Opportunity in Postindustrial America* (Cornell University Press, 1998)

Hey, Kenneth R., and Moore, Peter D., *The Caterpillar Doesn't Know* (Free Press, 1998)

Hill, Andrew D., *"Wrongful Discharge" and the Derogation of the At-Will Employment Doctrine*, Labor Relations and Public Policy Series no. 3, 1 (University of Pennsylvania, 1987)

Hindley, Brian, and Howe, Martin, *Better Off Out? The Benefits or Costs of EU Membership* (Institute of Economic Affairs, 2001)

Hix, Simon, *The Political System of the European Union* (Macmillan, 1999)

Hobhouse, Dominic, and Duncan, Alan, *Saturn's Children: How the State Devours Liberty and Prosperity* (Sinclair-Stevenson, 1995)

Hoffe, Otfried, *L'Etat et la Justice : John Rawls et Robert Nozick* (Librairie Philosophique Jean Vrin, 1988)

Hollingsworth, J. Rogers, and Boyer, Robert (eds.), *Contemporary Capitalism: The Embeddedness of Institutions* (Cambridge University Press, 1997)

Hooghe, Lisbet, *Territorial Politics—A Zero-sum Game? EU Cohesion Policy and Competing Models of European Capitalism*, European University Institute working paper 98/41 (1998)

Hooghe, Lisbet, and Marks, Gary, *The Making of a Polity: The Struggle over European Integration*, European University Institute working paper 97/31 (1997)

Hopner, Martin, *Corporate Governance in Transition: Ten Empirical Findings on Shareholder*

Value and Industrial Relations in Germany, discussion paper 01/05 (Max Planck Institute, 2001)

Hudson, Michael (ed.), *Merchants of Misery: How Corporate America Profits from Poverty* (Common Courage Press, 1996)

Hutton, Will, *The State We're In* (Cape, 1995; pb Vintage, 1996)

Inglehart, Ronald, Basaney, Miguel, and Moreno, Alejandro, *Human Values and Beliefs: A Cross-Cultural Sourcebook. Political, Religious, Sexual and Economic Norms in 43 Countries: Findings from the 1990–93 World Value Survey* (University of Michigan Press, 1998)

Institute for Public Policy Research, *Building Better Partnerships*, (IPPR, 2001)

Isles, Nic, and Palazzi, Marcello (eds.), *The European Model for Enterprise* (Industrial Society Learning/Capita, 2002)

Iversen, Torben, et al. (eds.), *Unions, Employers and Central Banks: Macroeconomic Coordination and Institutional Change in Social Market Economies* (Cambridge University Press, 2000)

Jabko, Nicolas, "In the Name of the Market: How the European Commission Paved the Way for Monetary Union," *Journal of European Public Policy* (Sept. 1999)

Jacquet, Pierre, and Pisani-Ferry, Jean, *Economic Policy Co-ordination in the Euro-zone* (Centre for European Reform, 2001)

Jensen, M., "The Modern Industrial Revolution: Exit and the Failure of Internal Control Systems," *Journal of Finance* 48, no. 9 (July 1993), pp. 831–80

Jensen, M., and Ruback, R., "The Market for Corporate Control: The Scientific Evidence," *Journal of Financial Economics* (1983), no. 11, pp. 5–50

Johnson, Chalmers, *Blowback* (Little, Brown, 2000)

Johnson, Debra, and Turner, Colin, *Trans-European Networks: The Political Economy of Integrating Europe's Infrastructure* (Macmillan, 1997)

Jones, Ci, and Williams, J. C., "Measuring the Social Return to R&D," *Quarterly Journal of Economics* (Nov. 1998)

Johnston, Carla Brooks, *Screened Out: How the Media Control Us and What We Can Do About It* (M. E. Sharpe, 2000)

Jowell, Roger et al. (eds.), *British Social Attitudes; the 16th Report. Who Shares New Labour Values?* (National Centre for Social Research, 1999)

Judis, John B., *The Paradox of American Democracy: Elites, Special Interests and the Betrayal of Public Trust* (Random House, 2000)

Judis, John B., and Teixeira, Ruy, *The Emerging Democratic Majority* (Scribner, 2001)

Kann, Mark E., *A Republic of Men* (New York University Press, 1988)

Kant, Immanuel, *Political Writings*, ed. Hans Reiss, trans. H. B. Nisbett (Cambridge University Press, 1970)

Karake Shalhoub, Zeinab A., *Organizational Down-sizing, Discrimination and Corporate Social Responsibility* (Quorum, 1994)

Katz, Harry C. (ed.), *Telecommunications: Restructuring Work and Employment Relations Worldwide* (Cornell University Press, 1997)

Kennedy, Alan, *The End of Shareholder Value: The Real Effects of the Shareholder Value Phenomenon and the Crisis it is Bringing to Business* (Orion Business, 2000)

Kersbergen, Kees van, *Social Capitalism: A Study of Christian Democracy and the Welfare State* (Routledge, 1995)

King, Lawrence Peter, *The Basic Features of Postcommunist Capitalism in Eastern Europe: Firms in Hungary, the Czech Republic and Slovakia* (Praeger, 2001)

References

Klein, Naomi, *No Logo* (Flamingo, 2000)

Kluth, Michael F., *The Political Economy of a Social Europe: Understanding Labour Market Integration in the European Union* (Macmillan, 1998)

Knack, S., and Keefern, P. "Does Social Capital Have an Economic Pay-off?" *Quarterly Journal of Economics*, 1997, 4, pp. 1251–88

Kovach, Bill, and Rosenstiel, Tom, *The Elements of Journalism: What Newspeople Should Know* and the *Public Should Expect* (Three Rivers Press, 2001).

KPMG, *Unlocking Shareholder Value, the Key to Success* (KPMG, 2001)

Kreisky, Bruno, "The Hidden Agenda of the Information Society," *International Studies* (1997)

Kroes, Rob, *If You've Seen One You've Seen the Mall: Europeans and American Mass Culture* (University of Illinois Press, 1996)

Krugman, Paul, *Peddling Prosperity* (W. W. Norton, 1994)

Kukathas, Chandran, and Pettit, Philip, *Rawls, a Theory of Justice and its Critics* (Polity, 1990)

Kuttner, Robert, *Everything for Sale: The Virtues and Limits of Markets* (Knopf, 1996)

Kuttner, Robert, *The End of Laissez-Faire: National Purpose and the Global Economy after the Cold War* (University of Pennsylvania Press, 1991)

Lafontaine, Oskar, 'The Future of German Social Democracy', *New Left Review* 227 (Jan.–Feb. 1998)

Landesmann, Michael A., and Pichelman, Karl (eds.), *Unemployment in Europe*, proceedings of a conference held by the Confederation of European Economic Associations, Vienna (Macmillan, 2000)

Lasch, Christopher, *The Culture of Narcissism* (W. W. Norton, 1979)

Leach, William, *Country of Exiles: The Destruction of Place in American Life* (Pantheon, 1999)

Lemann, Nicholas, *The Big Test: The Secret History of the American Meritocracy* (Farrar, Straus & Giroux, 1999)

Light, Donald, and May, Annabelle, *Britain's Health System: From Welfare State to Managed Markets* (Faulkner & Gray, 1993)

Link, Rosemary J., Anthony, A., et al., *When Children Pay: US Welfare Reform and its Implications for UK Policy* (Child Poverty Action Group, 2000)

Lipset, Seymour Martin, *American Exceptionalism: A Double-Edged Sword* (W. W. Norton, 1999)

Lipset, Seymour Martin, and Bendix, R., *Social Mobility in Industrial Society* (University of California Press, 1967)

Lipset, Seymour Martin, and Marks, Gary, *It Didn't Happen Here: Why Socialism Failed in the United States* (W. W. Norton, 2000)

Litan, Robert E., and Rauch, Jonathan, *American Finance for the 21st Century* (Brookings Institution Press, 1998)

Locke, John, *Two Treatises of Government* (Cambridge University Press, 1988)

Lodge, J. (ed.), *Institutions and Policies of the European Community* (Pinter, 1983)

Lynn, Matthew, *Birds of Prey: The War Between Boeing and Airbus* (Four Walls Eight Windows, 1997)

McAllister, Matthew P., *The Commercialization of American Culture* (Sage, 1996)

Macfarlane, Leslie J., *Socialism, Social Ownership and Social Justice* (Macmillan, 1998)

McQuaid, Kim, *Uneasy Partners: Big Business in American Politics 1945–1990* (Johns Hopkins University Press, 1994)

Madison, James, et al., *The Federalist Papers* (Penguin, 1987)

Majone, Giandomenico, *Regulating Europe* (Routledge, 1996)

Mandel, Michael, *The Coming Internet Depression* (Pearson Education, 2001)

Marchak, Patricia M., *The Integrated Circus: The New Right and the Restructuring of Global Markets* (McGill-Queen's University Press, 1991)

Marks, Gary, et al. (eds.), *Governance in the European Union* (Sage, 1996)

Marsden, Keith, *Towards a Treaty of Commerce* (Centre for Policy Studies, 2000)

Marshall, T. H., *Citizenship and Social Class* (Cambridge University Press, 1950)

Mazower, Mark, *Dark Continent* (Penguin, 1998)

Melchionni, Maria Grazia, *Altiero Spinelli et Jean Monnet* (Fondation Jean Monnet pour l'Europe, 1993)

Mellin, Phil, and Roper, Jon, *Americanisation and the Transformation of World Cultures: Melting Pot or Cultural Chernobyl* (Edwin Mellen, 1996)

Mény, Yves, "Five (Hypo)theses on Democracy and its Future," in Anthony Giddens (ed.), *The Global Third Way Debate* (Polity, 2001)

Micklethwait, John, and Wooldridge, Adrian, *The Witch Doctors: What the Management Gurus Are Saying, Why It Matters and How to Make Sense of It* (Heinemann, 1996)

Midgley, James, "Growth, Redistribution and Welfare: Towards Social Investment," in Anthony Giddens (ed.), *The Global Third Way Debate* (Polity, 2001)

Miles, David, "Testing for Short-Termism in the UK Stock Market," *Economic Journal* (Nov. 1993)

Mishel, Lawrence, Bernstein, Jared, and Schmitt, John, *The State of Working America 2000–2001* (Cornell University Press, 2001)

Misner, Paul, *Social Catholicism in Europe: From the Onset of Industrialisation to the First World War* (Darton, Longman and Todd, 1991)

Monks, Robert, *The New Global Investors* (Capstone, 2001)

Morris, Dick, *Behind the Oval Office* (Renaissance, 1997)

Mowery, David C., *U.S. Industry in 2000: Studies in Competitive Performance* (National Academy Press, 1999)

Mowery, David, and Rosenberg, Nathan, *Paths of Innovation: Technological Change in Twentieth-Century America* (Cambridge University Press, 1998)

National Institute for Economic and Social Research, *Britain's Productivity Performance, 1990–1996* (NIESR, 1999)

Nelson, Joel L., *Post-Industrial Capitalism: Exploring Economic Inequality in America* (Sage, 1995)

Nickell, Stephen, "The Distribution of Wages and Unemployment across Skill Groups," in Michael Landesmann and Karl Pichelman (eds.), *Unemployment in Europe* (Macmillan, 2000)

Nickell, Stephen, *The Performance of Companies* (Blackwell, 1995)

Nielsen, Ruth, and Szyszczak, Erika, *The Social Dimension of the European Union* (Handelshojskolens Forlag, 1997)

No Campaign, "The Economic Case against the Euro," *New Europe* (2001)

Nozick, Robert, *Anarchy, State and Utopia* (Harvard University Press, 1973)

Nuffield Trust, *Reflections on the Management of the NHS* (Nuffield Trust, 1985)

Nugent, Neil, *The Government and Politics of the EU*, 4th ed. (Macmillan, 1999)

Nye, Joseph S., "In Government We Don't Trust," in Anthony Giddens (ed.), *The Global Third Way Debate* (Polity, 2001)

References

O'Connor, Karen, *No Neutral Ground?* (Westview, 1996)

OECD, *Benefit Systems and Work Incentives* (OECD, 1999)

OECD, *Economic Outlook* no. 70 (OECD, Dec. 2001)

OECD, *Education at a Glance: OECD Indicators* (OECD, 2000)

OECD, *Growth Effects of Education and Social Capital in the OECD Countries*, working paper no. 263 (OECD, 2000)

OECD, *Health Data 1999: A Comparative Analysis of 29 Countries* (OECD, 1999)

OECD, *Human Capital Investment* (OECD, 1998)

OECD, *OECD Economic Survey of the Euro Area* (OECD, 2001)

OECD, *OECD Economic Surveys—France* (OECD, 1997)

OECD, *OECD Economic Surveys—Germany* (OECD, May 2001)

OECD, *OECD Employment Outlook 2000* (OECD, 2000)

OECD, *Taxing Wages in OECD Countries* (OECD, 1998–99)

Olufs III, Dick W., *The Making of Telecommunications Policy* (Lynne Rienner, 1999)

O'Mahoney, Mary, *Britain's Productivity Performance, 1990–1996* (NIESR, 1999)

Osterman, Paul (ed.), *Broken Ladder: Managerial Careers in the New Economy* (Oxford University Press, 1996)

O'Sullivan, Mary, *Contests for Corporate Control: Corporate Governance and Economic Performance in the United States and Germany* (Oxford University Press, 2000)

Palley, Thomas I., *Plenty of Nothing* (Princeton University Press, 1998)

Paraschos, Emmanuel E., *Media Law and Regulation in the European Union: National, Transnational and U.S. Perspectives* (Iowa State University Press, 1998)

Parkinson, J. E., *Corporate Power and Responsibility: Issues in the Theory of Company Law* (Clarendon Press, 1993)

Paul, Ellen Frankel, and Dickman, Howard (eds.), *Liberty, Property and the Foundations of the American Constitution* (State University of New York Press, 1989)

Perlstein, Rick, *Before the Storm* (Hill & Wang, 2001)

Petras, James, and Morley, Morris, *Empire or Republic?* (Routledge, 1995)

Pfeffer, Leo, *This Honorable Court: A History of the United States Supreme Court* (Beacon Press, 1965)

Pierson, Paul, "The Path to European Integration," *Comparative Political Studies*, vol. 29, no. 2 (1996)

Pinto, Arthur R., and Visentini, Gustavo (eds.), *The Legal Basis of Corporate Governance in Publicly Held Corporations: A Comparative Approach* (Kluwer Law International, 1998)

Pitt, Ivan L., and Norsworthy, John R., *Economics of the US Commercial Airline Industry: Productivity, Technology and Deregulation* (Kluwer Academic, 1999)

Pollack, Mark, "Delegation, Agency and Agenda-Setting in the European Community," *International Organisation*, vol. 51, no. 1 (1997)

Porter, Michael E., *On Competition* (Harvard University Press, 1996)

Porter, Michael E., *The Competitive Advantage of Nations* (Macmillan, 1998)

Porter, Michael E., and van Opstal, Debra, *U.S. Competitiveness 2001* (U.S. Council on Competitiveness, 2001)

Postman, Neil, *Amusing Ourselves to Death: Public Discourse in the Age of Show Business* (Methuen, 1985)

Powell, Martin (ed.), *New Labour, New Welfare State: The Third Way in British Social Policy*, (Polity, 1999)

Poynter, Gavin, *Restructuring in the Service Industry: Management Reform and Workplace Relations in the UK Service Sector* (Mansell, 2000)

Pries, Ludiger, *Accelerating from a Multinational to a Transnational Carmaker: The Volkswagen Consortium in the 1990s* (Institute of Sociology, University of Erlanger-Nurnberg, 1999)

Purdey, Jebediah, *For Common Things* (Knopf, 2000)

Putnam, Robert D., *Bowling Alone* (Simon & Schuster, 2000)

Ranade, Wendy (ed.), *Markets and Health Care: A Comparative Analysis* (Longman, 1998)

Rawls, John, *A Theory of Justice* (Oxford University Press, 1973)

Reich, Robert, *The Future of Success* (Knopf, 2001)

Reynolds, David, *One World Divisible* (W. W. Norton, 2000)

Rifkin, Jeremy, *The Age of Access* (Putnam, 2000)

Roberts, Richard, and Kynaston, David, *City and State* (Profile, 2001)

Robinson, John P., and Godbey, Geoffrey, *Time for Life* (Pennsylvania University Press, 1999)

Rosanvallon, Pierre, *The New Social Question: Rethinking the Welfare State* (Princeton University Press, 2000; first publ. in French as *La Nouvelle Question Sociale: Repenser l'Etat Providence*, Seuil, 1995)

Saint-Martin, Denis, *Building the New Managerialist State: Consultants and the Politics of Public Sector Reform in Comparative Perspective* (Oxford University Press, 2000)

Sandel, Michael, *Democracy's Discontent: America in Search of a Public Philosophy* (Harvard University Press, 1996)

Sassoon, Donald, *One Hundred Years of Socialism: The West European Left in the Twentieth Century* (I. B. Tauris, 1996)

Sauter, Wolf, "EU Competition Rules: Promoting and Policing the Internal Market," in Thomas C. Lawton (ed.), *European Industrial Policy and Competitiveness* (Macmillan, 1999)

Scharpf, Fritz, *Governing in Europe: Effective and Democratic?* (European University Institute, 1999)

Scharpf, Fritz, "The Joint Decision Trap: Lessons from German Federalism and European Integration," *Public Administration*, vol. 66, no. 3 (1988)

Schiller, Dan, *Digital Capitalism: Networking the Global Market System* (MIT Press, 1998)

Schiller, Herbert, *Information Inequality* (Routledge, 1996)

Schiller, Robert J., *Irrational Exuberance* (Princeton University Press, 2000)

Schmitter, Philippe C., *How to Democratize the European Union . . . And Why Bother?* (Rowman & Littlefield, 2000)

Schor, Juliet (ed.), *Do Americans Shop Too Much?* (Beacon Press, 2000)

Schweiger, Georg Christopher, *European Central Bank* (Minerva, 2000)

Seabrooke, Leonard, *US Power in International Finance: The Victory of Dividends* (Palgrave, 2001)

Sennett, Richard, *The Corrosion of Character* (W. W. Norton, 1998)

Sennett, Richard, *The Fall of Public Man* (Faber, 1993)

Sfez, Lucien, *Leçons sur l'égalité* (Presses de la Fondation Nationale des Sciences Politiques, 1984)

Shahin, Jamal, and Wintle, Michael (eds.), *The Idea of a United Europe: Political, Economic and Cultural Integration since the Fall of the Berlin Wall* (Macmillan, 2000)

References

Siedentop, Larry, *Democracy in Europe* (Allen Lane/Penguin Press, 2000)

Skidelsky, Robert, *John Maynard Keynes: Fighting for Britain* (Macmillan, 2000)

Slater, David, and Taylor, Peter S. (eds), *The American Century: Consensus and Coercion in the Projection of American Power* (Blackwell, 1999)

Slotkin, Richard, *Gunfighter Nation: The Myth of the Frontier in Twentieth-Century America* (Atheneum, 1992)

Smeeding, Timothy, *Financial Poverty in Developed Countries: The Evidence from the Luxembourg Income Study* (UNDP, 1997)

Smith, Mitchell P., "Autonomy by the Rules: The European Commission and the Development of State Aid Policy," *Journal of Common Market Studies* (March 1998)

Solinger, Ricky (ed.), *Abortion Wars* (University of California Press, 1998)

Sorkin, Michael (ed.), *Variations on a Theme Park: The New American City and the End of Public Space* (Hill & Wang, 2000)

Soskice, David, "Divergent Production Regimes: Coordinated and Uncoordinated Market Economies in the 1980s and 1990s," in H. Kitschelt, P. Lange, G. Marks, and J. D. Stevens (eds.), *Continuity and Change in Contemporary Capitalism* (Cambridge University Press, 1999)

Sparrow, Bartholomew H., *Uncertain Guardians: The News Media as a Political Institution* (Johns Hopkins University Press, 1999)

Spector, Robert, *Amazon.com: Get Big Fast* (Random House, 2000)

Steinbock, Dan, *The Nokia Revolution: The Story of an Extraordinary Company that Transformed an Industry* (Amacom, 2001)

Strauss, Leo, *Natural Rights and History* (Chicago University Press, 1953)

Streeck, Wolfgang, "Beneficial Constraints on the Economic Limits of Rational Voluntarism," in J. Rogers Hollingsworth and Robert Boyer (eds.), *Contemporary Capitalism: The Embeddedness of Institutions* (Cambridge University Press, 1997)

Streeck, Wolfgang, "Neo-voluntarism: A New European Social Policy Regime," in Gary Marks et al. (eds.), *Governance in the European Union* (Sage, 1996)

Tawney, R. H., *Equality* (Allen & Unwin, 1931; rev. 1938, 1952)

Teixeira, Ruy, and Rogers, Joel, *America's Forgotten Majority: Why the White Working Class Still Matters* (Basic Books, 2000)

Thatcher, Margaret, *Statecraft* (HarperCollins, 2002)

Thelen, Kathleen, "Why German Employers Cannot Bring Themselves to Dismantle the German Model," in Torben Iversen et al. (eds), *Unions, Employers and Central Banks* (Cambridge University Press, 2000)

Thornley, Andy, *Urban Planning under Thatcherism: The Challenge of the Market* (Routledge, 1991)

Tocqueville, Alexis de, *Democracy in America* (Cambridge, 1864)

Treasury, *The Myners Report* (HM Treasury, 2001)

Triplett, Jack E., *Economic Statistics, the New Economy, and the Productivity Slowdown* (Brookings Institution, 1999)

TUC Task Force on Promoting Trade Unionism, *Reaching the Missing Millions* (TUC, Aug. 2001)

Turner, Adair, *Just Capital: The Liberal Economy* (Macmillan, 2001)

Védrine, Hubert, and Moïsi, Dominique, *France in an Age of Globalization* (Brookings Institution, 2001)

Von Ark, Bart, et al. (eds.), *Productivity, Technology and Economic Growth* (Kluwer, 2000)

Wallace, William, and Smith, Julie, "Democracy or Technocracy? European Integration and the Problem of Popular Consent," in Jack Hayward (ed.), *The Crisis of Representation in Europe* (Frank Cass, 1995)

Walter, Andrew, *World Power and World Money* (Harvester Wheatsheaf, 1993)

Watson, Justin, *The Christian Coalition* (Macmillan, 1999)

Weiler, J. H. H., *The Constitution of Europe: "Do the New Clothes Have an Emperor?" and other Essays on European Integration* (Cambridge University Press, 1999)

Wenglinsky, Harold, *When Money Matters: How Educational Expenditures Improve Student Performance and How They Don't* (Princeton University Press, 1997)

Zepengauer, Mark, and Naiman, Arthur, *Take the Risk of Welfare* (Odonion, 1996)

Zweig, Michael, *The Working Class Majority: America's Best Kept Secret* (Cornell University Press, 2000)

Zweigenhaft, Richard L., and Domhoff, William, *Diversity in the Power Elite: Have Women and Minorities Reached the Top?* (Yale University Press, 1998)

Index

Index

Index

Index

Index

Moral Majority, 85–86, 88
Motorola, 222
Mowery, David, 119
multiculturalism, 58
multilateralism, 4, 8, 13, 269
  as EU responsibility, 15
  sovereignty issues and, 277
  see also interdependence; unilateralism
Murdoch, Rupert, 201
Murray, Charles, 194
mutual funds, 44, 103, 105, 110

Nader, Ralph, 84, 95, 97
NAFTA (North American Free Trade Agreement), 93
Nasser, Jacques, 220
National Bureau of Economic Research, 118
National Health Service (NHS), 196, 198–99, 213, 251
nationalization, 210–11
National Review, 74
National Rifle Association, 85–86
Nation of Adversaries, A (Garry), 140
NATO (North Atlantic Treaty Organization), 13, 167
NBC, 155, 156
negative integration, 252–53
neo-conservatives, 6
Netherlands, 16, 51, 133, 169, 235, 240, 256, 257, 259, 262
Network Rail, 212
New Deal, 11, 26, 30, 41, 47, 66–67, 70, 71, 84, 100, 101, 171, 175, 184
New Economy, 121–29
New Jersey, 40
New York Federal Reserve, 179
New York Stock Exchange, 208
New York Times, 157
NHS (National Health Service), 196, 198–99, 213, 251
Nickel and Dimed (Ehrenreich), 145
Nickell, Stephen, 234–35
Nixon, Richard M., 73, 74, 80, 81, 85, 94, 169–70, 172, 198
Nixon administration, 67
Nokia, 222–24, 226, 227, 232–33, 261
Nokia Revolution, The (Steinbock), 222–23
Norquist, Grover, 92
Norsworthy, John, 232
North American Free Trade Agreement (NAFTA), 93
Norway, 245, 261

Nozick, Robert, 48–49, 50, 54, 56, 61, 78

Oklahoma City bombing, 69, 93
Ollila, Jorma, 222, 224
one-nation conservatives, 53, 190, 192, 251
Organization for Economic Cooperation and Development (OECD), 147, 163, 193, 198, 199, 202–3, 233, 254, 275
Organization of Petroleum Exporting Countries (OPEC), 82, 170–71
O'Sullivan, Mary, 115, 203–4, 208
overclass, 134
Owen, Robert, 45, 47

Patent Office, U.S., 184
patriotism, 15, 60, 66, 267
Paulson, Henry, 129
Peddling Prosperity (Krugman), 88
pensions, 214–16, 256–57
Perot, Ross, 90
Pfeffer, Leo, 41
Pickens, T. Boone, 110
Piesch, Ferdinand, 224
Pitt, Ivan, 232
politics, money and, 4, 41, 81, 85, 151–52, 185, 281
Pollack case, 41
Porras, Jerry, 279
Porter, Michael, 121
Portugal, 145, 246
Postman, Neil, 157
poverty:
  in Europe, 255–56
  in U.S., 130, 133–34, 145–46, 148, 255–56
presidency, Madison's view of, 38
prisons, 22–23, 27, 96, 199
privacy issues, 263–64
private consumption rates, 235–36
private finance initiative (PFI), 212–13
privatization, 212–13, 247, 256
productivity:
  in Europe, 16, 118, 162–63, 200, 201, 223, 240
  in Great Britain, 200, 201, 202–3, 205
  in U.S., 11–12, 16–17, 20, 22, 73, 81, 82, 103, 111, 118, 121, 123, 163, 168
Progressive era, 30, 66, 70–71
property rights, 192
  conservative view of, 31, 33–41, 98
  European conception of, 31, 42–48
  shareholder value and, 103–4
Proposition 13, 83, 140
Protestants, 28, 33, 34, 42, 45, 66, 85

Index